D1349403

Henry Fielding: His Life & Works

HENRY FIELDING

Playwright, Journalist and
Master of the Art of Fiction

His Life and Works

By H. K. Banerji, M.A., B.Litt.

*Professor of English Literature at the Presidency
College, Calcutta*

New York

RUSSELL & RUSSELL

1962

FIRST PUBLISHED IN 1929
REISSUED, 1962, BY RUSSELL & RUSSELL, INC.
L. C. CATALOG CARD NO: 62—13825

PRINTED IN THE UNITED STATES OF AMERICA

PREFACE

THE history of Fielding's literary life has received less attention than it deserves, particularly during the present century. His critics in the past in paying their tribute of admiration to his great novels or in detracting from their merits have paid little attention to the other products of his genius. His plays, even the best of them, are now known only by name, and his contributions to the journals that he edited are practically forgotten. The two volumes of the *Miscellanies*, again, which Fielding published in 1743, contain many pieces which deserve to be better known than they are at present.

While giving the prominence they deserve to the novels I have endeavoured in the following pages to invite the attention of my reader to the merits of some of the other products of Fielding's genius. I have found it difficult to believe that these were mere potboilers, as his latest critic has described them. And during the quarter of a century that I have studied the works of one of the most versatile masters of English prose I have always felt that a knowledge of the plays, the pamphlets, the essays in the periodicals and other miscellaneous writings is essential to a true estimate of Fielding's genius.

These considerations have induced me to include in my critical study even ephemeral pieces which have met the fate they deserve. But while I mention these to make my survey of Fielding's literary achievements as comprehensive as possible, my ambition is to rescue much that is really great from the oblivion that threatens to overtake them.

In looking back upon the labours of nearly six years in Europe I recall a time of great happiness, and I take this opportunity of expressing my gratitude to the authorities of the Education Department of the Government of Bengal whose sympathy with my aspirations has made these labours possible. To the staffs of some of the great libraries of Europe—and particularly to those of the Bodleian and the British Museum—I owe a deep debt of gratitude for the kindness and assistance that I have received from them. To my teachers in Oxford, Professor H. F. B. Brett-Smith and Mr. L. Rice-Oxley, I am indebted more than to anyone else for the guidance and assistance they have given to me. Without this assistance my labours could not have been brought to this issue.

H.K.B.

Presidency College,
  Calcutta.
August, 1928.

CONTENTS

vii

CHAPTER I

FIELDING'S ART

AT the close of his life, when he had given his great
novels to the world, Fielding makes a confession
which is of great significance because it gives us a true
insight into the distinctive quality of his genius and reveals to us the secret of his magnificent artistic achievement.

"I must confess," he says in his Preface to *The Journal
of a Voyage to Lisbon*, "I should have honoured and
loved Homer more had he written a true history of his
own times in humble prose than those noble poems that
have so justly collected the praise of all ages; for, though
I read these with more admiration and astonishment, I
still read Herodotus, Thucydides, and Xenophon with
more amusement and more satisfaction."

This confession, it must be borne in mind, is made by
a man whose classical attainments in spite of Thackeray's
outburst over his master's "absurd brag of his two-penny
learning" in *Joseph Andrews*,[1] are now known to have
been so far above the average as to preclude any suspicion that the pronouncement was the result of an insuffi-
cient acquaintance with or inability to appreciate the
beauties of classical literature. Fielding's works supply
us with ample evidence to prove that he had studied the
Homeric epics with much care and delight and that he
had a scholarly appreciation of their manifold beauties.
Indeed, in the same preface in which he makes his con-

[1]Letter to Mrs. Brookfield, August 11, 1848, *A Collection of Letters of
W. M. Thackeray, 1847–1855*, London, 1887. p. 20.

fession he fully vindicates the greatness of his favourites, the epic poets, who, he says, "found the limits of nature too strait for the immensity of their genius, which they had not room to exert without extending fact by fiction."

We cannot fail to realize from the words of his confession that "true history" made an appeal to him which was greater than that of the finest epic poetry; and our knowledge of this fact supplies us with a master key to a true estimate of his genius and a just appreciation of his art. When we examine his writings, we cannot help being struck by the fact that except in one or two works of minor importance, Fielding resolutely confined his attention to the living world around him. As a playwright he seldom turned to classical or mediæval story or legend for the materials of his plots. The best known of all his plays, *The Life and Death of Tom Thumb the Great*, is a very effective satire on the extravagances of the heroic dramatists ; and again and again in his plays, as well as in his other works, he ridicules "the empty inflations," to use the picturesque words of a seventeenth-century novelist, "of minds apparelled in fustian." As a journalist and pamphleteer he brought to the political and social problems of his time a wealth of knowledge of the world and a practical common sense as great as that of Addison or Steele. He describes his first novel as "a comic epic poem in prose" in which "everything is copied from the book of nature," and he declares that his intention in writing the book is to hold the glass to thousands in their closets so that they may contemplate their deformity and endeavour to reduce it.[1] In *Tom Jones* he is even more emphatic in declaring his determination to picture the life of his times. He tells his

[1] *Joseph Andrews*, Book III, Chap. I.

reader that the provision that he has made for him in his book is no other than human nature, which he intends to present at first to the keen appetite of his reader "in that more plain and simple manner in which it is found in the country"; afterwards he is going to "hash and ragoo it with all the high French and Italian seasoning of affectation and vice which courts and cities afford."[1] He is convinced that his business is to present the facts of life as he has read them and leave it to his sagacious reader to consult the original book of nature to judge for himself how far his presentment of the facts agrees with the original. In *Amelia*, again, he expresses the same determination to describe human nature as it is, not as we would wish it to be.[2]

It is to be expected from an artist like this, who is so determined "not to o'erstep the modesty of nature," that he would have little patience with writers of fiction whose conception of their art was very different from his own, "those persons of surprising genius," as he sarcastically describes them in *Joseph Andrews*, "the authors of immense romances, or the modern novel and Atalantis writers."[3] The anti-romantic novel was created by positive minds like his that were anxious not so much to kindle and captivate the imagination as to depict real life, to describe characters such as one meets with in everyday life, and to judge motives of action. Again and again in his writings Fielding speaks contemptuously of romances "which are filled with monsters, the productions, not of nature, but of distempered brains."[4] He feels that he has much in common

---

[1] *Tom Jones*, Book I, Chap. I.   [2] *Amelia*, Book X, Chap. IV.
[3] *Joseph Andrews*, Book III, Chap. I.
[4] *Tom Jones*, Book IV, Chap. I, and Book XIV, Chap. I ; *Joseph Andrews*, Preface and Book III, Chap. I.

with writers like Congreve and Vanbrugh. But he has nothing but contempt for their imitators whose characters and descriptions often appear to him to be as absurd as Hogarth's pictures would be if he painted a rout or a drum in the dresses of Titian and of Vandyke. And if we have the leisure and the inclination to read much of the fiction that was produced in England during the sixteenth and the seventeenth centuries, we shall realize that there is some ground for Fielding's complaint that "true nature is difficult to be met with in authors," though in justice to our novelist's predecessors who cultivated the art of fiction it must be pointed out that on the whole there was more verisimilitude in their work than Fielding was prepared to give them credit for.

The pictures of the underworld of London that are given in Greene's *Black Book's Messenger* and the Conny Catching pamphlets or in Lodge's *Alarum Against Usurers* make the stories contained in these works of the novelists far more realistic than their more ambitious efforts in fiction. A work like *The Unfortunate Traveller* of the "ingenuous, ingenious, fluent, facetious Thomas Nash" is so full of realistic descriptions, and the novelist is so closely in touch throughout his work with the facts of everyday life, that even the fastidious Fielding must have found much of "true nature" in it. And in novels like Thomas Deloney's *Jack of Newbury* and *The Gentle Craft*, Henry Chettle's *Piers Plainnes Seaven Yeres Prentiship* or Nicholas Breton's *Miseries of Mauillia*, we have enough of realistic description and narrative to prove that towards the end of the sixteenth century novelists were beginning to recognize the importance of verisimilitude in fiction.

This approach to realism was undoubtedly facilitated to some extent by the popularity of the picaresque novels of Spain, and particularly of that epoch-making novel, *Lazarillo de Tormes*, which was published in the middle of the sixteenth century. The tendency of writers of the history of fiction, however, has been to exaggerate the influence of the Spanish picaresque novel on the development of English fiction. The greatest of the early realistic novelists that England produced, Thomas Nash, owed little or nothing to the Spanish picaresque novel. Greene and Lodge, again, seem to have been more indebted for the realistic narratives contained in their pamphlets to their own experiences in life and to English "beggar books" like Awdeley's *Fraternity of Vagabonds* and Harman's *Caveat to Common Cursitors* than to a novel like *Lazarillo de Tormes*. And though it is true that some writers of fiction like Henry Chettle, Richard Head, and Francis Kirkman derived much of their inspiration for the realism in their work from the Spanish novels, after all realistic novels were rather the exception than the rule in the sixteenth and seventeenth centuries, and these men were far from being the most gifted exponents of their art that England produced during the two centuries.

The lover of fiction who expects to find in the novels of John Lyly and Sir Philip Sidney much of that real life or true nature which meant so much to Fielding will be disappointed. The influence of Sidney and Lyly and that of the spirit which inspired the later artificial romances of chivalry remained a potent factor in shaping the destinies of the novel for a long time. As a matter of fact, English fiction in the seventeenth century has less realism than the fiction of the Elizabethan age. Two of the best known works of fiction that the first quarter of the seventeenth century produced, Lady Mary Wroth's *Urania* and John Barclay's *Argenis*, are entirely romantic; the first, a pale imitation of Sidney's *Arcadia*, while the second, though more lively and interesting, is confessedly an allegorical novel modelled on the earlier romances of chivalry.

About the middle of the seventeenth century the prevailing rage in fiction was the interminable heroic romance of France nourished in the Hôtel de Rambouillet and speedily acclimatized in England through the exertions of literary coteries like those over which Catherine Philips, "the matchless Orinda," and the Duchess of Newcastle presided. The most popular of these "languishing love romances," as Mrs. Barbauld describes them, were the *Cassandre* and *Cléopâtre* of La Calprenède and the *Grand Cyrus*, *Ibrahim*, and *Clélie* of Madeleine de Scudéry. Addison bears witness to their popularity in *The Spectator* when he names five of them as forming part of the fair Leonora's library[1] which has a collection of less than ten novels; and even as late as Fielding's own time the clever Mrs. Charlotte Lennox satirizes their continued vogue with the fair sex in her amusing novel, *The Female Quixote*.

This popularity of La Calprenède and de Scudéry not only resulted in a flood of translations of the French heroic romances, but the second half of the seventeenth century saw the appearance in England of numerous imitations of them. And though occasionally an effort was made to satirize the extravagances of the heroic novelists and the heritage of realism that had

[1] *The Spectator*, No. 37, April 12, 171

been bequeathed to English fiction by Thomas Nash
was handed down to succeeding generations in the
crude efforts made in the picaresque genre by novelists
like Richard Head and Francis Kirkman, the greater
part of the seventeenth century was a period of stag-
nation so far as the progress of realism in English
fiction was concerned. The English heroic novelists
of the seventeenth century waged war against verisimilitude with as much success as their French masters
had done. An able critic of the time of Fielding makes
the following severe but not unfair comment on their
extravagances.

"A deluge of impossibility overflowed the press," says
the anonymous author of *An Essay on the New Species
of Writing Founded by Mr. Fielding*. "Nothing was
received with any kind of applause that did not appear
under the title of a romance or novel; and common
sense was kicked out of doors to make room for
marvellous dullness. The style in all these performances
was to be equal to the subject—amazing. And may be
called with great propriety, 'Prose run mad.' This
obtained a long time. Every beau was an Orondates,
and all the belles were Statiras: Not a *billet doux* but
run in heroics or the most common message deliver'd
but in the sublime."

Indeed, if we turn over the pages of novels like
Roger Boyle's *Parthenissa*, Sir George Mackenzie's
Aretina or the dramatist John Crowne's *Pandion and
Amphigenia*, we shall soon be convinced that these
strictures are far from being too severe. These novelists
make no pretensions whatever to realism. They set
out deliberately to portray a world of glorified passion
and superhuman achievement, and "the soaring pitch"

of their language heightens the unreality of their interminable stories. In spite of the pomp and parade of their story-telling there is little that is really striking in their narratives. The monotony of the constant recurrence of substantially the same kind of adventure in their long drawn out narratives is infinitely fatiguing. This, added to their constant disregard for verisimilitude, the tiresome complexity of the intrigues with which they overload their plots, their frequent digressions of appalling length, and their long soliloquies and sentimental analyses on rigidly conventional lines, produce a kind of paralysis of the main story. Sir Walter Scott is by no means unduly severe when he describes them as "huge folios of inanity over which our ancestors yawned themselves to sleep."[1] There is in them an abundance of what Fielding would call "monsters in lace and embroidery" who strut about as kings and queens, princes and princesses, valiant knights, mysterious strangers and afflicted maidens. They are full of those very faults which one of the writers of them, the dramatist Crowne, condemns severely enough, although he had not the grace to avoid them.   Their authors, Crowne says, "bolster up a crooked invention with fungous words and putrid phrases" and make fiction "an hospital for lame conceits."

It is not at all surprising that an enthusiastic realist like Fielding should be severe on them. It is a relief to turn from them to novels like the *Incognita* of Congreve, *The Fair Jilt* or *Oroonoko* of Mrs. Aphra Behn, or even to *The New Atalantis* of the notorious Mrs. Manley. And when we add to these humbler efforts to evolve a newer type of novel the remarkable work of Fielding's

[1]Scott, *Life of Richardson.*

greatest predecessor in the art of fiction, Daniel Defoe, on whom the honour of being the father of the English novel has been bestowed by many admirers, we are inclined to cavil at his pronouncement regarding the lack of true nature in authors and to remark that his enthusiasm for a closer imitation of real and every-day life in works of fiction betrayed him into the ex-pression of an opinion that does less than justice to some of his contemporaries and immediate prede-cessors.

While it is true that Defoe is inferior to Fielding in many respects, particularly in skill in the construction of his plots and in the development of character, the elder novelist's realism is little less convincing than that of Fielding, whether it is attained through the exercise of his wonderful power of "lying like truth," as in *Robinson Crusoe*, or through the vivid portrayal of the underworld of crime and vice in novels like *Moll Flanders*, *Colonel Jack*, or *Roxana*.

To his contemporaries Richardson and Smollett he was less unjust, though it was a great mistake, of course, not to give them any credit for realism, if we are justified at all in assuming that Fielding was also thinking of his great contemporaries when he deplored the absence of true nature in authors. Richardson's choice of the epistolary method was unfortunate so far as the verisimilitude of his novels was concerned. How-ever interesting his plots may be, and however greatly we may be impressed by his knowledge of the human heart, it is impossible for us altogether to ignore the inherent improbability of the kind of letters that Richardson's heroines write. And when in his later novels the industrious printer at Salisbury Court took it upon himself to depict the world of fashion, the strange beings that he created were utterly unlike the men and women of the fashionable world of his own or of any time. A strange perversity of choice led him to confine his attention in his later novels to a class of people of whom he knew very little. Richardson's *Clarissa Harlowe* and *Sir Charles Grandison* fully vindicate the soundness of Fielding's contention that "a true knowledge of the world is gained only by conversation, and the manners of every rank must be seen in order to be known."[1]

As a realist, Smollett came closer to Fielding's ideal than Richardson did. His heroes, abandoned rascals as most of them are, have much more of "the stuff of life" in them than a hero like Richardson's Sir Charles Grandison has. His heroines are as charming as they are human, and his sailors are among the most interesting realistic characters that are to be found in eighteenth century fiction. Again, like Fielding the Scotch novelist has a very quick eye for the eccentricities and foibles of men; and in so far as the description of them reveals the inner man, Smollett is a portrayer of character. But Fielding's Scotch rival was pre-eminently a humourist in the wider as well as the Elizabethan acceptance of the term, "a describer of the eccentricities of human life," as Hazlitt calls him. His realism, splendid as it is in certain parts of his novels, is less convincing on the whole than that of Fielding or Defoe.

Fielding is first and foremost an observer of character. He observes and portrays the idiosyncrasies of men and women not only because they appeal to his sense of humour, but also because they reveal character.

[1] *Tom Jones*, Book XIV, Chap. I.

Peculiarities that are merely external, or those that are the result of accidental circumstances, have not that importance in his eyes that real idiosyncrasies of character have. It is character in all its shades that he is interested in primarily.

To the task that he set himself of portraying real life he brought all the resources of an extraordinarily gifted, practical genius which refused even momentarily to lose touch with the living world around him, which kept him constantly alert to receive and treasure up impressions of everything that was likely to add to his knowledge of human nature and of the motives of human action, and which led him to try to bring within his field of observation every region of life so that his knowledge might be as full and perfect as it is given to man to make it. The memorable words in which Dryden pays his fine tribute to the genius of Shakespeare may, without disparagement to the greatest of all observers of human life, be applied to Fielding, if we leave the superlatives out. His soul was large and comprehensive. All the images of nature were still present to him, and he drew them, not laboriously, but luckily; when he describes anything, you more than see it, you feel it too.

And it was in the fitness of things that such powers should find ample scope for exercise. Fielding had exceptional opportunities in life of developing his great natural gifts. His was a life of many vicissitudes, and it was in the course of his varied experiences that he acquired that wonderful knowledge of human nature which he reveals in his writings and which makes them so unique. The ancient family to which he belonged, his education at Eton and his school friendships

made it possible for him to gain that first-hand knowledge of the ways of "high" life which was such a great
asset to him in his work. But quite early in life the
increasing financial difficulties of his spendthrift
father, Colonel Edmund Fielding, gave him a taste of
poverty and threw him among all sorts and conditions
of men. Much of that intimate knowledge of the seamy
side of life of which he gives us such constant indications in his works must have been acquired when he
was earning a precarious livelihood in London and
tasting the joys of life with that unique relish to which
his cousin, Lady Mary Montagu, bears witness. He
fully realized that these experiences had played a very
important part in developing his powers and making
them so productive. More than once in his writings he
lays stress on what may appear to us to be a truth that
is obvious enough—that a real knowledge of the world
can be gained only by familiar intercourse with that
world. "No author," he says in *Tom Jones*, "ought to
write anything besides dictionaries and spelling books
who is not admitted behind the scenes of this great
theatre of nature."[1]

The practical temper which characterized his age
and which was such a conspicuous feature of his genius
helped him to collect the right materials for his work
and to make the best use of them. He observed the
deficiencies in the plots of the novels written by his
predecessors and he carefully prepared more perfect
designs for the edifices of his art. But his indebtedness
to his literary predecessors is small compared to what
he owed to the experiences of his own life and to the
world around him. It is a great tribute to the originality

[1] *Tom Jones*, Book VII, Chap. I.

of his genius and the realism of his art that his critics
seek the originals of his characters and the sources of
his plots with their wonderful wealth of incident not
so much in the works of the poets, dramatists, character
writers, satirists, and journalists who preceded him, as
in the people, the manners, and the events of the times
in which he lived. As Garrick said in the course of a
tribute paid to him shortly after his death—Nature
prompted him and he wrote.

CHAPTER II

BEGINNINGS OF LITERARY CAREER
EARLY DRAMATIC ADVENTURES

AMONG the earliest efforts at literary composition made by Fielding that have survived are two satires in verse. The first of these, a burlesque modernization of part of Juvenal's *Sixth Satire*, afterwards revised and published in the *Miscellanies* of 1743, is a somewhat rambling performance of a kind that is to be expected from a young man who has a scholar's taste for classical poetry which was doubtless acquired at Eton, where he had worshipped, as he tells us in *Tom Jones*,[1] with true Spartan devotion at "the birchen altar" of Learning. The poem was the outcome of a love affair with one Miss Sarah Andrew, an heiress of Lyme Regis, with whom he seems to have meditated an elopement which, however, was prevented by the vigilance of the young lady's guardian. It was originally sketched, as Fielding tells us in his Preface to the *Miscellanies*, before he was twenty, and "was all the revenge taken by an injured lover."

The other early effort, *The Masquerade*, probably the first of his published works, appeared during the last week of January, 1728.[2] It is an indictment in Hudibrastic verse of a form of amusement on which Fielding was particularly severe throughout his life. The verses were "inscribed" to Count Heidegger, re-

[1] *Tom Jones*, Book XIII, Chap. I.
[2] *The Craftsman*, January 27, 1728.

14

nowned in his day for his ugliness which Hogarth has immortalized, and for his skill in organizing the notorious masquerades of the time. The young satirist heaps abuse in unstinted measure on this gifted purveyor of the revelry and licence of the time, and the poem, which describes the author's impressions of a masquerade which he had attended "in the strange habit of a bard," has little to recommend it either in felicity of expression or raciness of satire.

These pieces were *jeux d'esprit*, and in 1728 Fielding did not depend upon his literary labours for his livelihood; and though he produced his first play soon after the publication of *The Masquerade*, it was not until 1730, after he had returned to London from Leyden, that he made any serious effort to earn his living by writing for the stage. His career at the University of Leyden, where he had continued the classical studies of his younger days with a remarkable application, if we are to believe his first biographer, Arthur Murphy,[1] came to an untimely end because funds were not available. But this did not prevent his father from "settling" an allowance of £200 a year on him which "anybody might pay who would." As a matter of fact, on his return to London he was forced, as he said with his usual good humour, to choose between the alternatives of becoming either a hackney coachman or a hackney writer. And the success which attended his first dramatic effort encouraged him to try his fortune as a playwright.

He made his début in the dramatic world under the auspices of the great masters of the Restoration comedy.

[1] "An Essay on the Life and Genius of Henry Fielding, Esq.," prefixed to Murphy's Edition of Fielding's Works. 1762.

As a follower of Wycherley and Congreve he introduces into his comedies many of the types that had now become more or less conventional in the established tradition of the Comedy of Manners. We have men of wit and fashion about town whose main business in life is "the undivided pursuit of lawless gallantry." We have women of various degrees of respectability, and sometimes of none, who wear their elegance as part of their dress, and who are quite willing, and more than willing, to be pursued by such gallants. We have rakes whose chief occupation in life is gambling, drinking, or swindling. We have aristocratic roués and their minions; coxcombs of different varieties and ranks, and prudes; young men from the country with more money than brains, whose one ambition in life is to be known in the gay world as men of wit and fashion; a number of good young women; a few Wisemores, Worthies, Constants, and Heartfrees; staid city men whose wives make dupes and something worse of them. These characters are familiar to us in the Restoration comedy.

And yet it is worthy of note that even in the earliest years of his dramatic life, when the influence of Wycherley and Congreve was supreme, when his powers were immature and his experience of life more or less limited, he was successful in creating characters that are very far from being wooden imitations of the types that make their appearance in the Comedy of Manners. Even when he preserves the outlines of the conventional type, there is often so much of real life in the character that the admirer of Fielding has a delightful foretaste of his more mature powers.

In his earliest attempts at portraying character he

attains a certain measure of success. We have some striking portraits in his early comedies which every admirer of his genius ought to study. We must bear in mind while we criticize these early portraits that Fielding was barely twenty years old when he commenced his dramatic career. His first play, *Love in Several Masques*, produced at the Theatre Royal in Drury Lane in February, 1728,[1] was well received, though it was contemporary with *The Beggar's Opera*, which "engrossed the whole talk and admiration of the town," and had succeeded *The Provok'd Husband*, another successful play which the great Vanbrugh had left unfinished, but to which Colley Cibber had added the last act.

Love in Several Masques has something of the sprightliness that characterizes the work of Wycherley and Congreve. Fielding follows the elder dramatists rather closely; and yet in one or two of his characters he shows his own hand clearly and effectively enough. In Sir Positive Trap he gives us an excellent portrait of the pigheaded country gentleman "made up of avarice, folly, an ill-bred surliness of temper, and an odd fantastic pride built on the antiquity of his family." The very lively touches by means of which the dramatist makes the picture more or less his own, as for example, Sir Positive's habit of referring eternally to the noble and ancient family of the Traps, his objection to dancing because it "begets warmth which is the parent of wantonness," his enthusiasm for "the good old English art of clear-starching" give a refreshing liveliness and piquancy to the portrait. We have another good portrait in the same play, that of "the empty,

[1] *The Daily Post*, February 16, 1728; *The Craftsman*, February 24, 1728.

gaudy, nameless thing," Lord Formal, who has made
the important discovery that reading vastly impairs the
lustre of his eyes and who on a "day of business" rides
down two brace of chairmen in paying his morning
visits to milliners, perfumers and fan shops, much to
the detriment of his complexion. This kind of satire,
however, directed against the inanity of the gilded and
perfumed fop, was not a new thing in dramatic literature, and Fielding's indebtedness to the elder dramatists in such portraits as these was very great indeed.

His second play, *The Temple Beau*, produced in
January, 1730, at the theatre in Goodman's Fields,
has some lively scenes though the plot is far from being
original. In Lady Gravely Fielding gives us his first
picture of a prude, a type of character that was destined
to engage much of his attention in later life. The other
characters in the play are more or less conventional,
with the exception perhaps of Young Pedant, the
bookworm, for whom the dramatist has evidently a
soft corner in his heart though he makes us laugh
heartily at his eccentricities. The best scenes in the play
are those in which we have glimpses into the young
Templar's ways of life, and Genest apparently had
these scenes in his mind when he pronounced *The Temple
Beau* to be equal to *The Miser* and superior to any other
play that Fielding has written.[1]

The Temple Beau, however, did not add much to
Fielding's fame as a dramatist, though it would be a
mistake to describe its production as a failure. Genest
tells us that it had a run of eleven nights and this,
after all, is not a bad record.[2]

[1]Genest, *Some Account of the English Stage*, Vol. III, pp. 275, 276.
[2]*Ibid.*

Fielding's next play, *The Author's Farce*, first produced at the New or Little Theatre in the Haymarket on
the 30th of March, 1730,[1] and afterwards revived "with
great additions and a new prologue and epilogue," as
the playbills announced, in Drury Lane in January,
1734, is something of a landmark in his literary career.
The play is in many respects a typical product of his
genius. In *The Author's Farce* he confines his attention
altogether to the real world around him and particularly to that part of it of which he had gained by this
time a good deal of rather unpleasant experience.
There is much in the character of the reckless, impecunious, and irrepressible hero of the farce that is
undoubtedly reminiscent of Fielding himself in the
early years of his dramatic career when, according to
a contemporary satirist, on the lean days he would
"appear rough, clad in coarse frieze and plastered down
with snuff," and shine forth on the prosperous ones in
such "gaudy instant trappings" that his friends would
find it difficult to recognize the playhouse bard in his
fine feathers.

The farce is a curious medley, but the plot is interesting and has more originality than he had hitherto
exhibited in his other works. The pictures that are given
in the play of the drudgery to which literary hacks
were condemned in Fielding's day are as interesting as
they are amusing. The scenes that describe the experiences of Luckless, the author, with the arbiters of his
destiny, who in the later version of the play appear as
Marplay Senior and Marplay Junior, or those others
that show us the wretched Dash, Blotpage, and
Quibble writing in the room in Bookweight the

[1] *The Daily Post*, March 26, 1730.

bookseller's house, are obviously taken directly from life.

Apart from the pictures given in the play of the many buffets of fortune that the impecunious tribe of playwrights and literary hacks generally had to undergo, the play is of special interest to us because Fielding more than once directs his satire against some well-known people of his time. The most notable of these attacks is that made on the Cibbers. Here we have the beginnings of a feud which on Fielding's side was pursued with relentless vigour almost as long as he had any strength left in him to carry it on. Apparently Colley Cibber had already incurred his displeasure, and the drift of the satire in this play enables us to guess the cause. In the first version of the farce he attacked both Cibber and Wilks in the characters of Marplay and Sparkish, comedians, but the "slight pique" against the latter of which he speaks some years afterwards in his Preface to the *Miscellanies* having worn off, Sparkish in the final version of the play makes room for Marplay Junior, the younger Cibber. In more than one scene in the play we have interesting glimpses into the relations between the needy playwright and his masters, the actor managers, between young Fielding struggling hard for recognition and a subsistence and his patrons, the Cibbers. The interview described in the sixth scene of the first act is evidently typical of what happened frequently.

"I have a tragedy for your house, Mr. Marplay," says Luckless.

Mr. Marplay, Junior, apparently speaking on behalf of his father replies, "Ha! if you will send it to me, I will give you my opinion of it; and if I can make any alterations in it that will be for its advantage, I will do it freely."

And in his expansive mood he vouchsafes interesting information to the wretched playwright.

"My father and I, sir," he says, "are a couple of poetical tailors. When a play is brought us, we consider it as a tailor does his coat: we cut it, sir—we cut it; and let me tell you, we have the exact measure of the town; we know how to fit their taste"—and much more in the same strain till his chair is brought to the door and he goes out, singing.

The latter part of this medley in which the hero's puppet-show is rehearsed is not so original as the first part. The election of an arch poet or poet laureate to the Goddess of Nonsense is declared in the final version of the play to be the chief business of the plot of the puppet-show, and this points to some inspiration received from Dryden's *Mac Flecknoe*; while the idea of a play within a play is perhaps borrowed from *The Rehearsal*. The puppet-show is named the Pleasures of the Town and in this part of the farce the dramatist ridicules the prevailing rage for pantomime, farce, and opera which John Rich at the theatre in Lincoln's Inn Fields and Handel at the Opera House in the Haymarket were feeding so sumptuously. Fielding hits out rather recklessly and indiscriminately. The notorious "Orator" Henley of Clare Market fame, Walpole's protégé and henchman and afterwards editor of *The Hyp Doctor*, Samuel Johnson, the author of *Hurlothrumbo*, and Eliza Haywood the novelist among others come in for a share of the dramatist's attentions. Attacks such as these doubtless laid the foundations of some of those bitter animosities which were destined to pursue Fielding throughout his life. Eliza Haywood, for example, speaks most bitterly of him many years afterwards in her novel, *The History of Miss Betsy Thoughtless*.

Fielding's next dramatic effort was a burlesque in two acts called *Tom Thumb, a Tragedy*, which was first put on the stage in the Little Theatre in the Haymarket as an afterpiece to *The Author's Farce* on the 24th of April, 1730.[1] It was very well received from the beginning. We have evidence of this in the paragraphs that appear in *The Grub-Street Journal* describing good houses, the presence of the Prince of Wales among the audience, and the jealousy of an unsuccessful poet against the author. The play had a long and successful run of at least thirty-seven nights, to which the publisher, John Roberts of Warwick Lane, bears witness in his advertisement[2] of the second edition of the original version, which was issued in less than two months after the first performance. This success encouraged Fielding to enlarge his original two-act burlesque and put it on the stage again in 1731. This version of the play, in three acts, contained a number of new characters and episodes and was named *The Tragedy of Tragedies, or The Life and Death of Tom Thumb the Great*.

Tom Thumb is the most notable of Fielding's dramatic efforts, though its first success, great as it was, was not quite as remarkable as that of *Pasquin*. This piece, however, possesses what the political plays do not, an interest quite independent of local historical fact. Its popularity was great and abiding enough to enable it to hold its own ground against the success of later

[1] *The Daily Post*, April 23, 1730.   [2] *The Craftsman*, June 20, 1730.

plays of the same class like Carey's *Chrononhoton-thologos* and Sheridan's *Critic*. In fact *Tom Thumb* was one of the few plays of Fielding which survived him on the stage, and it so far won immortality that it was described in 1855 as still holding the stage.

The play certainly deserved its success, and Austin Dobson's verdict that it is one of the best burlesques ever written is very far from being a too favourable one. It is an advance on *The Rehearsal*, the most notable of its predecessors in the same line, not only in the wider range of its satire, but also in its raciness and piquancy. The many extravagances of the heroic dramatists are ridiculed with a satiric power and ingenuity that appear to be inexhaustible, and there is hardly a line in the play that does not make an effective hit at the bombast and rant in the mighty lines of Dryden, Banks, Lee, Thomson, and other exponents of the heroic drama. From the opening rhapsody of the courtier, Doodle, on the auspicious day of Tom Thumb's triumph, a day on which "all nature wears one universal grin," to the last words in the play in which the dying king likens the tremendous debacle at the end to the kings, queens, and knaves in a pack of cards throwing each other down "till the whole pack lies scatter'd and o'erthrown," we have a rich succession of burlesque declamations, heroic outbursts of tragic or tender passion, and mock heroic similes, and for almost every line of this Fielding refers us to a passage in some heroic tragedy well known to the playgoers of his time. One or two examples will illustrate the effectiveness and piquancy of his satire and the richness of his humour.

The Queen, Dollallolla, has a few words with the

King when the latter proposes to bestow the Princess Huncamunca on Tom Thumb.

QUEEN. Though greater yet his boasted merit was,
　　　He shall not have my daughter, that is pos'.
KING.　Ha! Sayst thou, Dollallolla?
QUEEN. I say he shan't.
KING.　Then by our royal self we swear you lie.
QUEEN. Who but a dog, who but a dog
　　　Would use me as thou dost? Me, who have lain
　　　These twenty years so loving by thy side!
　　　But I will be revenged. I'll hang myself.
　　　Then tremble all who did this match persuade,
　　　For, riding on a cat, from high I'll fall,
　　　And squirt down royal vengeance on you all.
FOODLE (a Courtier). Her majesty the queen is in a passion.[1]

To this Fielding adds the following note by way of comment :

"An information very like this we have in the tragedy of Love where, Cyrus having stormed in the most violent manner, Cyaxares observes very calmly,

　　　Why, nephew Cyrus, you are moved."

Another characteristic note, on one of the opening lines of the play, "The mighty Thomas Thumb victorious comes," gives us the following information:

"Dr. B—y reads, The mighty Tall-mast Thumb. Mr. D—s, The mighty Thumbing Thumb. Mr. T—d reads, Thundering. I think Thomas more agreeable to the great simplicity so apparent in our author."

Or consider the following as an example of the dramatist's mock heroic similes. The choleric Lord Grizzle driven to rebellion by jealousy meets his fate

[1] *The Life and Death of Tom Thumb the Great*, Act I, Sc. iii.

on the battlefield and expires with the following
soliloquy,

> But, ha! I feel death rumbling in my brains:
> Some kinder sprite knocks softly at my soul,
> And gently whispers it to haste away.
> I come, I come, most willingly I come.
>   So when some city wife, for country air,
> To Hampstead or to Highgate does repair,
> Her to make haste her husband does implore,
> And cries, "My dear, the coach is at the door":
> With equal wish, desirous to be gone,
> She gets into the coach, and then she cries—"Drive on!"[1]

But it is impossible to convey an adequate idea of the
merits of this burlesque by merely quoting passages
from it. The admirer of Fielding's remarkable gifts
for satire should read not only the play itself, but the
notes which he appended to the later enlarged version
of the play in which he ridicules with many a bright
sally of genial wit the pedantry of some of the learned
scholars of his time.

Besides adding these notes to the revised version
of the play, Fielding altered the earlier version from
beginning to end. It is in the earlier version that the
ghost of Tom Thumb is killed by Lord Grizzle, an
incident which moved the great Swift to laughter for
the second time in his life, as Mrs. Laetitia Pilkington
tells us in her *Memoirs*[2]. Among other alterations made
in the play in the final version, this incident of the
killing of Tom Thumb's ghost was omitted in deference to the wishes of some critics, and the hero's ghost
was replaced by that of his father which appears in the

[1] *The Life and Death of Tom Thumb the Great*, Act III, Sc. ix.
[2] *Memoirs of Mrs. Laetitia Pilkington*, written by Herself, London, 1754
vol. III, p. 155.

third act of the play to make solemn announcements of
great dangers impending in accordance with the
established tragic conventions. But the play is poorer
for this change.

Tom Thumb and The Author's Farce had an exceptional
run on the stage, and Fielding took advantage of this
popularity that he had earned to bring out a comedy in
which he tried more serious satire than he had hitherto
done in any of his plays. The new comedy was originally named Rape, upon Rape, or The Justice Caught in his
own Trap, but the first title having given offence, it
was afterwards changed to The Coffee-House Politician.
The play was first put on the stage in the Little Theatre
in the Haymarket in June, 1730.[1]

The dramatist declares in his prologue that his
muse's endeavour now is to "combat vice cloth'd with
pow'r," and in this play we have the first glimpse of
Fielding the reformer. It is somewhat curious that he
should select as the first objective of his serious satire
the notoriously corrupt practices of the "trading justice,"
an office which he was to fill himself in his later life.
The character that gives the play its first title, that of
the dabbler in politics who neglects his own concerns
entirely in order to pursue his hobby, the original of
which Fielding doubtless found in Addison's excellent
picture of the political upholsterer in The Tatler, is
thrown more or less into the background by the more
striking and aggressive personality of Justice Squeezum.

As a comedy The Coffee-House Politician is in some
respects an advance on its predecessors. The plot
seems to have greater vigour in it, though in the matter
of the character sketches there is not much to choose

[1] The Craftsman, June 20, 1730.

between this and the earlier comedies. If the portrait of Squeezum makes a greater impression it is because it is painted more directly from life and owes less to the characters of the elder comedy.

And yet it can hardly be denied that Fielding allowed the spirit of satire to carry him too far in the accounts that he gives us of Squeezum's conduct. The travesty of justice made by Squeezum in some of the scenes in the play is too monstrous to be quite true to life. But while one feels that in these pictures the limits of probability are strained too much, one recognizes at the same time that the frailties and vices that the dramatist castigates are real enough, and it is because they are so that some of his portraits in these early comedies deserve more attention than they have received.

The stage history of *The Coffee-House Politician* was an unfortunate one. The first performance of the comedy had to be postponed for a week on account of the indisposition of one of the principal actors in the Little Theatre, and then after a brief run it had to be withdrawn temporarily because the actor was ill again.

In 1731, besides the enlarged version of *Tom Thumb*, Fielding produced two other plays at the Little Theatre in the Harymaket. These appear to have been written under the pressure of want, and Fielding apparently did not give as much time and thought to them as he had done to earlier plays like *The Temple Beau* or *The Author's Farce*. The first of these, *The Letter Writers, or A New Way to Keep a Wife at Home*, was a farce in three acts apparently written in haste to provide the Little Theatre with an afterpiece to *Tom Thumb*. It was produced in March.[1]

[1] *The Daily Post*, March 23, 1731.

In *The Letter Writers* we have practically all the usual features of the typical Restoration comedy faithfully reproduced—the staid city men duped by their handsome young wives and their gallants; the usual assignations, surprises and the resort to the closet with the resulting complications. In fact, the only spark of originality in the play is found in the portrait of Jack Commons, the university rake; otherwise it is more or less an echo of Vanbrugh's *Confederacy*, and the resemblances between the characters and the main action in the two plays seem to be much too close to be quite accidental. A play like this was not likely to be a success, and it had to be withdrawn after the fifth performance. Its place as an afterpiece to *Tom Thumb* was taken by *The Author's Farce*.

Fielding's next effort demands more of our attention because it is another landmark in his literary career. In *The Grub-Street Opera*, originally named *The Welsh Opera, or The Grey Mare the Better Horse*, produced in April, 1731, at the Little Theatre in the Haymarket, Fielding makes his first incursion into politics. Some of his recent biographers have advanced the view that in *Tom Thumb* he made an attack on Walpole in the mock-heroic picture that he gave of Tom's greatness. Even if the dramatist had the great minister in his mind when he portrayed the hero of his burlesque, the main interest of the piece is anything but political, and it is doubtful if the general public discovered any political allusions in the play.

In *The Welsh Opera*, however, the political references are unmistakable. The plot, such as it is, is a thin disguise, and to audiences in Fielding's days it must have been thinner still. What is most noticeable about the political satire is its audacity, though it must be remembered that Fielding was by no means singular in making almost open onslaughts of this kind on the frailties of the great.

The *Welsh Opera* had a fairly long run and was popular on account of its political references, though Fielding seems to have felt some misgivings in bringing it out and even postponed the first performance, which was announced to take place on the 7th of April, 1731. It first came on the stage as an afterpiece to *Tom Thumb*.[1] Later on it was occasionally put on the stage with *The Fall of Mortimer*, an historical play altered from the *Edward the Third* of Mountfort, in which the story of Mortimer's influence with the Queen Mother during the minority of Edward was made use of to launch out a violent attack on Walpole and Queen Caroline.

The success of the play and the hesitation and delay of the Government in taking action encouraged Fielding to enlarge his original piece considerably. He made many additions to the first act and almost altogether transformed the second and the third. The new version of the play was named *The Grub-Street Opera* to ridicule *The Grub-Street Journal*, which had now commenced its campaign of hostility to Fielding. It was severer on Walpole and the Queen, and among other improvements it contained some new songs, the best of these being the well-known "Roast Beef of Old England."

At first sight *The Grub-Street Opera* appears to be one of the most careless performances of Fielding—a slipshod attempt at stringing together a number of scenes which do not make a very convincing whole. In his introduction to the play, Scriblerus Secundus, a

[1] *The Daily Post*, April 17, 1731.

pseudonym which Fielding had adopted when he
produced *The Author's Farce* and which he had continued to use, makes some significant remarks about his
play. "As for plot, sir," he says, "I had writ an admirable
one; but, having observed that the plot of our English
operas have had no good effect on our audiences, so I
have e'en left it out. For the design, it is deep—very
deep."

What there is of plot in the play is simple and commonplace enough. It turns on the love affairs of men
and women servants in a country gentleman's family,
and particularly on the love affair of Robin and his
sweetheart, Sweetissa. The courses of these love affairs
do not run very smooth because Master Owen, the
son of the squire, who is much too fond of women and
very assiduous in his attentions to the maids in the
house, forges letters to set the lovers by the ears. He
not only succeeds in doing this, but makes the men-
servants quarrel violently. The misunderstandings are,
however, removed in the end.

It is the "design" which is behind this commonplace
story that gives the play its interest. In Sir Owen
Apshinken and his wife the dramatist gives us pictures
of the King and the Queen, satirizing their weaknesses
with as much freedom as he dared. In the character of
Master Owen Fielding portrayed the chief frailty of
the Prince of Wales, his fondness for women, with a
boldness which is characteristic of the times. For
example, when Molly Apshones, young Master Owen's
sweetheart, talks about her lover to her father, the
latter makes revelations to her the real significance of
which would not be lost upon the audience.

"I have heard," says Apshones, "that that gentle

gentleman, when he was at London, rummaged all
the playhouses for mistresses: nay, you yourself have
heard of his pranks in the parish; did he not seduce the
fiddler's daughter? Hath he not made mischief between several men and their wives? And do you not
know that he lusts after every woman he sees, though
the poor wretch does not look as if he was quite come
from nurse yet."[1]

Equally daring is the attack that is made on Walpole.
The butler in Sir Owen's household is given a name
which would leave no room for any doubt as to who
was aimed at. The scene[2] in which we have an account
of the butler Robin's encounter with William the
coachman, in the course of which the would-be combatants hurl abuse at each other, William threatening
to expose Robin's rogueries and thefts while the butler
accuses William of trying to supplant him, is an
effective satire on the quarrels of the great ministers,
and we have it on record that the town "particularly
approved these altercative and scolding scenes."

The play contains many references to current
political events and to the scandals in the private lives
of some of the great men of the time. Poor Robin is
assailed not only as a minister, but his private affairs
are dragged in for satire with a bold and thorough-
going effrontery. The servants in Sir Owen's household,
William the coachman, John the groom and Thomas
the gardener, are easily identified with William Pulteney, John, Lord Hervey, and Thomas Pelham-Holles,
Duke of Newcastle.

It appears that *The Grub-Street Opera* never reached
the stage. Genest suggests that there was a performance

---

[1] *The Grub-Street Opera*, Act II, Sc. i.   [2] *Ibid.*, Act II, Sc. iv.

in July though he does not mention the date; and the title page of the text of the play printed by J. Roberts in 1731 describes it as "acted at the Theatre in *The Haymarket*." The Preface to *The Welsh Opera*, however, tells us that the performance of the revised and enlarged play was "prevented by a certain influence which has been very prevailing of late years"; and advertisements of *The Welsh Opera* which appear in the *Daily Post Boy* and *The St. James's Evening Post* of June 26th, 1731, contain the following note at the end, which seems to indicate that the play was never acted. "This opera," the note says, "is the same as was intended to have been acted with some few additions under the title of *The Grub-Street Opera*, but was suppressed by some secret influence."

During the months of July and August, 1731, as *The Grub-Street Journal*, *The Whitehall Evening Post*, and other papers report, the High Constable, acting on a "presentment" delivered by the Grand Jury for Middlesex to the Court of the King's Bench at Westminster against *The Craftsman*, *Fog's Weekly Journal*, a number of pamphlets against the Government, and the play, *The Fall of Mortimer*, made more than one descent on the Little Theatre in the Haymarket and eventually succeeded in dispersing its company of young comedians. These descents must have prevented the performance of *The Grub-Street Opera*.

Fielding's first incursion into politics as a dramatist, therefore, ended in disaster, and as a result of the Government's attentions, the Little Theatre in the Haymarket was shorn of much of its glory because actors were now shy of appearing on its stage. By the end of the year the performance of plays had become comparatively a rare occurrence at the theatre, and it confined itself for some time to the kinds of entertainment—pantomimes, acrobatic displays, and dancing—which had been its chief attractions in the earlier years of its existence.

In these circumstances the obvious course for Fielding to follow was to make his peace with Wilks and Cibber, the managers of the Theatre Royal in Drury Lane, if he was to continue his dramatic career. And hitherto he had met with so much success that no thought of abandoning that career had yet entered his mind. As a matter of fact his breach with the authorities in Drury Lane had not been a very serious one. The "slight pique" against Wilks of which he speaks in his Preface to the *Miscellanies* of 1743 had already worn off, and Colley Cibber was not implacable. We have evidence of this in an advertisement in *The Craftsman* of the 8th of May, 1731, of a benefit night for Fielding on the 10th of May, on which both Wilks and Cibber appeared in Vanbrugh's *Relapse*. Before the end of the year Fielding had decided to throw in his lot with the authorities of the Theatre Royal. At the same time many of the actors who had been appearing in his farces in the Little Theatre came to Drury Lane with him.

CHAPTER III

TRIUMPHS AND REVERSES AS A PLAYWRIGHT
THE LICENSING ACT

FIELDING commenced his new career at Drury Lane with a farce called *The Lottery*, which was put on the stage on the first night of the new year. *The Lottery* is a bright little piece with some lively dialogue, an attractive heroine to whom Miss Raftor, afterwards the celebrated Mrs. Clive, did full justice, and an amusing if somewhat dubious *dénouement*. Chloe, the heroine of *The Lottery*, is an enterprising young lady who comes up to town and conducts herself as if she had already won a prize of £10,000 in a lottery. She soon gets a scoundrel for a husband on the strength of her imaginary fortune, but he resigns her with great goodwill to her lover as soon as he discovers his mistake about her fortune.

The story is amusing enough. But Fielding had a serious purpose in his mind when he wrote *The Lottery*, and this is brought home to us when we consider the change he made in a later version of the play. This change consisted of the addition of a graphic scene in which he exposed the scandals of the lotteries which were so popular at this time. This scene is laid in Guildhall, and all the paraphernalia of the state lotteries of the time—the wheel, the commissioners, the clerks, etc.—together with the victims of this form of licensed swindling are introduced into the play. The satire, of

34

course, is directed against the gross abuses connected with these lotteries which the Parliament countenanced as a means of raising revenue. The prizes in these lotteries had a curious way of going to someone connected with the Court or "to a lady in Germany." The scene to which we have referred, which shows the majority of the ticket holders drawing blanks, must have been a very effective exposure of the scandal. As a matter of fact, the tickets in these lotteries were usually first bought up by stockjobbers, and these people sold them to the general public, making large profits on them and practising with impunity all kinds of rogueries on their victims. In his play Fielding gives us a realistic picture of a stockjobber and shows up in a number of good scenes the sharp practices of these gentry.

The farce was a popular one as much on account of its main theme, which was of special interest to the public at the time, as for its own merits. Before the end of the year three editions of the play were issued by booksellers. Its career on the stage was a comparatively short one, though for "a trifle," as Genest calls it, twelve performances were not a bad record after all.

Fielding's next play was a much more ambitious effort. For a considerable length of time he apparently had with him a full-length comedy on which he seems to have bestowed much care and thought. About the middle of September, 1730, *The Craftsman* had announced a comedy from his pen which was supposed "to bear a great reputation." But for some reason or other Fielding had not put it on the stage, and the delay in doing this was a long one. From a letter written by

Fielding to Lady Mary Montagu probably in September, 1730, the extant fragment of which was first published in 1803 in Dallaway's edition of Lady Mary's *Works*[1], it appears that he submitted his play to his cousin for her opinion soon after he had finished it. *The Craftsman's* announcement seems to point to the fact that the play was being circulated privately among friends.

Fielding seems to have made no attempt to produce the play during the whole of the year 1731 in spite of the fact that Lady Mary had approved of it. Probably after his unfortunate experience of the career of his last comedy, *The Coffee-House Politician*, on the stage of the Little Theatre, he had felt that the company at that theatre would not be able to do justice to a full-length comedy, and this may have led him to put aside *The Modern Husband* and to continue his dramatic career with farces. The company at Drury Lane, which was now strengthened by some of the best actors from the Little Theatre, offered a splendid opportunity to the dramatist, and this apparently determined him to try his fortune with his comedy, though he seems to have felt some misgivings about its reception as the words of the prologue to the play indicate. It was put on the stage about the middle of February, and the hisses with which it was received on its first night showed that if Fielding had any misgivings, they were well founded. In spite of this unfavourable reception, however, the play continued to be put on the stage at Drury Lane, and was actually acted fourteen times before it was withdrawn. It was a complete failure,

[1] *The Works of the Right Honourable Lady Mary Wortley Montagu, including Her Correspondence, Poems, and Essays*, London, 1803, Vol. I, p. 108.

though the company that acted it was a very good one, including as it did the Cibbers, Wilks, Mullart, Mrs. Cibber, and Mrs. Charke, in fact, the best actors and actresses of the time.

It is much to the credit of the audience that the chief objection to the play was to the sordid scenes in which Fielding dwells on his main theme, the selling of the wife, Mrs. Modern, to the noble voluptuary, Lord Richly, by the husband. The woman who plays her part so willingly in the sordid affair, the husband who helps her without any hesitation to degrade herself to the lowest depths, the rich voluptuary who is so thoroughly convinced that every woman has her price and acts accordingly, are all portrayed with a realism which is as ugly as it is unsparing. Fielding tries to justify his repulsive portraits by laying special emphasis on his moral purpose. He tells us in his prologue to the play that his object is to show how detestable "modern vice" is, and that

> At length, repenting frolic flights of youth,
> Once more he flies to nature and to truth.

This claim is made good to some extent in the pictures that he gives in his play of some of the worst evils in society; and though some of the characters in *The Modern Husband* bear a close resemblance to the gallants and men of fashion who make their appearance in the Restoration comedy, unlike the elder dramatists, Fielding does not set out to create an unreal world, that "Utopia of gallantry" which Lamb describes so well, in which the characters are "mere sports of a witty fancy." It was his unsparing and sordid realism that turned his audience against him. He was accused of over-stepping the bounds of decency, and the question that arises is whether his moral purpose justified him in representing evil in all its loathsome deform i

Even if from the moralist's point of view we hesitate to condemn the play altogether, there can be little doubt that as a work of art, and particularly of dramatic art, it was a mistake. *The Grub-Street Journal* was not very far out when, in pronouncing judgment, it pointed out that "no poet ought to rake into human nature and compound characters from the excesses of each of our passions or the intemperance of some of our humours in order to entertain his audience with something new."[1]

Fielding's next ventures as a playwright were also unfortunate. Two plays from his prolific pen, *The Old Debauchees* and *The Covent Garden Tragedy*, were put on the stage together on the 1st of June, 1732.[2] Both efforts were unworthy of his genius, though the first was not such an outrageous performance as the second. The failure of *The Modern Husband* apparently had not been a lesson to Fielding to deter him from offending against good taste.

The Old Debauchees, however, is not a particularly objectionable play on the whole, though the subject and the treatment of it are not what they should be. Some of the more sober among the contemporaries of Fielding, dramatists like George Lillo or Colley Cibber, for example, would have hesitated to handle such a theme. But Fielding felt no such hesitation. The sensation created by the trial of a Jesuit priest named Girard

---

[1] *The Grub-Street Journal*, March 30, 1732.
[2] *The Daily Post*, May 31, and June 1, 1732.

of Toulon who was accused of practising sorcery on a
beautiful girl named Catherine Cadière in order to
seduce her had, according to the newspapers of the
time, nearly subsided when Fielding decided to try
his hand on the subject. The revelations made at the
trial of the priest had been taken full advantage of by
the newspapers, pamphlet writers, "engravers and
drawers" of the time. Before *The Old Debauchees* was
produced an anonymous ballad opera on the subject
named *The Wanton Jesuit* had been performed at the
Little Theatre in the Haymarket.

Fielding now turned to this popular subject and
tried to revive and increase its popularity by laying
Molière's *Tartuffe* under contribution to embellish
the story. The result was, in the words of Genest, "a
pretty good comedy in three acts"[1] which met with
some success on the stage though the newspaper press
was inclined to look askance at it. *The Grub-Street
Journal* described it as "the most coarse, vicious, insipid
trumpery that ever was hatched."[2]

The Old Debauchees, however, is a clever and witty
play, though the language is intemperate and coarse.
The jest in the effective climax of the plot, the exposure
of an amorous priest by means of a clever trap laid for
him, is very far from being original; but the plot itself
and its climax are handled skilfully. The satire against
the wiles of priestcraft and sacerdotal corruption is
scathing, but probably Fielding's audience did not
find it difficult to forgive him for this. The coarseness
of the language was more difficult to forgive, and the
modern reader of the play will probably feel that the

---

[1] J. Genest, *Some Account of the English Stage*, vol. III, p. 335.
[2] *The Grub-Street Journal*, July 20, 1732.

audience was not too severe on the dramatist when it
signified its disapproval of such language.

Among the characters in the play we have good portraits of repentant and unrepentant sinners in the priest-
ridden Jourdain, the father of the charming heroine of
the play, and in the unregenerate old debauchee, Laroon.

The companion piece to *The Old Debauchees*, *The
Covent Garden Tragedy*, met with a more complete and
more deserved failure on the stage. The play is ostensibly a burlesque of Ambrose Philips' *Distrest Mother*, a
tragedy of no great merit so closely modelled on
Racine's *Andromaque* as to be almost a translation.

This burlesque is greatly inferior to *Tom Thumb*.
Fielding made a great mistake when he chose the underworld of brothels as the scene of his mock heroic
action. In doing this he dragged his art down to the
lowest depths of degradation, and it is no wonder that
his audience revolted against this kind of prostitution
of the drama. *The Covent Garden Tragedy* was damned
very thoroughly and had to be withdrawn. *The Grub-
Street Journal*, in speaking of the performances of *The
Old Debauchees* and *The Covent Garden Tragedy*, says
that the plays were greeted with "the universal detesta-
tion of the town,"[1] and this was quite true so far as
The Covent Garden Tragedy was concerned.

Apart from the fact that the play reflects no credit
on Fielding's taste, *The Covent Garden Tragedy* is anything but a great burlesque. In his sarcastic prolegomena to the piece in which Fielding tried to have his
fling at his enemies who had attacked him in *The Grub-
Street Journal*, he tells us that his principal characters,
Lovegirlo, Captain Bilkum, Kissinda, and Stormandra,

[1] *The Grub-Street Journal*, July 20, 1732.

are imitations of Pyrrhus, Orestes, Andromache, and
Hermione of *The Distrest Mother*. The satirist, however,
was rather unfortunate in his choice of the play on
which he based his burlesque. *The Distrest Mother*,
though by no means a great play, is not absurd enough
either in the action or the style to make a very satisfactory butt for the satirist. And though in the story of the
relations between his Lovegirlo and Kissinda, Stormandra and Captain Bilkum, Fielding ridicules the
romantic story of Pyrrhus' infatuation for Andromache
and Orestes' love for Hermione as related in *The Distrest Mother*, in other respects Fielding's play goes rather
wide of its mark. He makes little effort to parody the
rant and the high-flown sentiment of *The Distrest
Mother*, but seems to be more anxious to rake up some
of the scandals of the day for satire.

The Covent Garden Tragedy lowered Fielding in the
estimation of the public even more than *The Modern
Husband* had done. Guilty as he was of a serious offence
against good taste in his choice of characters and scenes
in the play, he probably offended even more by the
coarseness of the language that he used. Even the
epilogue contains expressions that are most unfortunate. The humour that the piece contains, even the
effective jest of Lovegirlo's tragic wound turning
out to be a wound received by his coat only, and
Stormandra's supposed suicide fizzling out to the
hanging of her gown to the curtains of her bed, cannot
extenuate the dramatist's offence. The few mock heroic
similes that the play contains make a very feeble appeal
on behalf of the dramatist, and the modern reader of the
play and admirer of Fielding's genius wishes that *The
Covent Garden Tragedy* had never been written.

His enemies took full advantage of these excesses
and the promoters of the two plays, *The Old Debau-*
chees and *The Covent Garden Tragedy*, were assailed
from different quarters, *The Grub-Street Journal* leading
the attack. The dramatist and the authorities at Drury
Lane tried to defend themselves by challenging their
accusers to instance passages and scenes which could
be objected to on account of their profaneness or in-
decency; and they even went so far as to make the
astounding plea that "the scene of a bawdy house may
be shown on a stage without shocking the most modest
woman."[1]

But though they attempted to brazen out their
offence, Fielding and his friends seem to have realized
the weakness of their cause. No attempt was made to
put *The Covent Garden Tragedy* on the stage again, and
the dramatist proceeded to prune his *Old Debauchees*
to make it more acceptable to the public, and in this he
seems to have succeeded. He made a special effort to
recover some of the ground he had lost. He worked
hard, and in less than a month after the withdrawal of
The Covent Garden Tragedy its place on the Drury
Lane stage was taken by a clever adaptation of Molière's *Le Médecin malgré lui*.

Fielding's attention seems to have been drawn at this
time to the great French dramatist through a literary
project in which he seems to have had a hand. During
the second half of the year 1732 a series of translations
of Molière's comedies was published by John Watts,
who had brought out many of Fielding's plays, and it is
more than likely that our dramatist was one of the several
gentlemen who, as the advertisements of "the select

[1] *The Daily Post*, July 31, 1732.

collection" announced, "joined and consulted together about every part of it."[1] If, then, he had already tried his hand at the translation of Molière, it could not have been very difficult for him to bring out a good adaptation of one of the plays of the French dramatist in a short time. This new play which he named *The Mock Doctor, or The Dumb Lady Cur'd* is not merely a translation of *Le Médecin malgré lui*, though in his Preface to the play Fielding describes it as such. He worked directly on the orignal and made no use of Lacy's or Mrs. Centlivre's imitations of Molière's play. He introduced some excellent jokes of his own into the piece, and wrote out two or three new scenes to please Miss Raftor who thought her part, that of Gregory's wife Dorcas, too short. In one of these, the thirteenth, he ridiculed, with a humour that is as innocent as it is rich, the pretensions and peculiar ways of Dr. Misaubin of St. Martin's Lane, a notorious French quack, who had already received the attentions of the newspapers of the time and had been introduced by Hogarth into his *Harlot's Progress*. The French physician's "little peel" was specially introduced into the play to ridicule Misaubin's famous specific for all diseases which Fielding also made fun of in his sarcastic dedication of the play to the doctor.

The three-act comedy of Molière is converted into an excellent ballad opera with a liberal sprinkling of songs between the scenes. Fielding is very successful indeed in reproducing in his play the rich humour and the liveliness of his original. The dialogue throughout the play is so natural and so good that one hardly suspects as one reads it that the greater part of it is

[1] *The Grub-Street Journal*, July 6, 1732.

a reproduction of the language of Molière. One very noticeable feature of Fielding's play is that there is much less coarseness in it than in the original. Our dramatist's late experiences had made him careful, and in *The Mock Doctor* he seems to be anxious to avoid the mistakes of the past. The play succeeded on the stage on its own merits, though the enemies of Fielding tried to make out that its success was due altogether to the excellence of the acting. Theophilus Cibber and Miss Raftor indeed did full justice to the principal parts, those of Gregory and his wife Dorcas, the Sganarelle and Martine of the original, and Fielding acknowledges this in his Preface to the published version of the play.

This success encouraged Fielding to turn to Molière again for his theme. *The Miser*, an adaptation of *L'Avare*, was put on the Drury Lane stage about the middle of February, 1733,[1] and this play was even a greater success than *The Mock Doctor* had been. In fact, *The Miser* was the only other play of Fielding besides *Tom Thumb* that continued to be popular on the stage after the novelist's death.

In *The Miser* Fielding allowed himself much more liberty to deviate from his original than he had done in *The Mock Doctor*. The first three scenes of the play are Fielding's own, and throughout the comedy he so often rewrites the scenes of the original completely that *The Miser* is anything but a translation of Molière's comedy. In the advertisements of the play in contemporary newspapers and on the title page it is described as "a comedy *taken* from Plautus and Molière," whereas *The Mock Doctor* had been described as "a comedy *done* from Molière." Fielding introduces some changes in

[1] *The Daily Post*, February 17, 1733.

the *dramatis personæ*, though the principal characters in the two plays are substantially the same. Only, Molière's amiable and charming Marianne becomes a calculating and heartless coquette in Fielding's play.

In *The Miser* the humour and gaiety of Molière are reproduced with the same success as in *The Mock Doctor*. And though the dialogues in the former play are more original, where Fielding does follow Molière he shows the same naturalness and ease in his dialogue that he does in the earlier play. In *The Miser*, again, he leaves out much of the coarse language and indelicate incident and allusion of the original. All these features of the play contributed to its popularity, and its success was so great that it completely outshone the earlier versions of *L'Avare* by Shadwell and Ozell.

Fielding had now recovered much of the ground he had lost in public esteem by his earlier mistakes, and at the time that *The Miser* was at the height of its popularity he put on the stage at Drury Lane a little farce to serve as an afterpiece to *The Miser* for a benefit night to Miss Raftor on the 6th of April, 1733. This piece, called *Deborah, or A Wife for You All*, was apparently written in haste for the benefit performance. It was never published and seems to have been acted only once. The play bills described it as "a new farce of one act by the author of *The Miser*."

After the success that Fielding had gained by his adaptations from Molière he was inclined to rest on his laurels for a while, for during the rest of the year he produced nothing new except the farce named above. In the meanwhile the affairs of the Theatre Royal were approaching a crisis. The three older patentees of the theatre were all gone by the middle of the year 1733. Wilks had died in September, 1732. Booth, who had been ill for some time, had sold half his share in the patent to Highmore; and when he died in May, 1733, Mrs. Booth sold the other half to Henry Giffard, the manager of Goodman's Fields. About the same time Colley Cibber sold his entire share in the patent to Highmore.

These changes left Highmore in control of affairs at Drury Lane. Giffard was busy with his own theatre, and Mrs. Wilks' agent, Ellis, was more or less a nonentity. Highmore and the younger Cibber thoroughly disliked each other, and now that the former was left in control of affairs and was trying to rule with a high hand, Theophilus Cibber, who considered himself ill-used both by his father and Highmore, stirred up a revolt among the actors at Drury Lane. In the autumn of 1733 most of the members of the Drury Lane Company, with the notable exception of Mrs. Clive—the Miss Raftor of other days—and one or two others, left the Theatre Royal under the leadership of the younger Cibber and engaged the Little Theatre in the Haymarket for the ensuing season.

But the revolt of their company was not the only trouble of the authorities at Drury Lane. Rival attractions, and particularly the popularity of operas and a new rage for Italian singing, seemed to threaten Drury Lane with disaster even more than the dissensions among the actors did. There were at this time two rival companies in London drawing crowded houses to operas, Handel's Company at the Opera House under the patronage of the King, and another company at the theatre in Lincoln's Inn Fields which Rich had recently abandoned. To add to these rival attractions,

Rich had started a new playhouse which was called the Theatre Royal, Covent Garden.

On his return to London Fielding made up his mind to throw in his lot with the authorities at Drury Lane. He took up his old play, *The Author's Farce*, again because its main theme and allusions were a very piquant commentary on the state of affairs in the theatrical world in the beginning of the year 1734. By the middle of January he had revised the play and made considerable alterations some of which have been noticed already. The comedian Sparkish of the earlier version of the play now made room for Marplay Junior, as Fielding wanted to have his fling at the younger Cibber who had been the cause of so much trouble at Drury Lane. This he did very effectively in a new scene—the sixth of the first act in the final version—in which we have a very interesting conversation between Luckless the author, his friend Witmore and Mr. Marplay Junior.

With *The Author's Farce* was put on the stage about the middle of January, 1734[1], a new play by Fielding called *The Intriguing Chambermaid*. This was written specially for Mrs. Clive who was now the most prominent member of the company acting at Drury Lane. In an epistle prefixed to the published version of the play Fielding pays enthusiastic compliments to this lady, extolling her gifts as an actress and praising her for the many virtues of her character.

The Intriguing Chambermaid is an interesting comedy in two acts adapted from Regnard's *Le Retour imprévu*. Its main theme is the unexpected return of an elderly gentleman to his house in which the gay and fashion-

[1] *The Daily Journal*, January 15, 1734.

able companions of his pleasure-loving son are making themselves happy. Fielding does ample justice to the humour of the situation, though the idea, of course, is not altogether his own.

One notable feature of the comedy is the satire that it contains. In the characters and conversation of Lords Puff and Pride Fielding denounces the ways of the fashionable world, and the satire is severe as it usually is when he deals with this subject. Apart from this satire and the very lively and attractive portrait of the servant girl Lettice, the play is conventional enough in its plot and the majority of its characters, though it has a number of lively and vigorous scenes. These gave enough scope to Mrs. Clive, who played the part of Lettice, to exhibit her remarkable gifts to advantage and to ensure the success of the play.

Fielding now exerted himself with great goodwill to help the distressed actors in Drury Lane and proceeded to revise one of his earliest dramatic efforts in order to put it on the stage. This was a comedy called *Don Quixote in England*, which, as he tells us in his Preface to the revised version of the play, "was begun at Leyden in the year 1728; and, after it had been sketched out into a few loose scenes, was thrown by, and for a long while no more thought of." He had not produced it all this time because the elder Cibber and Booth had dissuaded him from doing so.

He now revised his play thoroughly and added some political scenes to it. By the time, however, the play was ready for the stage a new authority had come to rule in Drury Lane in the person of Charles Fleetwood who had bought Highmore's and Mrs. Wilks' shares in the Drury Lane patent. The new management of the theatre found

its most formidable rival in Rich's new theatre in Covent
Garden, and in order to secure a triumph over Rich with
his own weapon Fleetwood substituted Fielding's *Don
Quixote in England*, which was being rehearsed at Drury
Lane, for a pantomime entertainment.

In March the rebel members of the Drury Lane
Company came back, but for some time no effort was
made to bring Fielding's play on the Drury Lane stage.
The dramatist, therefore, decided to produce it at the
Little Theatre in the Haymarket, and here it was "acted
with great applause" about the middle of April.[1]

Don Quixote in England is a play that has received less
attention than it deserves. Though Fielding was indebted
to Cervantes for his principal characters, he contributed
enough from his own genius to the play to make it one of
the most original of his comedies. The scenes are laid in a
country inn where the eccentric conduct of Don Quixote
creates situations that have a novelty in them which is
very refreshing after the conventional episodes of some
of the earlier plays of Fielding. The Knight of the Woeful
Figure and his squire are delineated in the true spirit of
Cervantes, and the humour of the creator of Don Quixote
is skilfully reproduced within the limits that Fielding allowed himself in his play. But Don Quixote and Sancho
are not the only striking characters in this interesting
comedy. In Squire Badger we have one of the most successful of Fielding's early portraits of the country gentleman, and as one studies the character one realizes that in
this Somersetshire squire we have the first sketch of the
immortal Squire Western. Some of the other characters
in the play, Guzzle the innkeeper, for example, or Brief
the lawyer, or Drench the physician, though sketched in

[1]Genest, *Some Account of the English Stage*, Vol. III, p. 435.

outline only, are good portraits and foreshadow the inn-
keepers, lawyers, and doctors of the novels.

But probably the play owed its success less to the excellence of its character sketches or its humour than to its
"political" scenes as they have been called. *Don Quixote in
England* was produced on the eve of an election, and this
gave a special interest to the scenes in which Fielding
launched a satire against the corruption that was such a
disgraceful feature of the parliamentary elections of the
time. The dramatist in dedicating his play to Lord Chesterfield says: "I fancy a lively representation of the calamities brought on a country by general corruption might
have a very sensible and useful effect on the spectators."
The most notable constituent of this "general corruption" was bribery, and Fielding directs his satire principally against this evil. Another noteworthy feature of the
play is the number of good songs it contains, the best of
these being the hunting song beginning, "The dusky
night rides down the sky," and an improved version of
the "Roast Beef of Old England" which he had first introduced into *The Grub-Street Opera*.

After the production of *Don Quixote in England* Fielding wrote no new plays during the rest of the year 1734.
As a matter of fact he was away in the country most of the
time, probably in Salisbury, where he found the wife who
was to call forth a splendid devotion in him, and bring
much happiness into his life in spite of its many vicissitudes and troubles. In the little village of Charlecombe,
about two miles north of Bath, he was married on the 28th
of November, 1734, to the beautiful Charlotte Cradock of
Salisbury with whom he had fallen in love four years before and whose charms he had eulogized in numerous
love poems, some of which were published in the *Miscel-*

lanies of 1743. The entry in the register of St. Mary's Church at Charlcombe describes both Fielding and Charlotte Cradock as "of the parish of St. James in Bath," and this, together with the fact of a remote country, church being selected for the celebration of the marriage, seems to point to an elopement.

In January, 1735, Fielding was in London again and in this month[1] he produced at Drury Lane a brisk little farce called *An Old Man Taught Wisdom*, afterwards renamed *The Virgin Unmask'd*. Like *The Intriguing Chambermaid* this play was written specially for Mrs. Clive. It is a short one-act piece liberally interspersed with songs. What there is of plot in it is simple enough. A man who has prospered in the world is anxious to marry his only daughter to the most worthy man among his poor relations. He invites these relations to his house, but his daughter who is a forward young lady treats her suitors "skittishly" as Miss Godden, one of the biographers of Fielding, describes it, and elopes with a footman.

There is a good deal of real humour in the play, and in the different suitors of Lucy the heroine Fielding portrays a number of amusing characters. One of these, however, Bookish, the student from Oxford, gave offence to the audience because the dramatist had made him say to the heiress, "I shall throw myself at no woman's feet, for I look on myself as the superior of the two." The character was hissed because the words were considered to be an insult to the fair sex. Fielding submitted to this vagary of the audience and removed the character altogether from the play. Another character, the lawyer Wormwood, had also given offence apparently, because in the printed version of the play the character is described as "omitted in

[1] *The London Evening Post*, January 16-18, 1735.

the representation." These changes and some other minor ones in the dialogue and the songs made the play more acceptable, and the altered version continued to be popular on the stage for a long time.

Fielding's next effort as a playwright was a full length comedy named *The Universal Gallant, or The Different Husbands*, which was put on the Drury Lane stage during the second week of February, 1735.[1] And now Fielding had to face the third great failure in his dramatic career. We have an account of the reception given to the play on the first night in a contemporary theatrical paper, *The Prompter*, which was conducted by the versatile Aaron Hill and his friend William Popple, who at this time were inclined to be friendly to Fielding. "I had likewise an opportunity," says the "author" of the *Prompter* of February 18, 1735, "of observing much more *impartiality* than I expected in the behaviour of the audience, for till almost the third act was over they sat very quiet, in hopes it would mend, till finding it grew still *worse* and *worse*, they at length lost all patience, and not an *expression* or *sentiment* afterwards passed without its *deserved censure*."

This failure could not have been due to bad acting, for the company that performed the play was an excellent one including as it did Quin, the Younger Cibber, Mills, and Mrs. Heron. Nor would it be fair to the audience to ascribe the failure, as Fielding does in his Advertisement to the published version of the play, to "an inveterate prejudice" against him, or to the vagaries of some young gentlemen about town who "made a jest of damning plays." *The Prompter* bears witness to the impartiality of the audience and there is no reason why its evidence should not be accepted.

[1] *Fog's Weekly Journal*, February 8, 1735.

The Universal Gallant is the dullest of Fielding's comedies and its failure was deserved. The dramatist's grievance to which he gives expression in the Advertisement referred to above that his play was condemned unheard was an imaginary one. Nor is one inclined to attach much importance to the suggestion that has been made by some that the failure was in part due to the caustic remarks on the frailties of women that the play contains. It is true that Fielding deals with these frailties rather severely in this play, but satire of this kind was far from being a new thing on the stage, and characters like Lady Raffler the prude or Mrs. Raffler the woman of easy virtue were by no means uncommon in contemporary drama and fiction.

There is hardly anything in the plot or in the situations in *The Universal Gallant* to relieve the pervading dullness of the comedy. The dialogue is unusually heavy and flashes of wit rather rare. What action there is in the play turns on the one hand on the jealousy of a suspicious husband which drives the wife to a sullen estrangement from him; and on the other, on the excessive confidence of an easy-going husband which gives the wife ample opportunities for intrigue. The characters are all more or less conventional, and Fielding seems to have little to contribute from his own genius and powers of observation to make them more interesting. The universal gallant, Captain Spark, and the prude, Lady Raffler, are a little more interesting than the other characters, but even these are in no sense great characters. The suspicious husband, Sir Simon Raffler, is occasionally amusing, but the portrait is thoroughly conventional.

Fielding seems to have taken this failure of his play very much to heart, and he was the more depressed by it because now that he had a wife to support success in his profession was a far more important consideration to him than it had been formerly. Both in his Advertisement and in his Prologue to the play he makes a feeling protest against the inhumanity of preventing a man from earning his livelihood in an honest and inoffensive way.

Just at this time, however, Fielding's immediate pecuniary difficulties were removed by an inheritance which came to Mrs. Fielding under her mother's will which was proved on the 25th of February, 1735. This inheritance, which Murphy says "did not exceed fifteen hundred pounds," enabled Fielding to take his wife away from the uncertainties of an author's life in London to a good home in East Stour in Dorsetshire where his mother's estate, still in the hands of trustees, was situated. Here he lived the life of a country gentleman for some months, and Murphy gives us a graphic account of his improvidence and folly and tries to make out that the future novelist wasted his substance recklessly, encumbering himself with a large retinue of servants all decked out in costly yellow liveries and "squandering his little patrimony in entertainments, hounds, and horses."[1]

Murphy's account obviously contains many exaggerations, and the unreliability of his statements has been demonstrated. But that Fielding was lavish in his hospitality and spent more of his wife's fortune than he should have done is probable enough. Indeed, the fact that in something less than a year after he had set up as a country gentleman he is back again in London working hard as a playwright seems to indicate that the greater part of his wife's fortune was spent, although it is quite likely that

[1] "An Essay on the Life and Genius of Henry Fielding, Esq.," prefixed to Murphy's Edition of Fielding's Works.

he returned to town because he was getting tired of country life.

But apparently the whole of his wife's fortune was not spent yet, because on his return to London he took the Little Theatre in the Haymarket on lease, and seizing the opportunity that now presented itself as a result of the factions among the actors in London he formed the "Great Mogul's Company of Comedians," so called after the name given by the playwrights to the elder Cibber whose arbitrary ways Fielding had already satirized in *The Author's Farce*. In his new undertaking he had as his partner James Ralph, an old friend, whom Tom Davies in his *Life of Garrick* describes as a "poacher in dramatic poetry"; but if we are to believe Davies, Ralph "had no other share in the management than viewing and repining at the success of his partner."[1]

The last two years of Fielding's dramatic career saw the production of two of his most successful plays, *Pasquin* and *The Historical Register for the Year* 1736. The applause with which the election scenes in *Don Quixote in England* had been received had revealed to Fielding a new field for the exercise of his powers of satire, and he now proceeded to make use of the stage of the Little Theatre in the Haymarket as a platform for the prosecution of a vigorous political campaign against the ministry. Improving on Gay's "local hits" at the politicians of the day, he carried political satire to such daring lengths and made his plays such a formidable weapon in the political warfare of the times that in the end the ministry determined to take action.

Pasquin, or *A Dramatic Satire on the Times* seems to

[1] *Memoirs of the Life of David Garrick, Esq.*, by Thomas Davies. London, 1781, Vol. I, p. 232.

have been put on the stage of the Little Theatre in the Haymarket in the first week in March, 1736, as an advertisement of the play in *The Grub-Street Journal* of the 8th of April describes it as "having been already acted thirty nights successively." Its success was very great indeed, greater than that of any other play he had produced so far. Its first run lasted for more than forty nights, and the Little Theatre is said to have attracted numerous and enthusiastic audiences "from Grosvenor, Cavendish, Hanover, and all the other fashionable squares, as also from Pall Mall and the Inns of Court."[1] *The Prompter* bears witness to its "vogue with all sorts of persons,"[2] and Mrs. Pendarves, afterwards Mrs. Delany, writing to Dean Swift on the 22nd of April, 1736, says, "When I went out of town last autumn, the reigning madness was Farinell; I find it now turned on *Pasquin*, a dramatic satire on the times. It has had almost as long a run as *The Beggar's Opera*; but in my opinion, not with equal merit, though it has humour."[3]

In May the newspapers announce the sixtieth performance of the play, and by this time the Great Mogul's Company at the Little Theatre had begun to call itself "Pasquin's Company of Comedians." We have also the evidence of contemporary prints to prove the popularity of the play. One of these, supposed to be designed by Hogarth, depicts the stage of the Little Theatre and on it a scene from the fifth act of *Pasquin* in which the foes of Queen Common Sense are portrayed as triumphant. Pope is introduced into this picture in a side box on the

---

[1] *An Apology for the Life of Mr. T . . C . . Comedian.* Supposed to be written by himself. London, 1740, p. 92.
[2] *The Prompter*, April 2, 1736.
[3] *Mrs. Delany's Autobiography and Correspondence*, edited by Lady Llanover London, 1861, Vol. I. p. 554.

left side of the theatre and the artist makes him say, "There's no whitewashing this stuff." Another print, named "The Judgment of the Queen o' Common Sense, Address'd to Henry Fielding, Esq.," shows the dramatist receiving an overflowing purse from the Queen of Common Sense who at the same time presents a halter to Harlequin.

Pasquin bears a considerable resemblance to *The Author's Farce*, though, of course, the earlier play has nothing in it corresponding to the political scenes which are the outstanding feature of the later satire. The device of a play within a play is once again made very happy use of by Fielding. *Pasquin* begins with the rehearsal of a comedy called "The Election" consisting of a series of broadly humorous scenes in which the flagrant and open bribery at elections and the shameless immorality of fashionable life are satirized. The satire, severe as it is, is enlivened by many a sally of genial wit, and the dramatist makes no effort to obscure his allusions. The prologue to the comedy declares that the author will "maul" both Whig and Tory, the Court and the Country party, without fear and favour. As in *Don Quixote in England*, bribery, "direct and indirect," is the principal theme of the political satire, and Trapwit, the author of the comedy, declares that the play is an exact representation of nature. In regard to plot, the comedy has hardly any worth the name. When Trapwit, the author of the piece, is asked what action or fable or design he has, he answers, "Oh! you ask who is to be married? Why, sir, I have a marriage; I hope you think I understand the laws of comedy better than to write without marrying somebody."[1] As a matter of fact the scenes in the comedy are strung together loosely in very much the

[1] *Pasquin*, Act I, Sc. i.

same way as the scenes in Fielding's other political plays
are. What "connected" action there is in the play turns
on the election tactics of the candidates belonging to the
Court and the Country party. The former is represented
by Lord Place and Colonel Promise who bribe openly,
and this the playwright Trapwit declares to be one of his
"strongest" jokes; while Sir Henry Foxchace and Squire
Tankard, the representatives of the Country party, bribe
indirectly. The mayor of the borough, whose sympathies
are with the latter, is induced in the end to vote for and return the Court candidates although they are in a minority;
and the comedy ends with the marriage of Colonel Promise to the mayor's daughter in strict conformity with
the playwright's conception of the laws of comedy.

But the political scenes do not constitute the only noteworthy feature of Mr. Trapwit's comedy. The social satire that the play contains is almost equally good. Fielding, as usual, is severe on the fashionable world and exposes its frailties and vices relentlessly. At the same time
he ridicules the taste of the theatre-going world, its preference of pantomime and Italian singing to the regular
drama. The popular Farinelli is mentioned more than
once in *Pasquin* and the French dancers, "the only people that support the house," come in for their full share of
the dramatist's attentions. The student of literature, however, will probably find the most interesting feature of
Mr. Trapwit's comedy in a number of exquisite little
touches in which the humours of stage life behind the
scenes are depicted. These touches give us interesting
glimpses into the conditions prevailing in the theatrical
world in Fielding's time.

The second part of *Pasquin*, the tragedy called "The
Life and Death of Common Sense," is an extravaganza

very much like the puppet-show in *The Author's Farce*. There is more of a plot in the tragedy than in the comedy that precedes it. The main theme of the former is a conspiracy against the rule of Common Sense, and the prime movers in this are the representatives of religion and of the learned professions of law and medicine. These conspirators prefer Queen Ignorance to Queen Common Sense as their sovereign. Fielding makes use of this allegory to satirize the inordinate claims set up by the Church, to expose the inequalities and hardships that the existing laws countenanced, and to ridicule the quackery practised in the name of medical science. The satire is vigorous throughout and *Pasquin* is inclined to be particularly severe on the Church.

As the action of the tragedy develops in the rehearsal we have many charasteristic incidents that give us interesting glimpses into the humours of dramatic life behind the scenes. Most amusing accidents happen to some of the numerous ghosts that "rise" in the play. One appears without being properly "floured" because the stage barber has gone to Drury Lane "to shave the Sultan in the new entertainment." Another ghost, that of Queen Common Sense, rises before the queen is dead. Again, a battle on the stage between the armies of Queen Common Sense and Queen Ignorance is such a tame affair that Fustian the author of the tragedy insists on its being fought properly, which is done after repeated attempts. At a critical moment in the action of the play it is discovered that "the mob" has disappeared, and Law while straying outside the playhouse passage is snapped up by a lord chief justice's warrant. The comic effect produced by these exquisite touches is immeasurably heightened by the very effective burlesque of heroic declamation

which the dramatist constantly indulges in. Indeed,
though the play is not quite as full of burlesque declamations and mock heroic similes as *Tom Thumb* is, where
Fielding does try his hand at them, he shows much of his
old skill. The priest Firebrand's rhapsody on omens is as
good a burlesque declamation as any in *Tom Thumb:*

> Avert these omens, ye auspicious stars!
> Oh Law! oh Physic! As last even, late,
> I offer'd sacred incense in the temple,
> The temple shook—strange prodigies appear'd;
> A cat in boots did dance a rigadoon,
> While a huge dog play'd on the violin;
> And whilst I trembling at the altar stood,
> Voices were heard i' th' air, and seem'd to say,
> "Awake, my drowsy sons, and sleep no more"
> They must mean something![1]

In satirizing the prevailing rage for pantomime, rope
dancing, and tumbling in *Pasquin* Fielding handled
Harlequin and Covent Garden so severely that Rich had to
retaliate to save his face. He did this by bringing out in
his theatre early in April when *Pasquin* was rising on the
crest of the wave of its popularity a farce called *Marforio*
in which he tried to give a reply to his "witty brother"
Pasquin. Marforio, according to Genest, was acted only
once and apparently the revenge that Rich aimed at was
not a very satisfactory one. But Fielding punished Rich
for his presumption in thinking of revenge, and this was
done in a dramatic "entertainment" called *Tumble-Down
Dick, or Phaeton in the Suds*, a clever parody of a pantomime called *The Fall of Phaeton* which had succeeded on
the Drury Lane stage on account of its good music and
some novel "machinery."

[1] *Pasquin*, Act IV, Sc. i.

Tumble-Down Dick is ostensibly a continuation of *Pasquin*, and the playwright Fustian and the critic Sneerwell of the latter play make their appearance once again to comment on the new piece which is ironically described as "a dramatic entertainment of walking, in serious and foolish characters, interlarded with burlesque, grotesque, comic interludes, called Harlequin a Pickpocket." The parody ridicules the popular form of the pantomime in which scenes introducing the Greek gods and heroes alternated with the tricks of Harlequin as in *The Fall of Phaeton*, for example. Fielding depended for his burlesque effects mainly on the transformation of the serious characters, the divinities of his original, *The Fall of Phaeton*, into characters of low comedy. For example, the Phœbus of the Drury Lane play becomes a London watchman, Clymene an oyster wench, and for a dance of the Hours is substituted a jig by a group of rakes and loose women at King's Coffee House. The chief business of the action, if action it can be called, is to ridicule Harlequin and his tricks, and Rich's shortcomings and frailties come in for their full share of the dramatist's attentions.

Fielding published his farce on the day on which it was first performed, the 29th of April, and the published version of the play contained a dedication to John Lunn, Esquire, the name by which Rich was known on the stage. The dedication is a little masterpiece of satire and is more interesting than the play itself. In this Fielding congratulates Rich for having brought the so-called "entertainment," that is to say, the kind of pantomime which was the chief attraction of Rich's theatre, into fashion, thanks him for his satire on *Pasquin* and concludes with an eulogy of his "whole merit" which the public might see "all at once" whenever he condescends to "peform" the Harlequin.

During the rest of the year no new play from Fielding's pen was produced in any of the London theatres, and our dramatist was content to give to his audiences at the Little Theatre old favourites like *Tom Thumb* or Carey's *Chrononhotonthologos*, and promising new pieces like George Lillo's *Fatal Curiosity* or Jack Juniper's *The Deposing and Death of Queen Gin*. *Pasquin*, of course, continued to be played from time to time and *Tumble-Down Dick* was also produced many times as an after-piece to greater plays.

The next year Fielding tried his hand at burlesque once more, and as Fleetwood was now ready enough to produce a play written by the famous author of *Pasquin*, the new piece which was called *Eurydice, or The Devil Henpeck'd* was put on the Drury Lane stage on the 19th of February.[1] In this one-act farce Fielding's satire ranges over a fairly extensive field, though its main objective seems to have been the public taste in music, its preference for Italian singing. The dramatist is severe as usual on the vices of the fashionable world and makes his beaus, Spindle and Weazel, thoroughly contemptible. The classical story of Orpheus and Eurydice is the basis of the burlesque, in the course of which some of the characters of classical mythology are converted into low comedy types in very much the same way as they are in *Tumble-Down Dick*. In portraying Orpheus Fielding seems to have had the famous Farinelli in his mind, and Eurydice evidently represents the fine lady of the fashionable world in Fielding's own day. The scene is laid in the lower world, and almost all the characters in the farce are spirits. There are

[1] *The London Daily Post*, February 19, 1737.

occasional sallies of wit in the play, but on the whole it has little that is new or striking. Fielding made the mistake of repeating the device of the play within the play without any variation, and the comments of the playwright and the critic on the farce, as they have hardly anything in them that is novel or particularly piquant, are apt to be tiresome.

The career of *Eurydice* on the stage was an unfortunate one, as on the first night of its appearance there was a disturbance in the theatre caused by the audience in the pit rising against the footmen in the boxes who had for some time been particularly objectionable in their behaviour and had grossly abused the privilege they had enjoyed for some years of occupying the boxes till their masters and mistresses appeared. On the second night of the play also there was a disturbance and *Eurydice* was withdrawn after this. The audience objected to the character of Captain Weazel, the spirit of the military beau in the play, as an insult to the army.

Fielding does not seem to have been much distressed by this failure, and shortly afterwards he endeavoured to carry it off as a joke by writing a farce on the hissing of the play; and when many years afterwards he published *Eurydice* in his *Miscellanies*, he kept up the joke by inserting on the title-page of the play the words, "As it was d—mn'd at the Theatre-Royal, Drury Lane."

It was not long after the failure of *Eurydice* at Drury Lane that Fielding produced another great political play by which, as Colley Cibber describes it in his *Apology for his Life*, the dramatist "like another Erostratus set fire to his stage by writing up to an Act of Parliament to demolish it."

The Historical Register for the Year 1736, as this play

was named, seems to have been put on the stage of the
Little Theatre during the last week in March, 1737. The
earliest newspaper reference to it that has been discovered
so far is that of *The Daily Journal* for the 6th April, 1737,
which advertises a performance of the play on the 11th of
April as the ninth.

It was on the whole not badly received on the first night,
though it appears that some of the more pointed allusions
in the first version of the play to the famous dispute between the second wife of the younger Cibber and Mrs.
Clive over the part of Polly in *The Beggar's Opera* were
hissed and Fielding had to remove them from the play.
The subsequent career of *The Historical Register* on the
stage, however, was a very prosperous one.

Like Fielding's other political plays *The Historical
Register* is a medley in which the preponderating elements
are social and political satire. It is a much shorter play
than *Pasquin*, containing three acts only and has even less
of plot or "connected" story than the latter play. But both
the political and social satire in *The Historical Register* are as
good as they are in *Pasquin*. As a matter of fact the political
satire in *The Historical Register* is bolder, and Fielding attacks Walpole more openly now than he had done in
Pasquin. In his Dedication to the Public prefixed to the
published version of the play he declares with an irony
which is as effective as it is genial that "had not all mankind been either very blind or very dishonest, he need
not have publicly informed them that *The Register* is a
ministerial pamphlet, calculated to infuse into the minds
of the people a great opinion of their ministry."

In *The Historical Register* Fielding makes use once
again of the device of a play within a play and introduces
an author named Medley and two critics, Sourwit and

Lord Dapper, to comment on the piece in the usual strain.. Mr Medley's play begins by way of prologue with an Ode to the New Year which is an excellent parody of the laureate Cibber's usual vapid style in odes. The first act contains an amusing scene which discovers five politicians in council, "the ablest heads in the kingdom, and consequently the greatest men" who decide to levy a tax on ignorance and go out to raise it, this being "the full account of the whole history of Europe comprised in one scene."[1]

In the second act we have the best scene of the play, a very happy satire, after the manner of Lucian's *Sale of Creeds*, on the frailties of mankind and on the fashionable auctions of the day. Fielding introduces Christopher Cock, the celebrated auctioneer of the time, into this scene under the name of Hen. The lots that are put up for auction are particularly interesting. For example, there is "a most curious remnant of political honesty" which is excellent material for a good cloak; there are "three grains of modesty" for which no one bids; there is "all the wit lately belonging to Mr. Hugh Pantomime, composer of entertainments for the playhouses"; there is "a very clear conscience which has been worn by a judge and a bishop" which is also laid by because there is no bid for it. In fact every item in "the catalogue of curiosities which were collected by the indefatigable pains of that celebrated virtuoso, Peter Humdrum, Esq.," is worthy of attention, and Fielding's ingenuity and humour are seen at their best in this magnificent scene.

From this the dramatist passes on to theatrical affairs, and the two Cibbers, as usual, come in for their share of his attentions. The younger Cibber is introduced as a de-

[1] *The Historical Register for the Year* 1736, Act I, Sc. i.

mented Pistol who with the help of his friends collects a mob to whom he puts the question whether his wife should play the part of Polly Peachum in *The Beggar's Opera*; and when the mob hisses, Pistol is described as accepting that as a declaration of the public desire that Mrs. Cibber and not Mrs. Clive should act the disputed part.

The satire against the elder Cibber is more severe. He appears in the play as Ground-Ivy, an obvious reference to his position as laureate, and in much the same strain as he had done in *The Author's Farce* Fielding satirizes Cibber's practice of "improving upon" the plays of the great masters. The liberties that he had taken with Shakespeare's *King John* are made the basis of some excellent and thoroughly deserved satire.

The play concludes with a very audacious scene which introduces four "shabby fellows," patriots of different types, who condole with one another on their miserable poverty when Quidam, whose identity is such an open secret that Fielding declares in his dedication of the play to the public that "he who maketh any wrong application thereof might as well mistake the name of Thomas for John, or old Nick for old Bob," enters and pours out gold on a table. The patriots snatch up this money, and Quidam playing on a fiddle leads them in a dance, in the course of which the money falls out through holes in the pockets of the patriots. Walpole and his minions, some of them renegades from the Opposition, are attacked so very boldly in this scene that one cannot help believing that Fielding and his friends were expecting the fall of the ministry, of which expectation he gives us some broad hints in a farce called *Eurydice Hiss'd, or A Word to the Wise*, which he produced at the Little Theatre about a fortnight after the first performance of *The Historical Register*.

This farce is a satiric comment, which is remarkably good humoured considering the subject, on the conduct of the Drury Lane audience in hissing his *Eurydice* a month before. Fielding endeavours to turn the tables against the theatre-going public by making their damnation of *Eurydice* the subject of his new farce. He makes Spatter, the supposed author of the play, say, "I have chose this subject very cunningly; for, as the town have damn'd my play, for their own sakes they will not damn the damnation of it."

Eurydice Hiss'd purports to be a continuation of *The Historical Register* inasmuch as the critics Sourwit and Lord Dapper are once again brought upon the stage. But the two plays have little in common beyond the attack that is made on the ministry in both. Pillage in *Eurydice Hiss'd* is described as "a very great man," and in one part of the farce in which he is represented as holding his levee the political references are unmistakable. Tom Davies, who at this time was a member of the company appearing at the Little Theatre, tells us in his *Life of Garrick* that Fielding brought the minister upon the stage in a levee scene, and a correspondent writing to the *Daily Gazetteer* of the 7th of May, 1737, declared that "Fielding impudently compared the Government to a farce and kept up the allegory throughout."

These persistent attacks on the Walpole administration and the phenomenal success of *Pasquin* and *The Historical Register* at last roused the ministry to action. Fielding's campaign against the much assailed Government was known to be countenanced by the leaders of the Opposition, and the popularity of his political plays with the general public was so great that Walpole and his advisers had hesitated to take drastic measures to put an end to his activities. They were seeking an opportunity that would enable them to conceal effectively the personal considerations moving them to action and this opportunity came while the town was still talking about the success of *The Historical Register*. In May, 1737, Giffard, the manager of the theatre in Goodman's Fields, in the hope evidently of receiving some kind of reward for his good offices in which, as Coxe tells us in his *Life of Walpole*,[1] he was not disappointed, took the unusual step of handing over to Walpole a dramatic piece called *The Golden Rump* which was based on some scurrilous and obscene articles which had appeared in Chesterfield and Lyttelton's newspaper called *Common Sense*. Davies in his *Life of Garrick* tells us that the farce was "a most outrageous satire against the king, the royal family and many of the highest and most respected persons in the kingdom." *The Golden Rump* fell into the hands of Walpole at such an opportune moment that it has been suggested that the Prime Minister's good fortune was something more than a mere accident, and that the whole transaction was a carefully laid plot, and Walpole himself had instigated the writing of the play. Horace Walpole, however, ascribes the farce to Fielding and tells us that he found an imperfect copy of it among his father's papers after his death.[2] Horace Walpole's assumption in regard to the authorship of *The Golden Rump* hardly deserves any serious consideration, as Fielding was not likely to give to another theatre a political farce which would certainly have taken away from his own house the

[1] *Memoirs of the Life and Administration of Sir Robert Walpole*, by William Coxe. 1798, Vol. II, p. 516.
[2] Horace Walpole, *Memoirs of the Last Ten Years of the Reign of George II*. Vol. I, p. 12.

audiences on which he was depending for the support of his company. Whoever the author was, Walpole determined to make use of the play to convince the Parliament of the necessity of legislation to put a stop to such excesses. He made extracts from the play of the treasonable and profane passages in it, and these were submitted to some prominent men belonging to both the political parties. They were read in Parliament and produced the desired effect. Leave was immediately given to bring in a bill which would provide for the supervision of all theatrical entertainments by a licensing authority. As a matter of fact the opinion had been gaining ground for some time that Government should make a special effort to regulate the activities of the stage. Bills had been brought forward in 1733 and 1735, the second one by Sir John Barnard, who had complained of the mischief done by the London theatres "by corrupting youth, encouraging vice and debauchery, and greatly prejudicing trade." But both bills had been withdrawn.

The new bill, which was an amendment and extension of the Vagrant Act of Queen Anne's reign, passed rapidy through both the Houses though there was some opposition to it. Pulteney opposed it in the House of Commons, and the Earl of Chesterfield made one of his best speeches against it in the House of Lords, declaring that the proposed legislation would affect the liberty of the Press and that the measure was a tax upon the chief dependence of men of letters, their wit. By a reference to the story of the ban imposed on Molière's *Tartuffe* Chesterfield with caustic and happy wit made it clear to the House that the Opposition understood that Fielding's attacks on the ministry were the real cause of the Government's new bill. But the ministry had timed their measure so well and

Walpole's tactics were so good that in spite of the opposition the bill passed through both Houses in less than a fortnight after its first reading and received the royal assent on the 21st of June, 1737.

The Licensing Act, as the new measure was called, prohibited under a penalty of £50 the acting of any play in any other place than a house of entertainment authorized by letters patent from the Crown or until the play was licensed by the Lord Chamberlain. Other provisions of the bill ordained that copies of all plays that were intended to be produced should be submitted to the Lord Chamberlain two weeks before their performance. All theatres not within the verge of the Court were restricted to the City of Westminster and the liberties thereof.

The Licensing Act answered the expectations of the ministry very well though, of course, the writing of scurrilous plays did not cease. Out of the six London playhouses three were closed, and these were the Little Theatre in the Haymarket and, by a curious irony of fate, the two houses in Lincoln's Inn Fields and Goodman's Fields in which Giffard's companies had been playing, though the Government, apparently in return for the services he had rendered, winked at his artful evasion of the provisions of the new Act when he made a practice of presenting his repertoire of plays between concerts of vocal and instrumental music for which ostensibly he reopened his theatre in Goodman's Fields.

If the immediate aim of the Licensing Act was to put an end to Fielding's activities as a writer of political plays, this end was also fully achieved. Fielding's dramatic career was now ended, though *The Historical Register* and *Eurydice Hiss'd* were not the last of his plays to be put on the stage. As a matter of fact the most notable of his early successes like *Tom Thumb* or *The Miser* continued to be acted for a long time after the Licensing Act was passed; and in the years 1742 and 1743 he was driven by his financial straits to produce plays which had never been acted before.

But these efforts were spasmodic, and after the year 1737 he did not make any serious effort to write a new play. Apparently he had come to the conclusion that his dramatic career had come to an end with the passing of the Licensing Act, and before the year was out he had practically turned his back on a profession in which he had made a reputation for himself among his contemporaries. His biographers have speculated a good deal over the reasons which prompted him to abandon the profession of the playwright at a time when, according to his own confession, he ought to have entered upon it. One is tempted to believe that the consideration which weighed most with Fielding in his final decision was the uncertainty of the playwright's position so far as the earning of a steady income was concerned.

It is true that in the course of his dramatic career he had found fortune anything but an unkind mistress on the whole. He had been fortunate in securing a foothold in the profession quite early in his life; and we have reason to believe that his income as a playwright, at any rate after the "prolific Mr. Fielding" had become known in town, was a good one on the whole. In his later years he speaks of £50 as a small remuneration for a play, and it would be legitimate to conclude from this that his takings, though uncertain, were considerable sometimes.

At the same time it must not be forgotten that he had encountered notable reverses in the course of his dramatic career, and reverses had come again and again when he had tried his hand at the regular, full-length comedy. Apart from the fact that he had never shown any remarkable originality in his comedies, their failure was also due to a certain lack that he had displayed of those gifts of imagination which are essential to the highest dramatic art. His most notable early successes had been gained in the domain of burlesque; but later on in his dramatic career he had introduced questionable elements into his burlesques as, for example, into *The Covent Garden Tragedy* or *Eurydice*, and this had led to disastrous consequences. These unfortunate experiences had driven him to new fields in search of dramatic adventure.

The success of *Pasquin* and *The Historical Register* had revealed to him in a way that none of his previous plays had done where his strength lay. Untrammelled by the influence of any dramatic predecessor he had appeared before the world as a satirist of contemporary manners, and had won greater successes on the stage than he had ever done before. We may speculate, as some of his biographers and critics have done, whether he would have won further triumphs in the new field of his dramatic activities, and whether such triumphs would have won for him a place in the ranks of the great dramatists that England has produced. Some of these critics have inclined to the belief that he would never have risen to real greatness as a dramatist and have expressed the opinion, which can scarcely be defended, that the years of his dramatic life were wasted years. Speculation apart, one notable fact about his subsequent fortunes as a playwright that invites comment is that the few efforts that he made after the passing of the Licensing Act to produce farce and comedy met with little success.

The first of these later efforts was a sequel to *The Virgin*

Unmask'd which the audience in Drury Lane in a captious mood had hissed on its first appearance. *Miss Lucy in Town*, as the new ballad farce was called, was written in collaboration with an unknown dramatist, and Fielding had a very small share in its composition, as he tells us in his Preface to the *Miscellanies*. It was first produced at Drury Lane on the 6th of May, 1742, and apparently it ran on the boards without mishap for about a fortnight.

It is surprising that the play was not hissed on the first night. It was produced on the same stage on which *The Covent Garden Tragedy* had been damned on account of its low scenes and the sordidness of its main theme, and so far as these features are concerned *Miss Lucy in Town* is hardly an improvement on the earlier play. The hoyden of *The Virgin Unmask'd* is once again the heroine of the play, and the one episode of the new farce is a visit that she pays with her husband Thomas, the footman of other days, to London where they find lodgings in the "house" of a Mrs. Haycock. The irrepressible Lucy, now more a hoyden than before, attracts the attention of some of the clients of her landlady, but fortunately she is taken back to the country before she has become too proficient in the art of playing the fine lady.

The career of the farce on the stage was rather abruptly interrupted. Apart from the almost open attack made in the play on the disreputable Mrs. Haywood the novelist in the character of the proprietress of the house in which Lucy and her husband find lodgings, the play contained a reflection on "a particular person of quality" who apparently recognized a portrait of himself in the character of Lord Bawble, one of the aristocratic customers of Mrs. Haycock. A protest seems to have been made, and the

Lord Chamberlain or his licenser Chetwynd prohibited further performances of the farce. But the Drury Lane authorities sent in their counter protest and the prohibition order was withdrawn. In October the farce was put on the stage again with only this change that Mrs. Haycock was now renamed Mrs. Midnight.

The next year another of Fielding's plays was put on the stage. Garrick had expressed to him his wish to appear in a play written by him, and Fielding, as he tells us in his Preface to the *Miscellanies*, was "as desirous of putting words into his mouth as he could appear to be of speaking them." He now offered to Fleetwood a play named *The Good Natur'd Man* which he had begun many years before but never finished, and the manager of the Theatre Royal agreed to produce it. Fielding then proceeded to revise the unfinished play, and the work had progressed as far as the writing out of the parts for the different actors when he began to be doubtful about the wisdom of producing it. The comedy had many defects because he had given himself "too little time for the perfecting it" when it was first written, and now he felt that the time that Fleetwood had given to him to get his play ready for the stage would not be sufficient to enable him to rewrite the play. Moreover, he found that the part he had designed for Garrick was a comparatively insignificant one. He decided, therefore, not to proceed further with his revision of *The Good Natur'd Man*, but gave his attention to another play, *The Wedding Day*, an earlier effort, which he describes in his Preface to the *Miscellanies* as "the third dramatic performance he ever attempted." One of its leading characters, Millamour, intended originally for Wilks, offered a rôle in which Garrick could do justice to himself.

Fielding now proceeded to revise *The Wedding Day* for production and he worked hard to get it ready for the stage by the time appointed. But before he could make much headway in his work many domestic troubles, and particularly the serious illness of his wife, put an end to all his literary labours for the time. He was compelled, therefore, to send his comedy to the theatre for rehearsal before it had undergone thorough revision. It was produced at the Theatre Royal on the 17th of February, and kept the stage for six nights through the good offices of Garrick and Fleetwood; but it was a complete failure. Rumours had been circulated that the play was indecent; and Fielding's previous record had induced people to give credence to them. Indeed, the licenser had been censured for being too remiss in the discharge of his duties, though he had objected to certain passages which the dramatist had removed from his play. On the last night of its short run on the stage, which was the author's benefit night, only five ladies were present in the boxes.

These rumours were largely responsible for the failure of the play, and the actual coarseness of some parts of it substantiated these rumours to a certain extent. And yet it can scarcely be maintained that *The Wedding Day* is a particularly objectionable play. It is certainly not quite so serious an offence against good taste and propriety as some of his other plays are. Its want of originality must also be held responsible to some extent for its failure. Though the plot of the comedy is an interesting one, the characters are all more or less closely modelled on those of the Restoration Comedy, and the dialogues are larded with the wit-traps of Wycherley and Congreve to an extent that is hardly a credit to the originality of Fielding's genius. Nor does the dramatist exhibit more originality in the situations that he develops, and the dénouement is more dubious than effective.

The Fathers, or The Good Natur'd Man, Fielding's other play which had never been produced, had an adventurous career before it reached the stage nearly a quarter of a century after the novelist's death. As the advertisement to the published version of the play informs us, it had been submitted to Sir Charles Hanbury Williams, the friend of Fielding's school days at Eton, and for many years all trace of it was lost. The advertisement to the play also tells us the story of its discovery some time after Sir Charles' death. One Mr. Thomas Johnes of Cardigan having received the manuscript copy of the play as a present from Sir Charles' son sent it to London for Garrick's opinion, and the great actor at once recognized it to be Fielding's long lost comedy for which inquiries had been made in vain.

It was now decided to produce the play, and Garrick and Sheridan revised and retouched it here and there, the former writing a prologue and an epilogue to the piece. It was produced at Drury Lane on the 30th of November, 1778[1], and Sheridan and Garrick as well as Fielding's brother John exerted themselves to make the production a success. Sheridan even withdrew his own *School for Scandal* for a time to ensure the success of Fielding's comedy and provided new scenery and costumes for its production. The play was well received, and the three benefit nights given to Fielding's family were all successful, though there was a feeling abroad that the cast did not do full justice to what was believed to be the best comedy that Fielding had ever written.

Though this opinion was not a mistaken one, the

[1] *The Public Advertiser*, November 30, 1778.

comedy in spite of the symmetry of its construction and a certain amount of vivacity here and there is on the whole far from being a great play. The plot is anything but original, and for his character sketches Fielding was not indebted to Terence alone as Genest suggests. Most of the characters in the play are modelled on those of the Comedy of Manners, and the dramatist follows the traditions of the elder comedy much too closely. The situations have nothing striking in them; and though there is some humour in the play, its general tone is grave and didactic. The serious troubles that had come into his life at the time he was revising the play for Garrick and Fleetwood left their impress on it and Fielding was inclined to moralize too much.

CHAPTER IV

THE CHAMPION

IN putting an end to his activities on the stage and dispersing the Great Mogul's Company of Comedians the Licensing Act left Fielding without a profession and ostensibly without any means of earning his livelihood. He had now to make a fresh start in life, as it were, and he decided to study law and to try his fortune at the bar. With commendable promptitude he entered himself a student of the Middle Temple in Michaelmas Term, 1737, in the thirty-first year of his age.

He devoted himself to his legal studies with undivided attention for nearly two years, and during this time he seems to have written nothing more important than a short essay on Conversation and perhaps a few articles in *Common Sense*. In the winter of the year 1739 his pecuniary resources were apparently at a low ebb and he was compelled to take recourse to his pen again. In the month of November he reappeared in the literary and political world, this time as a journalist and as an observer and critic of men and manners. *The Champion* or *British Mercury* was started by him and his friend James Ralph with very much the same aim that had led the elder essayists to establish *The Tatler* or *The Spectator*, and it was evidently the intention of the editors of *The Champion* to conduct it on very much the same lines. In more than one number of their paper they acknowledge their indebtedness to the elder essayists, and declare with a charming *naïveté* that their ambition is to emulate the success of *The Tatler* or *The Spectator*.

The Champion appeared, like *The Tatler*, on three days in the week, on Tuesdays, Thursdays, and Saturdays. It was a morning paper in the beginning, but after it had been in circulation for about five months it became an evening paper "because many of the country papers had begun to enrich themselves with its spoils,"[1] and its second title was changed into *The Evening Advertiser*. Its usual contents were the leading article, letters from correspondents, columns of domestic and foreign news, short paragraphs headed "Rumours" and "Puffs," and a "Journal of the War."

The first number of the paper came out on the 15th of November, 1739, and in this the "author," following the example of his great predecessors, assumed the name of Captain Hercules Vinegar, borrowed apparently from a cudgel player who had been performing in Hockley in the Hole, Clerkenwell, some years before. The name was soon a familiar one to the reading public, and the audacious Mr. Pasquin of the palmy days before the Licensing Act reappeared in the political and social world laying about him manfully with his mighty club, a picture of which adorned the first page of the paper, and which had "a very strange and almost incredible quality belonging to it of falling, of its own accord, on every egregious knave who came in its way."[2] The blows, whether meant for the shoulders of the old cynic Sir Robert or those of poor Colley Cibber, were always effective, and so long as Fielding's active connection with it continued, the paper in spite of its frequent personalities preserved a dignity of tone and a sense of decorum which prevented it from degenerating into a receptacle of personal scurrilities. The utmost length to which it went was the abuse that it

[1] *The Champion*. April 10, 1740.   [2] *The Champion*, December 8, 1739.

heaped on Thomas Pitt, the principal writer in the ministerial organ, *The Daily Gazetteer*, on whom *The Champion* delighted to practise its skill in the use of strong language. But even in these attacks on "Ralph Freeman," as Pitt called himself in *The Daily Gazetteer*, *The Champion* hardly ever overstepped the bounds of decency.

Though it is not possible to ascertain with absolute certainty the exact share of Fielding in the contributions to *The Champion*, he has given us sufficient hints to enable us to identify the greater part of his work. In June, 1741, was published a collection in two volumes[1] of the articles and miscellaneous paragraphs that had appeared in *The Champion* up to the 19th of June, 1740, and this compilation contains an "Advertisement" which tells us that "all the papers distinguished with a C or an L are the work of one hand; those mark'd thus * * or sign'd Lilbourne, of another, to whose account, likewise, except a few paragraphs, the Index of the Times, is to be plac'd." These paragraphs under the heading "Index to the Times" were selections from the news and other items that had appeared in *The Champion*.

Though Fielding never definitely asserted that the articles signed with a C or an L were his, the subjects dealt with in the contributions so distinguished the evidence of the style, and the frequent recurrence of some expressions and grammatical forms which are the characteristic marks of his language, leave little room for doubt as to who was responsible for them. In one of the articles signed with a C, which undoubtedly was written by him, he tells us that to pacify his bookseller he "was forced to condescend to agree, that in order to make his

[1] *The London Daily Post*, June 18-26, 1741.

paper appear like a *Spectator*, it should for the future be adorned with a capital letter at the end as well as a motto at the beginning."[1]

Of the articles published in the two volumes of 1741, nearly all of which are signed, the majority are from the pen of Fielding. The first four have no distinguishing marks, but they are unmistakably his. Ralph contributed his first leading article to the fifth number of *The Champion*, and in the collection in the 1741 volumes each leading article from his pen seems to be regularly marked with his distinctive signs, the two stars and "Lilbourne." Besides Fielding and Ralph there were other occasional contributors to the paper.

From the end of the month of June, 1740, Fielding's interest in *The Champion* seems to have waned. The original issues of the paper preserved in the Hope Collection in the Bodleian Library, which take us down to the middle of November, 1740, show that after the month of June a much smaller number of leading articles than in the preceding seven months have Fielding's distinctive marks, the letters C and L; and from this time onwards unsigned articles become far more frequent. In the collection preserved in the British Museum, which contains one issue—that of September 2nd—of the year 1740 and thirty-four issues of the year 1741, none of the leading articles in the paper is signed with a C or an L. Fielding himself tells us in his Preface to the *Miscellanies* of 1743 that "as long as from June, 1741," he had desisted from writing one syllable in *The Champion*. And it appears from the disappearance of his name, as Miss G. M. Godden notes in her Memoir of the novelist[2] from the

---

[1] *The Champion*, March 1, 1740.
[2] Miss G. M. Godden, *Henry Fielding, a Memoir*, London, 1910, p. 116.

minutes of the meetings of the partners in *The Champion* after the 29th of June, 1741, that he severed his connection with the paper about this time.

The articles that he contributed to *The Champion* are, as a rule, reflective, satiric, or didactic. There is not much of that portrayal of character and piquant narrative that we have in the Coverley papers of *The Spectator* which contributed so much to the success of that periodical. As Austin Dobson says, *The Champion* is hard reading, and a kind of lassitude broods heavily even over Fielding's contributions to the paper, though at his best he rises almost to the level of the finest writing in *The Tatler* or *The Spectator*. Dr. Nathan Drake, no mean authority on the subject, in his *Essays on Periodical Papers between the Close of the Eighth Volume of the Spectator and the Commencement of* 1809, expresses the opinion that nothing so good as Fielding's essays to *The Champion* had appeared since the eighth volume of *The Spectator* except the essays in *The Freethinker*. Fielding's work certainly exhibits something of that variety of subject and treatment that is such an attractive feature of Addison's or Steele's contributions to *The Tatler* or *The Spectator*. We have moral discourses, satires on contemporary manners, scathing indictments of social and political evils, a few visions and allegories, occasional character sketches, and personal attacks on people against whom he had a grievance, though in these last Fielding carefully avoided any references to the private affairs of his adversaries.

He seems to have given too much of his time and thought to didactic and reflective essays, and the result of this is that his splendid gifts for humorous and satiric composition do not find adequate expression in his papers. *The Champion* would have been a much greater periodical if these gifts had been allowed to assert themselves more than they did. For example, if we had more essays written in the spirit in which his well-known Lucianic vision is composed in which he laughs at the weaknesses of men and women with such delightful humour and portrays himself and Colley Cibber, or more character sketches like those of the members of the Vinegar family, or a few more papers describing the proceedings of Captain Vinegar's Court of Censorial Enquiry, *The Champion* would be much more widely read than it is now.

His essays, such as they are, are of great interest to us because they give us the results of his observation of life in the shape of comment and criticism of the world around him. They demand our attention because they supplement the information that we derive from his plays about his ways of thought. They mark a stage in the growth of his powers of observation and of his knowledge of the world. Some aspects of contemporary life that he deals with in his plays are touched upon again in *The Champion* for comment and reflection, and the insight that we gain into his outlook on life at this time is a very good introduction to the study of his novels. We are guided, as it were, into the tracks of his thought, we begin to take an interest in the types of character that he was most interested in, and our attention is drawn to the social and political questions which were to occupy so much of his attention in the novels and in the later journals that he edited.

A few examples will illustrate this. Among other evils in society which he marks out for special condemnation, one that constantly engages his attention in the novels, is pride of birth and rank. This satire against "high" people must have been very effective in its own day, coming as it did from a man of his rank in society. In his plays we have portraits, somewhat lightly sketched, like that of Sir Positive Trap in his first comedy, or those of Lords Puff and Pride in *The Intriguing Chambermaid*, which are intended to be satires on this frailty in man. We are perhaps justified in believing that in the earliest years of his life in town this type did not attract and hold his attention in the same way as certain other kinds of character did, the rake, the spendthrift, or the prude, for example. As time went on and his knowledge of the fashionable world increased, he saw more and more of this pride of birth and rank in men. In *The Champion* we have many indications that he was closely studying the ways of people in whom this weakness was conspicuous. Observations like the following are a very piquant commentary on some of the portraits presented to the world in his plays:

"Hereditary honour, considered abstractedly, without any regard to the designs for which it was instituted, will appear perhaps as ridiculous as any opinion which time and authority have given a sanction to. And this (however politic their intentions were, who designed, by offering a reward even to the latest posterity of heroes, to incite all men to virtue, and their posterity in particular to emulation) hath certainly been, sometimes, carried into a most extravagant absurdity: For what can be more monstrous than to see the illiterate, the coward, the villain or the fool valuing himself, and valued by others, because his forefathers have been learned, brave, honest or wise; that is, in other words, the very reverse of himself?"[1]

Again, among the many weaknesses and frailties of the

[1] *The Champion*, November 17, 1739.

fair sex to which he gives his attention in the plays and the novels, prudery always calls forth some of his most biting satire. In the plays he gives us some excellent portraits of the prude, his best presentations being Lady Gravely in *The Temple Beau* and Lady Raffler in *The Universal Gallant*. The careful distinctions that he makes between the different varieties of prudery show how carefully he had studied this frailty in women. In *The Champion* he indicates to us clearly and forcibly his feelings towards prudes of the more blatant type. In one of his later contributions to the paper to which we have already referred in which he makes use, for the purposes of satire, of his favourite Lucianic device, he describes a vision of spirits passing from this world to the next. They come to Charon's boat, but before they are allowed to get in, Mercury orders them to divest themselves of their encumbrances and strip. Among other persons who come to the banks of the river Styx there is a prude. Fielding describes her and her encounter with Mercury in a kind of language which leaves no doubt in our minds as to what his feelings were towards the prude.

"A lady of a most austere countenance," he says, "then addressed herself to Mercury, and protested that she would never part with her virtue, that she had preserved it without the least flaw for forty years in the upper regions, tho' she had had the misfortune to live in the impurest times, when women were grown so intolerably forward, that it was the most shocking thing in the world to—— She was going on, when the examiner stopping her short, cry'd out, take your virtue with you and be d—mn'd, but leave that horrible grim face behind."[1]

[1] *The Champion*, May 24, 1740.

The patriots and politicians who come in for such scathing satire in some of the plays are again the subjects of his ridicule in *The Champion*. The charge brought against them is the same, bribery and corruption.

"The art of politics," he says in one paper, "is not unlike the art of fishing. Indeed a politician may very properly be called a fisher of men: I shall therefore consider him in this light; and, as the chief excellency of both consists in choosing proper baits, I shall lay down some instructions, whereby the politician may know how to bait his hook as well as the fisherman."[1]

And he proceeds to name the several kinds of fish which a politician should angle for, and the baits with which they are to be taken.

He returns to the charge again and again, though in one of his papers he pretends with a happy touch of irony to be ill qualified for political writing and very much afraid of the pillory. Indeed, though the political activities of *The Champion* formed the special province of Ralph, and the public were assured that Dr. Lilbourne would "dose them as often as it was requisite," Fielding was constantly tempted to encroach on his colleague's domain. The principal objective of the attacks, of course, was the great Walpole himself, and Fielding used all his ingenuity in devising novel and effective methods of attack. In one paper he gravely announces "lectures on state logic by Robin Brass in which the whole art and mystery of ministerial inveighing, amusing, perplexing, evading, deceiving, bullying, corrupting, spunging, and squandering, will be first theoretically propounded; and then experimentally demonstrated."[2] In another paper he comments with great freedom on the name Robin or

[1] *The Champion*, December 15, 1739.   [2] *The Champion*, April 29, 1740.

Robert and declares that he will not determine whether robbery came from Robin or Robin from robbery. Another number of *The Champion* describes in vigorous language the condition to which Old England has been reduced by being under the treatment of a quack doctor who has dosed his victim with "aurum potabile" so constantly that "the poor wretch, from one of the finest, stoutest, healthiest, bravest fellows that perhaps was ever seen, is now become a most miserable object, and is indeed almost one entire mass of corruption."[1]

But his attacks are not always masked under a very transparent allegory or the much used device of a suggestive fictitious name for the person aimed at, a name like Robin Brass, for example, or Forage or His Honour. Sometimes he spoke quite plainly, and the freedom and boldness of the language that he used are surprising.

"I own," he says in the course of one of these open onslaughts, "there is something very ridiculous in the image of several millions of people, complaining bitterly against the insults and oppression of one man. What an idea must we conceive of this man, but that he is another Hercules, or rather a Captain Gulliver in a nation of Lilliputians! But suppose the fact so much on the contrary, that this man should be one of the meanest and every way most contemptible in his country. ... If this ever should be the case, what could we conclude but that men are harnessed as well as horses, and like them may be drove by the meanest urchin."[2]

But these quotations give an imperfect idea of the vigour and persistency of Fielding's attacks on the ministry. His political papers in *The Champion* should be read if the admirer of Fielding desires to know how great the

[1] *The Champion*, June 17, 1740.   [2] *The Champion*, May 8, 1740.

services were that he rendered to the Opposition. The vigour of the language, the picturesque variety of the devices that are made use of in launching the attacks, and the sound common sense that characterizes these papers, make them quite worth perusal, though the political controversies that gave birth to them may not have a very strong hold on the interest of the modern reader.

Another person whom Fielding attacked persistently in *The Champion* was Colley Cibber. Though the famous actor-manager was in the good graces of the Government and had considered it incumbent upon him to defend the Licensing Act in the *Apology for his Life*, Fielding's animosity to him was almost wholly personal. The Cibbers, father and son, had never found any favour in the eyes of Fielding, and the antipathy was a deep-rooted one. He had singled them out from among the people belonging to the theatrical world for some of his most unwelcome attentions. As the chief authority in Drury Lane during the earlier years of Fielding's dramatic career Colley Cibber's behaviour towards the young playwright had evidently been anything but considerate, and Fielding in revenge had ridiculed him, as we have seen, with special delight in some of his plays, notably in *The Author's Farce* and *The Historical Register*. For a long time Cibber had made no effort to retaliate. But when he wrote his famous *Apology for his Life* he could not resist the temptation of having his fling at his adversary. In describing the events that had led up to the Licensing Act he dwelt with savage delight on Fielding's indiscretions and referred to the concluding stages of his dramatic career in caustic language, and there was enough truth in his account to make the references particularly galling to Fielding. He spoke of Fielding as a "broken wit who knew that as he was in

haste to get money, it would take up less time to be in-
trepidly abusive, than decently entertaining; that, to
draw the mob after him, he would rake the channel and
pelt their superiors." Upon this principle, according to
Cibber, "he produc'd several frank and free farces, that
seem'd to knock all distinctions of mankind on the head:
religion, laws, government, priests, judges and ministers
were all laid flat at the feet of this Herculean satirist!
This Drawcansir in wit that spared neither friend nor
foe! who to make his poetical fame immortal, like another
Erostratus, set fire to the stage, by writing up to an act of
parliament to demolish it."[1] He did not name Fielding
at all in the course of this invective and he pretended to
despise the offending plays so much that he said that he
would not give the particular strokes of Fielding's ingenuity a chance to be remembered.

The *Apology* was published in April, 1740, and there
was enough in the idea and execution of the work to give
Fielding an excellent opportunity of retaliating on his
old enemy for this new provocation. He devoted quite a
number of articles in *The Champion* exclusively to Colley
Cibber and his *Apology*. Indeed, the matter did not end
there; as in his later work, too, he does not miss any opportunity of making fun of Colley Cibber and his *Apology*.
Though his readers must have felt that they had a surfeit
of jokes at the expense of Cibber, the humour of the
papers in which Fielding has his fling at Cibber is delightful, and some of them, particularly the one that contains an account of the trial of Col. Apol in Captain Hercules Vinegar's Court of Censorial Enquiry, are among
the best in *The Champion*. He makes fun of the title and
idea of the book, and with delightful irony deprecates the

[1] *An Apology for the Life of Colley Cibber, Comedian*, Chap. VIII.

author's modesty in calling it an *Apology for his Own Life* and not "an Apology for the Life of One who hath played a very comical part which, tho' theatrical, hath been acted on a much larger stage than Drury Lane."[1] In another paper one of the correspondents of *The Champion* is made to express the opinion that "however that illustrious person the most inimitable laureat may wind up as a man, he will certainly end as an author with a very bad life."[2] Some of Cibber's rather absurd statements in the *Apology* are held up to deserved ridicule, and in one paper Fielding gives his readers an excellent parody of Cibber's efforts at fine writing and his empty rhetorical flourishes.[3] Again, he makes fun of Cibber's mistakes in grammar and orthography which, though frequent enough, were not so outrageous as Fielding tries to make out.[4]

His most effective hits at Cibber, however, were made in two papers in which we have his humour at its best. One contains an attack on Cibber's language in the *Apology* and makes fun of him for his bad grammar and sublime style which Fielding says come upon the reader like a blunderbuss and carry everything before them. In this paper Colley Cibber under the name of Col. Apol is arraigned before Captain Hercules Vinegar's Court of Censorial Enquiry on a charge of having made an assault upon and murdered the English language with a certain weapon called a goosequill, value one farthing, which he had held in his left hand. The account of Col. Apol's examination is an excellent burlesque of legal phraseology, and the prisoner's statement before the Court in which the language of the *Apology* is delightfully parodied is one of the best *jeux d'esprit* we have in *The Champion*.

[1] *The Champion*, April 22, 1740.   [2] *The Champion*, April 1, 1740
[3] *The Champion*, May 6, 1740.   [4] *The Champion*, April 22, 1740.

"Sir," he says, "I am as innocent as the child which hath not yet enter'd into human nature of the fact laid to my charge. This accusation is the forward spring of envy of my laurel. It is impossible I should have any enmity to the English language, with which I am so little acquainted; if therefore I have struck any wounds into it, they have rolled from accident only. I confess in my book that when I am warmed with a thought my imagination is apt to run away with me, and make me talk nonsense. Besides, if the English language be destroyed, it ought not to be laid to my charge, since I can evidently demonstrate that other literati have used the said language more barbarously than I have."[1]

The passage in which the other memorable attack is made on the elder Cibber occurs in the course of Fielding's delightful account of his Lucianic vision, certainly the best vision described in *The Champion*. "I was meditating," Fielding says in the paper which contains this account, "on the hard fate which beauty generally meets with, when my eyes were diverted by an elderly gentleman with a piece of wither'd laurel on his head. As soon as he was stripped, we observed a little book which he had bound close to his heart. I read the words Love in a Riddle[2] very plain, but he was obliged after many entreaties to leave it behind him. I was surprised to see him pass examination with his laurel on, and was assured by the standers by, that Mercury would have taken it off, if he had seen it."[3]

But though these personal attacks and controversial papers are excellent reading, and some of them real masterpieces of this particular kind of composition, they do

[1] *The Champion*, May 17, 1740.
[2] A pastoral produced by Cibber at Drury Lane in 1729.
[3] *The Champion*, May 24, 1740.

not make up the whole account of the good work that
Fielding did for *The Champion*. His serious and didactic
papers, though heavy reading on the whole, contain
much that deserves attention, and they are of special interest to us not only because they throw more light on his
views on important matters than his plays do, but also because we derive from them much valuable information
about his ethical standards and his religious convictions.

Among the serious papers must also be included those
in which he pays enthusiastic tributes to some of the men
of genius of his time. His eulogies on the work of Hogarth and George Lillo the dramatist deserve particular
mention. George Lillo, a very lovable man, was a *persona
grata* with Fielding, and the latter's admiration and
friendship for the man led him to estimate his dramatic
genius too highly, though the tribute paid in *The Champion* to the character of the man is in no sense extravagant
or partial.[1] To the merits of Hogarth Fielding bears witness in an eloquent passage, and the eulogy is one of the
earliest tributes paid to the genius of the great satirist.

"I esteem," he says, "the ingenious Mr. Hogarth as
one of the most useful satirists any age hath produced. In
his excellent works you see the delusive scene exposed
with all the force of humour, and, on casting your eyes on
another picture, you behold the dreadful and fatal consequence. I almost dare affirm that those two works of his
which he calls the Rake's and the Harlot's Progress, are
calculated more to serve the cause of virtue, and for the
preservation of mankind, than all the folios of morality
which have been ever written; and a sober family should
no more be without them, than without the *Whole Duty
of Man* in their house."[2]

[1] *The Champion*, February 26, 1740.   [2] *The Champion*, June 10, 1740.

The majority of Fielding's serious papers to *The Champion*, however, are devoted to moralizing, and though as a rule he is eloquent and impressive as a preacher of lay sermons he does not "enliven his morality with wit" to the same extent that the elder essayists do in *The Tatler* or *The Spectator*, though occasionally, as for example, in his remarks on swearing[1] or on "roasting,"[2] he shows something of the lightness of touch of Addison or Steele.

In his serious papers besides dealing with abstract subjects like virtue, charity, or self knowledge, Fielding satirizes the ignorance of the age, and particularly that of the learned professions, in very much the same strain in which he had held it up to ridicule in *Pasquin*.[3] He exposes the incompetence, greed and ignorance of magistrates in a very interesting paper in which we have some extracts from "the Voyages of Mr. Job Vinegar."[4] He describes in vigorous language the vices and frailties of men and women belonging to the fashionable world.[5] In more than one splendid paper on charity he makes eloquent appeals on behalf of debtors and denounces the practice of imprisonment for debt in powerful language. "How agreeable," he says in one paper, "the making such numbers of subjects not only useless to, but a burden on the community, may be to a wise or a polite nation, or the inflicting such misery on so many for sometimes no offence, may be to a human or a Christian people, I will not determine. The wisdom and goodness of our common law suffer'd this only in cases of violent trespasses, or for debts due to the king, till the Devil found means by slow degrees, and by several statutes,

[1] *The Champion*, January 17, 1740.   [2] *The Champion*, March 13, 1740.
[3] *The Champion*, December 25, 1739.   [4] *The Champion*, March 20, 1740.
[5] *The Champion*. January 29, 1740.

which gave this satisfaction, as it is call'd, first in account, afterwards in debt, etc., to introduce this prototype of Hell more generally."[1]

But of all the serious papers that he contributed to *The Champion* the best are those on charity and on the office and duties of the clergyman. Apart from their intrinsic merit, they are of very great interest to the admirer of Fielding's novels because they deal with matters to which the novelist attached the greatest importance and on which he had bestowed his deepest thought. According to him, want of charity among men is one of the greatest evils in society, and the great theme to which he recurs constantly in his writings is this want of "the most Christian virtue" among men. In *The Champion* he tells us what his conception of true charity is and who are the most proper objects of it.[2] He declares that he does not know a better general definition of virtue than that it is a delight in doing good. When he pleads for charity among men, we feel that there is a world of observation and experience behind his words which give them their remarkable power of appeal. It is one of those subjects that have the power to inspire his genius to make its noblest effort. And the reader of his papers on charity can hardly fail to notice that when he writes on this subject, he drops his usual tone of good-humoured banter and addresses himself to his reader in deep earnestness. The following passage from one of his papers will illustrate this:

"I declare, that henceforth, a hole in a man's stocking shall make no flaw in his reputation, unless the stocking be a very fine one, or the wearer rides in a chair. I do likewise, in the humblest manner, address myself to all ladies

[1] *The Champion*, February 19, 1740.
[2] *The Champion*, February 16, 1740, and April 5, 1740.

of quality, entreating them that their ladyships would be pleased never in the presence of any of their sex who are not of quality, to admire at the rustic constitutions of persons who can get up early in the morning, nor ever to mention such words as clerks of the kitchen, bills of fare, pyramids of desserts, rich wines, or any of the necessaries of great tables, nor condemn the beastliness of hackney chairs, rose diamonds, paste necklaces, coarse lace, thin edgings, colour'd stockings, frippery lutestrings or any other plain ornaments of beauty."[1]

There is such frequent recurrence to this theme in *The Champion* that we can scarcely fail to realize that Fielding looked upon charity as the basis of all that is good and noble in man's character. He makes it plain to us in his papers that in estimating the true worth of a man and the beauty and nobility of his character he placed the virtue of charity in the forefront. And it would be well for us in passing judgments on the characters in his novels if we keep clear before our minds the standards that he sets before us in his splendid papers on charity in *The Champion*. The insight that we obtain into his moral standards from utterances like the following ought to assist us considerably in doing justice to some of his characters in the novels.

"I own," he says in one of his papers on charity, "I am one of those who think there is some merit in misfortunes, especially when they are not balanced with guilt. I look on indiscretion with pity, not abhorrence, and on no indiscretion with so much pity as that of extravagance, which as it may bring men into the greatest calamities of this life; so may it arise from the goodness, the openness, and the generosity of the heart; qualities which naturally

[1] *The Champion*, February 19, 1740.

enlarge in every man's eye the idea of his possessions, as avarice lessens it."[1]

The most striking portraits that Fielding has painted in his novels are those of the country squire and the clergyman. From the pictures of country squires that he has given to us in his plays we know how greatly he excelled in portraying this particular class of men. As regards the clergy, beyond the general satire that he indulges in against the Church in *Pasquin* and a slight sketch of a country clergyman in *The Grub-Street Opera*, he has little to say about them in his plays. In *The Champion*, however, he tells us at some length what his conception of the clergyman's vocation is and what are the virtues and qualifications that are expected to be found in him.

"A clergyman," he says, "is a successor of Christ's disciples. A character which not only includes an idea of all the moral virtues, such as temperance, charity, patience, etc., but he must be humble, charitable, benevolent, void of envy, void of pride, void of vanity, void of rapaciousness, gentle, candid, truly sorry for the sins and misfortunes of men and rejoicing in their virtue and happiness."[2]

In an earlier paper he gives us a portrait of the good country clergyman painted, as he tells us, from life, and this is evidently a rudimentary study of the immortal Parson Adams. He gives us another picture also, that of the clergyman who is a disgrace to his order. This is painted with vigorous and realistic touches, and we find many of the imperfections and weaknesses that he speaks of here held up to condemnation in a very effective manner in some striking characters in his novels. There is a

[1] *The Champion*, February 16, 1740.   [2] *The Champion*, April 19, 1740.

picturesque vigour in his words which proves that there is much observation and experience behind them.

"Let us suppose then," he says, "a man of loose morals, proud, malevolent, vain, rapacious, and revengeful; not grieving at, but triumphing over the sins of men, and rejoicing, like the devil, that they will be punished for them; deaf to the cries of the poor; shunning the distress'd; blind to merit; a magnifier and spreader of slander; not shunning the society of the wicked for fear of contamination, but from hypocrisy and vainglory; hating not vice but the vicious; resenting not only an injury, but the least affront with inveteracy. Let us suppose this man feasting himself luxuriously at the tables of the great, where he is suffered at the expense of flattering their vices, and often too as meanly submitting to see himself and his order, nay often religion itself, ridiculed, whilst, that he may join in the Burgundy, he joins in the laugh, or rather is laughed at by the fools he flatters."[1]

[1] *The Champion*, April 19, 1740.

CHAPTER V

FIRST EFFORTS IN FICTION

THOUGH his contributions to *The Champion* did not cease altogether after Fielding was called to the Bar on the 20th of June, 1740, he seems to have devoted the greater part of his time and energies to his profession. We know very little of his life as a barrister except that he had chambers at No. 4 Pump Court, that he attended the Western Circuit and was most assiduous in his attendance at Westminster. But his labours were not rewarded with even a modest measure of professional and financial success. Unfortunately, soon after he entered on his new profession he became a victim to gout and this was fatal to his practice.

In the beginning of the year 1741 we find him busy with his pen, and this indicates that he was far from being engrossed in work in the law courts. Early in January he published a poem of considerable length named *Of True Greatness* which is of interest because it foreshadows some of the ideas which underlie his greatest satiric work, *Jonathan Wild*. It is a panegyric in heroic couplets on some of his friends in the political world, notably on George Bubb Dodington, who was assailed at this time by the ministerial Press on account of his secession to the Opposition. In an interesting preface to the poem Fielding makes common cause with the rather dubious object of his admiration and complains of the injuries that he had himself received at the hands of his enemies. *Of True Greatness* was afterwards reprinted in the *Miscellanies* of 1743.

In the same month Fielding made another poetic effort in a strain more suited to his genius. *The Vernoniad*, the main purpose of which was to celebrate the exploits of Admiral Vernon in his expedition against Porto Bello in 1739 and to denounce Walpole, is an elaborate attempt to burlesque the classical epic style, and incidentally to ridicule the pedantry of learned commentators of the day, though the young satirist himself exhibits something of the pedantry he ridicules. The title page of the poem, an amusing jargon of Greek and English letters, informed the reader that *The Vernoniad* was the first book of a poem originally written by Homer, and now done into English from a manuscript "lately found at Constantinople." The notes which were appended to the supposed translation exhibit something of the ingenuity but not the humour of the notes to *Tom Thumb*. Fielding never specifically acknowledged *The Vernoniad* as his work, though an extant order in his handwriting given to John Nourse the bookseller to deliver fifty copies of the poem to Mr. Chappelle, one of the proprietors of *The Champion*, which Roscoe printed in his edition of the novelist's works, places the question of the authorship beyond doubt.

Soon after this Fielding appears to have published anonymously a political pamphlet named *The Crisis*, a kind of election manifesto in the form of a sermon addressed to the public on behalf of the Opposition. Though nowhere acknowledged by him as his, this pamphlet, the full title of which is, *The Crisis: A Sermon, on Revel.* xiv. 9, 10, 11. *Necessary to be preached in all the Churches in England, Wales, and Berwick upon Tweed, at or before the next General Election*, has been ascribed to him on the evidence of its style and on the authority of Nichols who in his *Literary Anecdotes* tells us that he had in his posses-

sion a copy of it on the title page of which a former owner
had noted the following words, "This sermon was written by the late Mr. Fielding, author of *Tom Jones*, etc., as
the printer of it assured me."[1]

The same year in December appeared the striking
pamphlet named *The Opposition, A Vision*, afterwards acknowledged by Fielding as his in the Preface to the *Miscellanies*. In this pamphlet we have an indication of his
disaffection towards his party and its leaders in the
graphic picture that is given, by way of a vision, of a waggon loaded with immense trunks labelled "Grievances,"
"Public Spirit," "Motions for 1741–2," and with passengers. This waggon, which is drawn by asses, is stopped
by the coach of a fat gentleman who causes the asses to be
unharnessed and turned into a "delicious meadow." As
this fat gentleman proceeds on his way many passengers
from the waggon clamber up behind his coach. The
satire, of course, was directed against place hunters
among the members of the Opposition.

The year 1742, particularly the winter, was a time of
great distress and anxiety for our novelist, as he tells us in
his Preface to the *Miscellanies* of 1743. To add to the
anxieties arising from his financial difficulties, his wife
and child were both seriously ill and the latter died of this
illness in March. It was at this time of sickness and distress that he began his career as a novelist.

The world owes a very great debt to the pecuniary
difficulties that nearly overwhelmed Fielding at this time.
They drove him back to literature and compelled him to
try his hand at various kinds of literary work till he was
able to discover the field in which his genius was destined
to win its greatest triumphs. But his pecuniary distresses

[1] J. Nichols, *Literary Anecdotes of the Eighteenth Century*, 1814, VIII, 446.

were not solely or even mainly responsible for the immortality that he attained. We know that it was the spirit of burlesque in Fielding that produced *The History of Joseph Andrews*, and it has been truly remarked that if *Pamela* had never been written it is more than possible that English literature would never have known *Joseph Andrews*, *Tom Jones*, or *Amelia*. With *The History of Joseph Andrews*, however, Fielding made a conquest of a new kingdom, as it were, over which he was destined to rule in undisputed supremacy.

Richardson published his great and extraordinary novel anonymously in November, 1740. The history of the origin of *Pamela, or Virtue Rewarded* is an interesting one. At the request of the booksellers Rivington and Osborne the smug and prosperous printer of Salisbury Court, who was well qualified for the work by the training he had given himself in early life when he was the confidant and amanuensis of numerous young women, undertook to compile a series of familiar letters on "the useful concerns in common life," and while he was engaged in this work he bethought him of a story that he had heard of a young and beautiful girl, the daughter of honest and pious parents, who while working as a servant in a great family had been sore beset by the attempts made on her virtue by her mistress's son, but had risen superior both to her humble station in life and her dangerous situation, and had finally persuaded her would-be seducer to make her his wife. On this story from real life, as he tells Aaron Hill in one of his letters to him, Richardson founded his first novel, and he created a heroine over whom his contemporaries went into raptures. Lady Mary Montagu, who was no admirer of Richardson's character, bears witness to the extraordinary success of the novel,[1] and Horace Walpole in one of his juvenile letters, from which Miss Anna Seward quotes at the beginning of the next century, describes the popularity of *Pamela* in picturesque language. "The late singular novel," he writes, "is the universal and only theme—Pamela is like snow, she covers everything with her whiteness."[2] "Sylvanus Urban" in the *Gentleman's Magazine* for January, 1741, excuses himself for not reviewing what everybody has read, "it being judged in town," he says, "as great a sign of want of curiosity not to have read *Pamela* as not to have seen the French and Italian dancers."

The success of the novel was indeed phenomenal. Not only did the story in spite of its prolixity and monotony captivate the popular imagination, but the morality of the book, of which Richardson made a great parade on the title page as well as in his preface and in two commendatory letters with which he endeavoured to impose on the public, was applauded to an extent which it did not deserve. Dr. Slocock, chaplain of St. Saviour's, Southwark, recommended it from the pulpit, clergymen dedicated their theological treatises to the novelist, and the great Pope declared that it would do more good than volumes of sermons. It was translated into French and Italian, and Lady Mary Montagu tells us that "it was all the fashion at Paris and Versailles."[3] Dramatic versions of the novel were produced in the theatres in London and Paris, and within a year of its publication six editions of *Pamela* were issued.

[1] *Lady Mary Montagu's Letters and Works*, edited by Lord Wharncliffe, 1861, Vol. II, p. 200 (Letter to the Countess of Bute).
[2] *Letters of Anna Seward written between the years 1784 and 1807*, Edinburgh, 1811, Vol. V, p. 431.
[3] *Lady Mary Montagu's Letters and Works*, Wharncliffe's Edition, 1861. Vol II, p. 200 (Letter to the Countess of Bute).

But the applause, great as it was, was not quite unanimous. There were a few who were suspicious of the morality of the book, and there were booklets like *The Virgin in Eden, Anti-Pamela or Pamela Censured*, in which the morality of Richardson's novel was challenged. The good Dr. Watts, well known as a writer of hymns, complained of the indelicacy of some of the scenes.

Fielding was one of the few who laughed at the morality of *Pamela*, and he revolted as much against the author's mentality and his pretensions as a moralist as against the mawkish sentimentality of the novel itself. Constitutionally he was quite incapable of responding to the emotional appeal of *Pamela*. To him the virtue of Pamela appeared, as it has done to so many people since Richardson's days, as a strange mixture of innocence, prudery, and prudence, as something unnatural and absurd, and it aroused, as Austin Dobson says, "inextinguishable Homeric laughter" in him. And indeed after the "pomp and parade," to use Richardson's own words about the extravagances of novelists, of his morality in his preface and commendatory letters, to find the heroine in whom the novelist portrays the embodiment of his much lauded virtue making an excellent bargain with her "tickling commodity," a heroine who has always a shrewd eye on the main chance in spite of her simplicity and supposed ignorance of the ways of the wicked world, would be a discovery that would tickle the fancy of people whose sense of humour was much less keen than that of Henry Fielding. Mrs. Barbauld draws attention to some of the solecisms in *Pamela* in very pertinent language.

"The moral of this piece," she says in her *Life of Richardson* prefixed to her edition of the novelist's correspondence, "is more dubious than, in his lifetime, the author's friends were willing to allow. So long as Pamela is solely occupied in schemes to escape from her persecutor, her virtuous resistance obtains our unqualified approbation; but from the moment she begins to entertain hopes of marrying him, we admire her guarded prudence, rather than her purity of mind. She has an end in view, an interested end, and we can only consider her as the conscious possessor of a treasure which she is wisely resolved not to part with but for its just price."[1]

And a great many readers of Richardson's novel have felt that though they could perhaps forgive Pamela for admiring her master, it is impossible to forgive her for becoming his wife in the circumstances that ensue. The "*innocent* stratagems" that she makes use of in order to escape the snares which are laid for her virtue scarcely enhance our respect for her, particularly when we realize that she makes little effort to escape from his power. This conviction is fatal to the sympathy that might otherwise have been aroused for her.

But this dissatisfaction with Richardson's heroine and the consequent revolt against the morality inculcated in the novel do not make up the whole case against the novelist. It was a perverted and unhealthy taste which made him dwell continuously on a theme which could not fail to give offence if elaborated. In the accounts that are given in the novel of the numerous assaults made on Pamela's virtue Richardson betrays a pruriency of imagination that is as reprehensible as the unabashed coarseness of Fielding or Smollett.

The robust common sense of Fielding was up in arms against the false morality and against the sickly senti-

---

[1]Mrs. Barbauld, "Life of Samuel Richardson," prefixed to *The Correspondence of S. Richardson*, London, 1804, Vol. I, pp. lxiii-lxiv.

mentality of *Pamela*. But he was more inclined to laugh than to condemn. The laughter with which his whole frame was shaking demanded an outlet, and the spirit of burlesque that had asserted itself so often in the past was uppermost in him again. *Pamela* roused this spirit so effectually that he seems to have tried his hand at burlesque of the popular favourite more than once. In April, 1741,[1] by which time *Pamela* had run into three editions, appeared a very clever parody on Richardson's novel in the shape of a collection of rather gross letters preceded by a burlesque preface and two satiric commendatory letters ridiculing those that Richardson had prefixed to his novel. This somewhat disreputable performance bore the title, *An Apology for the Life of Mrs. Shamela Andrews*, and the title page declared that in this book "the many notorious falsehoods and misrepresentations of a book called *Pamela* are exposed and refuted; and all the matchless arts of that young politician set in a true and just light." The author's name was given as Conny Keyber and the book was printed for A. Dodd who had already published some works which had been ascribed to Fielding.

Ostensibly the occasion of the book is the presentation of a copy of *Pamela* by a certain Parson Tickletext to his friend Parson Oliver. At the time the book is sent Parson Tickletext writes a letter to his friend which overflows with lavish praise of the novel, and the good man desires his friend to present the book to his little god-daughter and also to give the maids in the house an opportunity of reading it; or if they cannot do that, to have it read to them, this being the only education Parson Tickletext and other admirers of the book intend henceforth to give

[1] *The Craftsman*, April 4, 1741.

to their girls. To this Parson Oliver replies that he is sorry the novel has so great a vogue, for, as he lives in the neighbourhood in which its events took place, he has a better opportunity than others of knowing the actual facts of the case, and he sends a number of letters to his friend to prove that the "lady," whose real name is Shamela and who is known to be the daughter of disreputable parents, is very far from being the innocent and virtuous woman she is represented to be. She is, in fact, a thoroughly abandoned character and the hero of the novel is a fool to be taken in by her. *An Apology for the Life of Shamela Andrews* concludes with a brief summary by Parson Oliver of the shortcomings of *Pamela,* and the criticisms that are made are as just as they are trenchant.

"The confederating," says Parson Oliver in his last letter, "to cry up a nonsensical ridiculous book, (I believe the most extensively so of any ever yet published,) and to be so weak and so wicked as to pretend to make it a matter of religion! Whereas so far from having any moral tendency, the book is by no means innocent."[1]

The great majority of the letters in *Shamela* are unusually gross ones and the performance reflects no credit on Fielding, if it is his work at all. Either for this reason or because they do not possess the necessary evidence Fielding's biographers and editors have not included *Shamela* among his writings, and Mrs. Barbauld does not mention this work at all in her *Life of Richardson*.

A close examination of *Shamela*, however, furnishes us with a good deal of evidence, and on the strength of this some recent biographers of Fielding, Wilbur Cross,[2] for example, have definitely ascribed the book to him. Rich-

[1] *An Apology for the Life of Mrs. Shamela Andrews*, London, 1741, p. 56.
[2] *The History of Henry Fielding.* Vol. I, p. 304.

ardson believed Fielding to be the author of *Shamela*.[1]
Horace Walpole was also of the same opinion, as he wrote
the words "By Fielding" on his copy of *Shamela* which is
now in the collection of Mr. A. S. Rosenbach of Philadelphia. And in a letter which Thomas Dampier, who
was afterwards sub-master of Eton and Dean of Durham,
wrote to some friends in Geneva on the 30th of July,
1741, he says that Fielding wrote *Shamela* to burlesque
Pamela.

The internal evidence of the book also seems to point
to Fielding as its author. The style is very much like
Fielding's and the forms "doth" and "hath" which he
invariably uses occur constantly in the letters in *Shamela*.
Some of the names in the book, like Squire Booby, Parson Oliver,[2] Parson Tickletext,[3] and the name of the supposed author, Conny Keyber,[4] undoubtedly suggest
Fielding's connection with the work. Some of the mala-
propisms of Mrs. Jewkes in *Shamela* are the same as
those of Mrs. Slipslop in *Joseph Andrews*. Many years
afterwards one of the numerous jokes perpetrated at the
expense of Fielding's last novel was the advertisement of
a parody on *Amelia* and this parody was named *Shamelia*.
After carefully weighing all this evidence Mr. R. Brim-

[1]Mrs. Barbauld, *Correspondence of S. Richardson*, Vol. IV, p. 285 (Letter
to Mrs. Belfour).
[2]Oliver was the name of the incumbent of Motcombe, near East Stour in
Dorset, who, according to Murphy, had charge of the education of Fielding
when a boy. The same authority says that he was the original of Parson
Trulliber.
[3]The only clergyman who appears in Fielding's plays is named Parson
Puzzletext. Puzzletext is chaplain to the Welsh squire, Sir Owen Apshinken,
in *The Grub-Street Opera*.
[4]Keyber is the name of the gentleman in *The Author's Farce* to whom
Luckless sends his play. Conny is evidently an abbreviation of Conyers, the
Christian name of Dr. Middleton, principal librarian of the University of
Cambridge, whose dedication of his *Life of Cicero* to Lord Hervey is parodied
in the dedication of *Shamela* to "Fanny."

ley Johnson, who has recently brought out a reprint of
Shamela,[1] is quite satisfied, as many others are, that the
reasons for attributing *Shamela* to Fielding are sound and
convincing.

If *An Apology for the Life of Mrs. Shamela Andrews*
was written by Fielding, this, as we know, was not the
only effort that he made to ridicule *Pamela*. The name
given to the first parody as well as certain expressions
that are used in some of the letters in *Shamela* suggest
that when the book was written Fielding was under the
impression that *Pamela* was the work of Colley Cibber,
and we can imagine the delight he would feel in getting
another opportunity of having a fling at his old enemy.
He used all his ingenuity to make his parody striking and
effective, and deliberately went much further than Richardson had done in the pruriency of his imagination, and
described in unusually coarse language all the details of
Shamela's encounters with her would-be seducer. A
work like this was bound to attract a certain class of
readers and evidently their number was not small, for a
second edition of the book was issued before the end of
the year.

Meanwhile, the success of Richardson's novel had
called forth numerous imitations and one or two sequels.
Richardson himself complained afterwards of sixteen of
these "scandalous engraftments." One of the most ambitious of these, *Pamela's Conduct in High Life*, appeared
in September, 1741[2], and this worthless performance induced Richardson to write in self-defence his own sequel
to his story which was published in December.[3] This

[1] *An Apology for the Life of Mrs. Shamela Andrews*, with an Introduction
by R. Brimley Johnson, The Golden Cockerel Press, 1926.
[2] *The General Evening Post*, September 10-12, 1741.
[3] *The Champion*, December 10, 1741.

continuation of the story contained nothing in the shape of new interest in the development of action or plot, and the two volumes in which Richardson endeavoured "to depict Pamela in her exalted condition" were utter failures. He still professed to conceal his identity by announcing on the title page of the third and fourth volumes of *Pamela* that they were written by the "editor" of the two first. But by this time or early next year the authorship of *Pamela* was no longer a secret.

It would be interesting if we could ascertain definitely that Fielding decided to make a second attempt at burlesquing *Pamela* (assuming that *Shamela* was written by him) when he came to know that the novel was the work of Richardson and not of Colley Cibber. This would give us a clue as to when he commenced writing *Joseph Andrews* and it would also account for, to some extent, the renewal of the attack on *Pamela*, though the persistency of his attacks on Colley Cibber's *Apology* shows that he could pursue the same author with ridicule for quite a long time.

If we argue that Fielding determined to make a fresh attack on *Pamela* when he discovered that Colley Cibber was not the author of the novel, then Fielding must have begun to write *Joseph Andrews* about the end of the year 1741 when he was confined to his house in Spring Gardens, Charing Cross, by his gout of which he speaks in his Preface to the *Miscellanies*. But it is quite likely that the novel was begun earlier. The last months of the year 1741 were full of troubles for him, and when we think of these we may be inclined to feel doubtful if the novel could in these circumstances be finished in two months.

The History of the Adventures of Joseph Andrews and of his Friend Mr. Abraham Adams was published by Andrew

Millar on the 22nd of February, 1742[1] in two duodecimo volumes. The title page described the novel as "written in imitation of the manner of Cervantes, author of *Don Quixote*," and Fielding's name did not appear on it.

In his carefully written Preface to the novel Fielding declares that he is giving to the world a kind of writing which he does not remember to have seen attempted hitherto in the English language, and he proceeds to explain at some length what his conception of the comic romance is and how far burlesque is admissible in such a work. Incidentally he gives his reader an exposition of his theory of humour. He declares that life everywhere furnishes the observer with the ridiculous; that the only source of the true ridiculous is affectation, and affectation proceeds from one of two causes, vanity or hypocrisy. He points out that though Aristotle declares that villainy is not the proper subject of ridicule he does not say what is; nor does the Abbé Bellegarde, who has written a treatise on the subject, trace it to its foundation.

Fielding's exposition, though couched in plausible language, is not very satisfactory, and he did not follow in his writings the principles that he enunciated when he commenced his career as a novelist. But the Preface as well as the introductory chapters to the first three books of *Joseph Andrews* are little masterpieces of critical composition.

The title page of *Joseph Andrews*, as we have pointed out, described the novel as written in imitation of the manner of Cervantes. The affinity between the two novelists is seen in many things. For example, in both we have the keenest perception of that which is ridiculous in the characters and actions of men, and the debt that Fielding

[1] *The Daily Gazetteer*, February 22, 1742.

owes to the Spanish novelist for his most elaborate study of character in *Joseph Andrews*, that of Parson Adams, is a considerable one. Both the novelists affect a certain drollery in their styles which frequently takes a mock heroic turn. They both give us considerable insight into the characters of certain classes of men and women, inn-keepers, ostlers, chambermaids, puppet-show men, and so forth; and in both we have a very refreshing geniality of temperament.

In some less important features of their novels also, as in the grouping of their chapters into different books or in the humorous or satiric descriptions of the contents of their chapters, or again, in the introduction of extrane-ous stories or episodes into their main narrative there are resemblances between the writings of Fielding and Cer-vantes.

But Fielding seems to have over-estimated his debt to the great Spanish writer who, as we know, was an early favourite with him. In so far as the essentials of its great-ness are concerned the kind of novel that Fielding created owed little to the genius of Cervantes. None of Fielding's works breathes that air of romance, that aspiration after imaginary good, that vague longing for something more than we possess that are such striking features of Cer-vantes' masterpiece. Again, each one of Cervantes' lead-ing characters has a kind of abnormal individuality of his own. As Hazlitt says, they do not so much belong to, as form a class by themselves.[1] They have little in common with the people around them, and their life is not the nor-mal life of the times.

Fielding set out to picture the ordinary life of the

[1]Hazlitt, *Lectures on the English Comic Writers*, Lecture VI, "On the English Novelists."

times. His ambition was to give faithful pictures of men
and women as they were to be found in the ordinary walks
of life. He had little use for that which was abnormal,
grotesque, or unnatural. His own experiences in life
supplied him with sufficient material for the purposes of
his art.

Since Fielding specifically acknowledges the influence
of a master in the evolution of his art in *Joseph Andrews*,
and as he refers in the course of his work to great writers
of fiction like Scarron, Le Sage, and Marivaux,[1] whose
novels present some resemblances to his own, his readers
and critics have endeavoured to find models for *Joseph
Andrews* in *Le Roman comique*, *Gil Blas*, *Marianne*, or *Le
Paysan parvenu*. It is true that there are certain features
of the picaresque novel in Fielding's work. *Joseph Andrews* is an epic of the road, its characters are mainly
those of the picaresque novel of Spain or France, and its
plot is neither very skilfully constructed nor very elaborate. In these respects and in the magnificent mock heroic
descriptions which are such a striking feature of the novel,
Joseph Andrews presents certain resemblances to novels
like *Le Roman comique* or *Gil Blas*; but the resemblances
are so superficial and slight that they do anything but
establish the fact that Fielding was indebted to any great
extent either to Scarron or to Le Sage, though he may
have borrowed some ideas from his great predecessors in
the art of fiction. He tells us in his Preface to *Joseph Andrews* that "everything in that novel is copied from the
book of nature, and scarce a character or action produced
which he has not taken from his own observations and
experience." If in writing *Joseph Andrews* he was indebted to any considerable extent to any previous writer it

---

[1] *Joseph Andrews*, Book III, Chap. I.

was to Marivaux; but the debt was not due to *Marianne*
as a German scholar has tried to prove.[1] The identification of Joseph as Wilson's son by means of the straw-
berry mole on his breast was not an idea borrowed from
Marianne, as it has been shown that the recognition
scene in *Marianne* from which the idea was supposed to
have been borrowed was not written by Marivaux but is
part of a later addition to the novel which was made after
the publication of *Joseph Andrews*.

The book to which Fielding seems to have been most
indebted was Marivaux's *Le Paysan parvenu*. This novel
had the interest of a comparatively recent publication
when Fielding began to write *Joseph Andrews*, as the five
parts of the French novelist's unfinished work were published during the years 1735 and 1736. But in the very
interesting catalogue preserved in the British Museum
of Fielding's library which was sold by auction soon after
the novelist's death the names of Marivaux's novels do
not occur at all. This circumstance, however, is not in itself significant of anything. As a matter of fact the catalogue contains the names of very few works of fiction, and
it is evident from Fielding's frequent references to Marivaux that he knew the writings of the French novelist
very well.

The main drift of Marivaux's story in *Le Paysan parvenu* is very different from Fielding's, but there are certain resemblances between some of the characters and
episodes in the two novels which seem to point to the fact
that Fielding found in the novel of the gifted and lively
but somewhat erratic French writer some ideas which he
was glad to make use of. Fielding's Joseph Andrews, like

---

[1] Erich Bosdorf, *Entstehungsgeschichte von Fieldings „Joseph Andrews,"*
Berlin, 1908, p. 40.

Marivaux's hero Jacob, is a young serving man whose
beauty and charm of manner make his mistress and other
women fall violently in love with him. Lady Booby greatly
resembles Jacob's mistress as Marivaux describes her,
"une femme qui passoit sa vie dans toutes les dissipations
du grand monde, qui alloit aux spectacles, soupoit en
ville, se couchoit à quatre heures du matin, se levoit à
une heure après midi."[1] Sir Thomas Booby and his lady,
like Jacob's master and mistress, are far from being an
affectionate couple. Betty, the chambermaid in *Joseph
Andrews* reminds one of Marivaux's Génevieve. Betty,
like Génevieve, falls in love with the handsome young
hero of the story, and like Génevieve again, receives the
attentions of her master. But probably Fielding's debt to
Marivaux is greatest in the account that he gives of Lady
Booby's infatuation for her handsome young footman,
and of the interviews she has with him. Marivaux describes a number of such interviews in which, however,
his hero Jacob, who finds favour in the eyes of more than
one woman far above his station in life, behaves very dif-
ferently from the immaculate Joseph. Marivaux's hero
is anything but backward in responding to the advances
made by his admirers and has no pretensions to the virtue
of Joseph. His conduct during his interview with his
mistress is very different from Joseph's.

"Je n'étois pas né indifferent," he says in describing
it, "il s'en falloit beaucoup; cette dame avoit de la fraicheur
& de l'embonpoint, & mes yeux lorgnoient volontiers.

"Elle s'en apperçut & sourit de la distraction qu'elle
me donnoit; moi je vis qu'elle s'en appercevoit, & je me
mis à rire aussi d'un air que la honte d'être pris sur le fait
& le plaisir de voir, rendoient moitié niais & moitié ten-

[1] *Le Paysan parvenu,* 1737, Première Partie, p. 10.

dre; & la regardant avec des yeux mêlés de tout ce que je dis-la, je ne lui disois rien."[1]

And in Jacob's other *tête-à-tête* with women like Madame de Ferval or Madame de Fecour who are in love with him there is the same gallantry in his behaviour and the same readiness to carry on the intrigue. One is tempted to believe that these affairs of Jacob suggested to Fielding the idea of Tom Jones' liaison with Lady Bellaston. Fielding's hero in *Joseph Andrews*, as we know, is very different; and, of course, the burlesque to which Fielding committed himself when he commenced writing the novel made it essential that he should be different from Marivaux's hero.

But, after all, Fielding's debt to other writers in the matter of his character sketches in *Joseph Andrews* is a comparatively insignificant one, and most of his portraits were painted directly from life. Notwithstanding the statement that he makes in his preface to the novel that his readers would find it impossible to guess at the originals of his characters, attempts have been made to identify some of them. The original of Parson Adams has been traced to an early friend of the novelist, the Rev. William Young, an excellent Greek scholar who was curate of East Stour from 1731 to 1740 and who afterwards collaborated with him in translating the Plutus of Aristophanes. To Richardson apparently belongs the credit of first making this identification. Murphy confirms this and relates a story about Young's absent-mindedness, the truth of which is not above suspicion. This identification has been generally accepted, and admirers of Fielding's novel have unearthed other stories about Parson Young to strengthen the case for the identification.

[1]*Le Paysan parvenu*, 1737, Première Partie, pp. 18-19.

Some years ago Mr. J. Paul de Castro communicated to *Notes and Queries*[1] the contents of an interesting document belonging to Mr. H. St. Barbe of Lymington, Hants, which seem to confirm the identification. Among other information that the document contains it tells us that Young was at one time a schoolmaster at Romsey. As Mr. de Castro has pointed out, this bit of information explains the authoritative pronouncements made by Parson Adams on public school education in the third book of *Joseph Andrews*, and it also accounts for Fielding's observation that Parson Adams thought a schoolmaster the greatest character in the world and himself the greatest of all schoolmasters.[2]

Parson Trulliber again has on the authority of Murphy been identified with the Rev. Mr. Oliver of Motcombe near East Stour who had charge of Fielding's early education. Another tradition connects Peter Pounce with the scrivener and usurer Peter Walter of Stalbridge Park near East Stour, who, according to Lawrence, filled the office of steward to several persons of distinction and made his fortune in the process. Fielding bears witness in *The Champion* to his adroitness in making additions to his estates and refers to his greed more than once in his writings.

As a matter of fact the majority of Fielding's critics have accepted the statement that he makes in his preface in regard to his characters and have not looked for the originals of these in the work of other novelists. His characters as a rule are so original that his portrait gallery has been the place in which many a novelist since his time has found the models for some of his best work in portraiture.

[1] *Notes and Queries*, 12 S. I. March 18, 1916, pp. 224-225.
[2] *Joseph Andrews*, Book III, Chap. V.

One of the great masterpieces in this gallery is the portrait of Adams who, if not the actual hero of *Joseph Andrews*, is certainly the greatest character in it. Parson Adams belongs to that eminent family whose ancestors can be traced to Falstaff and even further, the various members of which in different ages have attained immortality through the genius of playwrights, journalists, poets, and novelists who "tinged their virtues, frailties, or vices with extravagances to make them particularly their own, and to distinguish them from those of other men."

Adams is one of the favourite children of Fielding's genius, and the novelist brought to the portraiture an insight into human nature and a sympathy and enthusiasm which were bound to evolve a great character. And great in every respect the portrait is: great in its fidelity to life, in the grandeur and nobility of the conception, and in the individuality and distinctness with which it stands out from among the other great creations of the art of fiction. The majority of the gifted readers of Fielding, some of them great novelists themselves, have not hesitated to give the palm to Adams among the characters of English fiction. And the dissentient voices in the chorus of praise that has been sung through succeeding generations are few. Scott describes the portrait as one of the richest productions of the muse of fiction, which alone is sufficient to stamp the superiority of Fielding over all writers of his class.[1] Coleridge was of opinion that the author of *Waverley* had not produced Adams' equal.[2] Leigh Hunt's praise is even more enthusiastic. "Let everybody rejoice," he writes, "that there has been a man in the world called Henry Fielding to think of such a character, and

[1] Scott, *Lives of the Novelists:* "Fielding."
[2] Letter to Allsop, *Biographia Epistolaris*, 1911, Vol. II, pp. 184-185.

thousands of good people sprinkled about that world to answer for the truth of it."[1]   Indeed, so universal and unstinted has been the praise that has been given to the character that it is hardly possible to convey an adequate idea of it by the quotation of a few individual opinions.

The success of the portrait seems to be due above everything else to a just and harmonious combination of different and even conflicting elements in the character. Abraham Adams is full of eccentricities, and yet he is a man of strong common sense and very sound views on matters of moment. The comical effect of his eccentricities is considerably heightened by certain physical characteristics such as his pugnacity, his habit of snapping his fingers, or his carelessness in the matter of clothes. His habits and ways of life are certainly peculiar. And yet he is not really a freak of nature or an oddity. His impulsiveness and habitual absence of mind and preoccupation bring him perilously close to dishonesty and inconsistency, but we feel all the time that he is a thoroughly good and upright man. He orders his pot of beer and the pipe of which he is so fond or his food when he is hungry without giving a thought to the bill that has to be paid. He offers excellent advice to Joseph, but acts quite contrary to the precepts on which he holds forth with great eloquence. But though we come across numberless instances of inadvertencies and inconsistencies in his behaviour, we know that they are all the outcome of the simplicity of the man's nature, and a suspicion of his honesty or good faith never enters our mind. We laugh at him heartily as his creator does, at his simplicity, for example, when he imagines that he has only to step over to Parson Trulliber's house to fetch the money he needs, or at his pedan-

[1]Leigh Hunt, *Wit and Humour Selected from the English Poets*, 1846, p. 68.

try when he mystifies his landlord by his eloquent account of the voyages he has made without the assistance of a ship.

But we never feel any contempt for him. Scott notices that he is beaten a little too much and too often, but the cudgel lights on his shoulders without the slightest stain on his reputation. He is miserably poor and has little worldly wisdom, and people who possess what he lacks make him the butt of their ridicule or contempt. The country squire to whose house he is invited after being cruelly baited by his dogs adds insult to the injury by trying to "roast" him. Lady Booby seeks diversion for herself and her fashionable friends in "one of the most ridiculous sights they had ever seen, which was an old foolish parson who kept a wife and six brats on a salary of about twenty pounds a year."[1] But there is a native dignity in the man born of the sterling worth of his character which appears to the greatest advantage when the great and rich people of the world try to take advantage of his humble circumstances in life, and not all the discipline of of hog's blood, cudgels, cold water, aristocratic snobbishness, or cynicism can deprive him of that dignity. As Mr. Wilbur Cross says, it is the man practised in the ways of the world and not the idealist who is satirized in *Joseph Andrews*.[2] And Fielding holds up to admiration a character the chief beauties of which are absolute guilelessness, thoroughly disinterested benevolence, and a steadfast and fearless adherence to the cause of truth and righteousness. Lawrence's admiration for the character that he describes as "the grandest delineation of a pattern priest which the world has yet seen"[3] may be extravagant, but

[1] *Joseph Andrews*, Book IV, Chap. IX.
[2] *History of Henry Fielding*, Vol. I, p. 331.
[3] Frederick Lawrence, *Life of Henry Fielding*, London, 1855, p. 155.

there is no denying the fact that in Adams we have an exceptionally fine model of a country clergyman.

The majority of the other characters in *Joseph Andrews* pale into comparative insignificance by the side of Parson Adams. Only one or two can be compared to this masterpiece among the character sketches in vigour and distinctness of delineation. One of these is the portrait of the excellent Mrs. Slipslop. This character has been a source of inspiration to men of genius like Sheridan and Charles Dickens, whose portraits of Mrs. Malaprop and Mrs. Gamp are much better known than Fielding's Mrs. Slipslop.

The character of Mrs. Slipslop has received less attention than it deserves. There is a certain amount of coarseness in the delineation which gives the reader his first taste of the bizarre realism of Fielding's novels that has offended so many people. And in some of the characteristics that the portrait exhibits it goes dangerously near caricature. We must remember, however, that Mrs. Slipslop or Parson Trulliber are characters that make their appearance in his earliest effort at fiction, and we must make some allowance for the spirit of burlesque which prompted this effort. The humour with which the character is delineated, if somewhat broad, is extraordinarily good. Lady Booby's "waiting gentlewoman" is introduced to the reader as the daughter of a curate who has a very good opinion of her understanding, "as she has been frequently at London." She is "a maiden gentlewoman of about forty-five years of age, who, having made a small slip in her youth has continued a good maid ever since." She is "a mighty affecter of hard words" and her distorted and pompous vocabulary is rich in the most diverting lapses. Her person is described in some detail, and it is here that the novelist approaches caricature almost too closely. But, as in the case of Adams, the chief features in her character, her sensuality, her exacting sense of her dignity, her quick transitions from servility to insolence, are so human and lifelike that the portrait never really becomes a caricature even when Fielding speaks of the "tender advances" that she makes to Joseph, or of her disappointments, or of the visits that she pays to her stone bottle.

In the same way the satire in the portraits of Parson Trulliber and Mrs. Tow-wouse just stops short of caricature. The close-fisted and boorish clergyman is described as "one of the largest men you should see who could have acted the part of Sir John Falstaff without stuffing." His short stature, his loud and hoarse voice, his broad accent and the stateliness of his gait, "not unlike that of a goose," are all touches proper to caricature. But if there is a tendency towards caricature Fielding checks it in time, and in Parson Trulliber he gives us a very realistic picture of the country clergyman who is a disgrace to his order and almost the exact opposite of Parson Adams, utterly selfish and small-minded, a very coarse man whose rusticity is altogether repulsive.

In the portrait of Mrs. Tow-wouse, the wife of the master of the Dragon inn, the satire is keener and the novelist approaches caricature very closely indeed when he describes the wounded Joseph's shrewish hostess. "Her person," he says, "was short, thin, and crooked. Her forehead projected in the middle, and thence descended in a declivity to the top of her nose, which was sharp and red, and would have hung over her lips, had not nature turned up the end of it. Her lips were two bits of skin, which, whenever she spoke, she drew together in a purse. Her chin was peaked; and at the upper end of that skin which composed her cheeks, stood two bones, that almost hid a pair of small red eyes. Add to this a voice most wonderfully adapted to the sentiments it was intended to convey, being both loud and hoarse."[1]

But when he reveals her character in the course of his story, he moves away from his starting point, the neighbourhood of caricature, altogether. Mrs. Tow-wouse's shrewish temper, her transition from "a natural antipathy to vagabonds" to "pity for the misfortunes of a Christian" when she notices that Joseph is the friend of a gentleman, her instinct for business, and other very human features in her character are brought out in a series of episodes which show that Fielding had set out to picture a character true to life rather than an extravagantly comic personality almost unknown in real life.

It was the same sure instinct in laying hold of the facts of life that made him portray another very human character in Betty the chambermaid. If he received a hint from Marivaux for the portrait, it was a very slight one, and the outlines of the picture are Fielding's own, not Marivaux's. And Fielding brings out the innate generosity of the girl's nature much better than Marivaux does in his portrait of Génevieve.

He seems to have been more indebted to the French novelist for his picture of Lady Booby, though it is somewhat hazardous to speak of indebtedness, as the frailties of the fashionable woman that are described by both the novelists are the usual ones and they have been the constant theme of satirists and writers of fiction. Fielding, always severe on the frailties and vices of people belonging to the fashionable world, is almost bitter in his satire

[1] *Joseph Andrews*, Book I, Chap. XIV

in the portrait of Lady Booby, whose many frailties are shown as reaching their climax in a terrible malignity against those who stand in the way of the fulfilment of her desires.

The vices and follies of the fashionable world are satirized again and again in the novel, and one of his most severe denunciations is to be found in the history of Wilson's early life. Some readers of the novel have found in the story of Wilson's excesses as a young man of fashion about town a picture of the gay and reckless early life of the novelist himself. Though it is more than likely that Fielding wove into the story some of the experiences of his own life, it would be a mistake to identify the novelist too closely with Wilson. Those who have been tempted to do this have not made enough allowance for the malice of calumniators like Richardson or Horace Walpole, or the prejudice of others like Bishop Hurd who described him as a "poor, emaciated worn out rake" after he had met him in 1750.[1] It is always a hazardous thing to speculate about the circumstances of a man's life or about his character from the events narrated in a work of fiction, however certain we may be that the characters that figure in the events may to some extent be identified with the novelist, his relatives or his friends and acquaintances.

Fielding's contempt for the ways of the fashionable world finds expression again in the picture that he gives of the beau in *Joseph Andrews*. His antipathy to this tinsel ornament of society was a very strong one, and in his works he always speaks of the beau with the most sovereign contempt. This contempt is very noticeable in his description of Beau Didapper whose person, accomplish-

[1] *Memoirs of the Life and Writings of the Right Rev. Richard Hurd, D.D.,* by the Rev. Francis Kilvert, M.A., 1860, p. 45.

ments and conduct are held up to scorn in a way that no other character is in the novel.

Fielding's heroine in *Joseph Andrews* is not one of the great characters of the novel, though the portrait has a beauty of its own. Fanny is a thoroughly unsophisticated girl and much more of an *ingénue* than Pamela is, and it appears that Fielding intended the character to present a contrast to Richardson's heroine. Fanny's modesty, tenderness of heart, and purity make her a very attractive character, though many a reader of *Joseph Andrews* would perhaps regret that she is so often exposed to rude assaults on her virtue.

Fielding's hero, if Joseph can be called the hero of the novel, was in a sense forced upon him by the circumstances in which the novel had its origin. The novelist started with the idea of giving his reader a picture of male chastity that is able to resist all temptation, in order to ridicule that curious combination of purity, prudence, and prudery in Richardson's heroine which appeared so unnatural to him. There was some danger that he might end by making his hero a prig just as Richardson nearly succeeded in making his Pamela a prude. But Fielding was incapable of creating those "puppets out of frigid abstractions" that we come across so constantly in the pages of Richardson. As he progressed in his work, he made Joseph not only an interesting but a very human character, giving him his own physical beauty and strength, and endowing him with some of the finest qualities that a man can possess, honesty, courage, fidelity, tenderness, and unselfishness. If Joseph is not one of the great creations of Fielding's genius, and indeed the character could hardly be that considering the circumstances of its origin, the novelist's portrait is a very pleasing one.

The fact was that through the accident of the parody in which the novel had its origin the peculiar quality of Fielding's genius was asserting itself and marking out a new path in the domain of fiction. And he knew this. He begins his preface to his first novel by preparing his reader to expect a kind of writing not attempted hitherto by any English novelist. The idea of parodying Richardson was more or less abandoned in the initial stages of the work, though he had Richardson's novel in his mind all the time that he was writing his novel, as we can see from constant references to Pamela scattered throughout *Joseph Andrews*. As he progressed with his story he became deeply interested in the characters he had created, and he must have felt that a close adherence to the original idea of the parody would be a handicap to him in his attempt to write a successful novel. After he had written about ten chapters of it he seems to have made up his mind to tell his own story without pursuing any further his original intention of parodying Richardson's novel, though he had to return to it in the concluding chapters in order to close his work with some appearance of consistency. The spirit of burlesque which had prompted him to undertake the work was kept strictly under control so that he might not be surprised into making extravagant caricatures of real life. He recognized the danger himself.

"Though we have," he says in his preface to the novel which was apparently written after *Joseph Andrews* was finished, "sometimes admitted this (burlesque) in our diction, we have carefully excluded it from our sentiments and characters; for there it is never properly introduced, unless in writings of the burlesque kind, which this is not intended to be."

It is not very safe as a rule to pick out one particular ex-cellence of a successful work and say that it owes its title to greatness to this more than to others. In the case of Fielding's first novel, however, apart from the splendid character sketches, one feature stands out so conspicu-ously above others, and this has been recognized so unani-mously by critics to be the outstanding feature of the work that the palm has been given to it. In *Joseph An-drews* Fielding portrayed English life with a fidelity and vividness with which it had never been pictured before. Throughout the novel he never allows himself to lose touch with the realities of life. Hazlitt is a critic who sel-dom allows his enthusiasm for a favourite book to lead him into extravagant rhapsodies, and his tribute to Field-ing's realism is as enthusiastic as it is just.

"I should be at a loss," he says, "where to find in any authentic documents of the same period so satisfactory an account of the general state of society, and of moral, political and religious feeling in the reign of George II, as we meet with in *The Adventures of Joseph Andrews and his Friend Mr. Abraham Adams*. This work, in-deed, I take to be a perfect piece of statistics in its kind."[1]

This wonderful realism of the novel makes up for its want of a carefully constructed plot. Some of Fielding's contemporaries who were far from being enthusiastic about *Joseph Andrews* nevertheless paid their tribute to its magnificent fidelity to life. Gray, for example, found the incidents "ill laid and without invention," but he ad-mitted that the characters had a great deal of "nature," and the author of the novel showed himself "well read in

[1]Hazlitt, *Lectures on the English Comic Writers*, Lecture VI, "On the English Novelists."

stage coaches, country squires, inns and inns of Court."[1] Richardson, who described *Joseph Andrews* as a "lewd and ungenerous engraftment" on his story, and with a singular and perhaps affected obtuseness complained that Fielding had taken hints and names from that story, paid an unconscious tribute to his realism when many years later he deplored his "continued lowness."

"Poor Fielding!" he wrote to Lady Bradshaigh, "I could not help telling his sister that I was equally surprised at and concerned for his continued lowness. Had your brother, said I, been born in a stable or been a runner at a sponging-house, we should have thought him a genius, and wished he had had the advantage of a liberal education, and of being admitted into good company; but it is beyond my conception, that a man of family, and who had some learning, and who really is a writer, should descend so excessively low, in all his pieces."[2]

And yet Richardson had declared in his Preface to *Pamela* that "nothing properly speaking is low that suits well with the place it is raised to, that the passions of nature are the same, in the lord and his coachman, and all that makes them seem different consists in the degrees, in the means and the air whereto and wherewith they indulge them." But when his little soul overflowed with vexation at the success of *Tom Jones* and he brought the charge against his rival, others who were more or less prejudiced against Fielding were inclined to agree with him, and chief among these was Dr. Johnson, though the good doctor confessed that he had never read *Joseph Andrews*.[3]

[1] *The Letters of Thomas Gray*, edited by D. C. Tovey, London, 1900, Vol. I, p. 97. (Letter to West.)
[2] *The Correspondence of Samuel Richardson*, edited by Mrs. Barbauld, 1804, Vol. VI, p. 154.
[3] *Boswell's Life of Johnson*, edited by G. Birkbeck Hill, 1887, Vol. II, p.173.

He was somewhat obsessed with the stories that were current of Fielding's Bohemian ways of life and tried to convince himself and others that the novelist's success and delight in portraying "low" life were the outcome of those ways.

But the verdict pronounced by Richardson and Dr. Johnson is manifestly an unjust one. It is only in one novel of his, *Jonathan Wild*, that Fielding confines his attention to a particular class of people. The nature of his subject and his moral purpose made this inevitable. *Joseph Andrews* is sometimes described as a story of humble life, and this is true only in so far as it refers to the fact that the novelist gives in his work an importance to people in humble ranks in society which had seldom been done before. He seems to have felt that it was a great mistake to consider the lives of humble folk of interest to the novelist only so far as they are a part and parcel of the lives of people belonging to the higher ranks in society. But we are scarcely justified in going out of our way to try and account for the fact of his making a virtuous footman the hero of his tale and of introducing a number of "wretchedly low and dirty characters," as Richardson would have described them, by suggesting, as some have done, that it was the success of George Lillo's tragedy of common life, *George Barnwell*, that first made Fielding think of writing a novel that would deal mainly with scenes from humble life. Apart from the circumstances in which *Joseph Andrews* had its origin, which were responsible for the choice of the footman as the hero of the tale, Fielding was deeply interested in "the prodigious variety of life."

In this recognition of the principle that nothing was too low or too mean for the exercise of his splendid powers of observation and portraiture we have one of the distinctive features of Fielding's genius. Whether he is describing "the ticklish situation of a chambermaid at an inn," or waxing eloquent over the accomplishments of a footman, or giving us a full-length portrait of a waiting gentlewoman or the shrewish wife of an innkeeper, Fielding's humbler folk are portrayed with as much care, skill and success as his men and women belonging to the higher ranks in society. The criticism, if it can be taken seriously at all, that endeavoured to stigmatize his pictures of humble life as "low" was singularly inept. Every intelligent reader of Fielding since the days of Richardson and Johnson has felt that it was a very true and happy instinct that led him to seek and find the materials for his work as a writer of fiction in all grades and ranks in society. And this instinct not only enabled him to make his pictures of life comprehensive but also made some of them singularly impressive.

One of the principal serious themes in *Joseph Andrews* to which the novelist recurs constantly is want of charity among men, and Fielding's satire in the splendid chapter in the novel in which he describes the conduct of the passengers in the stage coach when the wounded and naked Joseph is discovered in the ditch[1] is all the more effective because it is a poor postilion who has compassion on the unfortunate hero when the others exhibit so much inhumanity and selfishness. Fielding again makes the lesson equally impressive when he describes how Adams was helped out of his difficulty by the generosity of a pedlar after he had made his appeal in vain to the prosperous Trulliber.[2]

[1] *Joseph Andrews*, Book I, Chap. XII.
[2] *Joseph Andrews*, Book II, Chap. XV.

K

The success of Fielding's first novel, though it did not equal that of *Pamela*, was nevertheless a notable one. The first edition of the book, which was published on the 22nd of February, 1742, and for which, according to the entries in Woodfall the printer's ledger, 1,500 copies were printed,[1] was apparently exhausted by June, as in *The Daily Post* of the 10th of that month occurs an advertisement announcing the second edition,[2] though the monthly magazines do not announce the second edition in their monthly register or catalogue of books till August.[3] The number of copies printed for the second edition, according to the entry in Woodfall's ledger,[4] was 2,000. A third edition of 3,000 copies was issued during the last week in March, 1743,[5] so that in little over a year three editions of the novel were published and altogether 6,500 copies of the book printed.

From the third edition a French translation of the novel was made the same year by a supposed "dame Angloise," but the real translator was the Abbé Pierre Desfontaines, who had already translated *Gulliver's Travels*. This French version was reprinted in Amsterdam in the following year.

Though no attempt was apparently made to depict Joseph Andrews "in his exalted condition," or to continue the story of Joseph in his married state, the novel was

[1] *Notes and Queries*, 7th Series II, November 6, 1886, p. 365 and 12 S. III, November 1917, p. 465.

[2] This was also advertised in *The London Evening Post*, Saturday, June 12 to Tuesday, June 15, 1742.

[3] *The London Magazine* and *The Gentleman's Magazine* for August, 1742.

[4] *Notes and Queries*, 7th Series II, November 6, 1886, p. 365 and 12 S III, November, 1917, p. 465.

[5] *St. James's Evening Post*, March 22–24, 1743. *The General Evening Post*, March 22–24, 1743.

popular enough to expose it to attempts at piracy. In the October following its publication the Attorney-General, Sir Dudley Ryder, was instructed to move for an injunction to restrain the sale of an unauthorized impression, but the first application for an injunction was not successful owing to a technical objection, as Sir Dudley Ryder tells his wife in a letter quoted in Lord Campbell's *Lives of the Chief Justices*.[1] But apparently an injunction was obtained soon afterwards.

All these things indicate that the novel was a popular one though it did not create the sensation that *Pamela* had done. Perhaps the fact that it was ostensibly a burlesque on a work over which the public had gone into raptures stood in the way of a greater popularity that it might have attained. Besides, it often happens that the immediate triumph won by an author who first makes an incursion into a new field is greater than that achieved by a mightier genius who follows close upon him.

The most puzzling fact about the reception of *Joseph Andrews* on its publication is the comparative paucity of references to it by the great literary men of the time. The contemporary monthly periodicals, in the columns of which one would look for notices or reviews of the novel, merely announce the book in their monthly register or catalogue of new publications. *The Gentleman's Magazine*, however, nearly a year after the publication of the novel printed an extract from *The Craftsman* commenting on certain statements that Fielding had made in his Preface to *Joseph Andrews*.[2] The same magazine in its issues for October, 1745, and May, 1746, makes rather feeble efforts at pleasantry in referring to the author of *Joseph*

[1] John, Lord Campbell, *Lives of the Chief Justices*, 1849, II. p. 260.
[2] *The Gentlemen's Magazine*, January, 1743.

Andrews and its principal character, Parson Adams, who apparently was now as well known as Pamela.

The great literary men of the day are not more communicative. No letters to Fielding expressing an opinion on his book have come to light yet; while of the opinions expressed in other letters the most notable are the captious comments of Gray to which we have already referred, and some more hostile criticism indulged in by Shenstone.[1] In Lady Mary Montagu's correspondence there is a letter which was written after the publication of *Tom Jones* in which she declares that she preferred *Joseph Andrews* to *Tom Jones*.[2] Richardson also curiously enough was singularly reticent for some years, and he did not make his hostile comments till *Tom Jones* was published, when the greater success of Fielding's masterpiece seems to have roused him to hostility even more than the parodies of his novel had done. As for others, Johnson confessed many years afterwards that he had never read *Joseph Andrews*. It is difficult to account for this, and almost equally unaccountable is the silence of Pope, Chesterfield, Horace Walpole, and many others from whom one would expect some expression of opinion. One explanation of this silence that has been offered is that until the publication of *Tom Jones* to the majority of people Fielding's first novel seemed at best little more than an extremely clever parody and burlesque which contained the diverting character of Parson Adams.[3]

And yet in spite of the want of a satisfactory record of

[1] *The Works of William Shenstone*, Second Edition, London, 1769, Vol. III, pp. 70-71.

[2] Letter to the Countess of Bute, October 1, N.S, 1749. *The Letters and Works of Lady Mary Montagu*, edited by Lord Wharncliffe, 3rd edition, 1861, Vol. III, p. 185.

[3] Frederic T. Blanchard, *Fielding the Novelist*, 1926, p. 17.

appreciation by great men there is little doubt that the novel was a success, and as the assignment of the copyright to Andrew Millar[1] shows, the pecuniary benefit that Fielding derived from his first novel, though nothing remarkable, was great enough to encourage him to persist in his literary labours.

[1]According to this document, which is preserved in the Forster Collection at South Kensington, Fielding received £199. 6s. for *Joseph Andrews*, the farce *Miss Lucy in Town* and his *Full Vindication of the Duchess Dowager of Marlborough*. A note on the reverse of the assignment informs us that the amount paid for *Joseph Andrews* was £183. 11s.

CHAPTER VI

THE MISCELLANIES

THE prevailing topic of interest in the spring of 1742, according to *The Gentleman's Magazine* for March, was a book of political memoirs of the aged Duchess of Marlborough. This early example of a class of writing with which the world seems to be flooded now was named *An Account of the Conduct of the Dowager Duchess of Marlborough from her first Coming to Court to the year* 1710 and was published during the second week in March.[1] In preparing her reminiscences for publication the great Sarah engaged the services of Nathaniel Hooke, author of a Roman history and a historian of some repute, to whom Fielding pays a graceful compliment in his *Journey from this World to the Next,* who "digested" these memoirs, as Horace Walpole describes it in one of his letters to Horace Mann, and is said to have been very liberally rewarded by his employer. The book was the occasion of an acrimonious controversy, and among other pamphlets that appeared giving the lie to the statements made in it was a particularly vindictive one by a "noble, old and spiteful" writer who called himself Britannicus. This pamphlet led Fielding to take up the cudgels on behalf of the wife of the military hero under whom his father had fought. His pamphlet, which was named *A Full Vindication of the Duchess Dowager of Marlborough: Both With regard to the Account lately Published by Her Grace, and to Her Character in general,* appeared about

[1] *The Craftsman,* March 13, 1742.

the middle of April.[1] It is a spirited defence of the old
duchess in whose bounty Fielding had probably shared
when *The Champion* had made its attacks on the ministry;
but the praise bestowed on the formidable and somewhat
dubious heroine of a long series of court intrigues is much
too lavish, and this has made some people question Fielding's sincerity and even to insinuate that the old duchess
rewarded her henchman for the advocacy of her cause.

The reward, if he received any at all, could not have
been a very liberal one and Fielding was still in pecuniary
difficulties. These financial straits seem to have driven him
to a literary project which after all did not produce any
encouraging results. On the 31st of May was published a
translation by Fielding and his friend Young of the *Plutus*
of Aristophanes, and the advertisements of this appearing in the papers announce that "this play is publish'd as
a specimen of an intended translation of all the comedies
(being eleven in number) of Aristophanes, by the same
gentlemen who intend to proceed in the work according
to the reception this play meets with from the public."[2]

The translation is a good one and is accompanied by
copious notes in which we have many a sally of bright wit
as in the notes to *Tom Thumb*. It is preceded by a dedication to Lord Talbot and an excellent preface in which the
translators make learned comments on the life and writings of Aristophanes. They promise in their opening sentences to give to the public "a very large dissertation on
the nature and end of Comedy" if they meet with sufficient encouragement from the public.

But this English version of *Plutus* in spite of its merits
was not much of a success financially, and Fielding and

[1] *The London Evening Post*, April 15–17, 1742.
[2] *The Champion*, May 4 and 29, 1742. *The Daily Post*, June 2, 1742.

his friend Young decided to abandon their original design of translating the eleven comedies of the great Greek dramatist. The "eternal want of pence" continued to vex him greatly, and he was compelled to seek other means of earning money. He tried his hand at the drama again, but both *Miss Lucy in Town* and *The Wedding Day*, as we have related already, were more or less unsuccessful. He next thought of eking out his slender resources by trusting to the generosity and support of his friends and acquaintances in a subscribed edition of *Miscellanies*. The idea of such a publication seems to have been in his mind for some time, as an advertisement of the proposals for the *Miscellanies* in *The Daily Post* of the 5th of June, 1742, declares that the publication of the volumes "hath been hitherto retarded by the author's indisposition last winter and a train of melancholy accidents scarce to be parallel'd." In this announcement the author promised to deliver the volumes "within the time mentioned in the last receipts, viz., by the 25th of December."

But the publication was again delayed owing to the continued illness of his wife, and it was not till the 7th of April, 1743, that the volumes began to be delivered to the subscribers.[1] For them the price was one guinea for sets printed on ordinary paper and two guineas for special sets in royal paper. It is evident from the long list of names of subscribers prefixed to all subscribed copies of the book that the enterprise was a financial success, as altogether 427 names appear on the list and 556 sets were subscribed, of which 214 were on royal paper. When the subscribers were supplied, the remaining copies were offered for sale to the public at 15s. per set, and *The Lon-*

[1] *The General Evening Post*, April 5–7, 1743, and *The London Daily Post and General Advertiser*, April 7, 1743.

don Magazine for April, 1743, evidently referred to this when it included in its monthly catalogue of books a "second edition" of *Miscellanies* by Henry Fielding in three volumes octavo.[1]

As announced in the advertisements, the first volume of the *Miscellanies* contained almost all the poems that he had written so far with the exception of *The Masquerade*, *The Vernoniad* and the songs and mock heroic verses of the plays. It also contained four essays, *On Conversation*, *On the Knowledge of the Characters of Men*, *On the Remedy of Affliction for the Loss of Our Friends*, and *On Nothing*. To these were added a translation of the first Olynthiac of Demosthenes, *A Dialogue between Alexander the Great and Diogenes the Cynic* and two other pieces of little importance. The second volume contained the very attractive but unequal and unfinished *Journey from this World to the Next*, the farce *Eurydice* and the ill-fated comedy, *The Wedding Day*. The third volume was devoted entirely to *The History of the Life of Jonathan Wild the Great*.

One of the most interesting features of the *Miscellanies* is the admirable Preface in which Fielding not only talks about the contents of the three volumes and describes the circumstances in which the more important among them had their origin, but gives us most interesting though all too brief glimpses into the circumstances of his life and his literary activities during the years immediately preceding the publication of the *Miscellanies*, and this Preface is of great biographical interest.

The poetical pieces contained in the first volume are of no outstanding merit. Most of them were written when

[1] The three volumes of this issue are in the British Museum. Vols. I and III have the words "The Second Edition" on the title page. See Bibliography.

Fielding was very young and, as he naïvely confesses in his Preface, were "the productions of the heart rather than of the head." The first three pieces, *Of True Greatness*, of which we have already spoken, *Of Good Nature*, a poem written in very much the same strain and addressed to the Duke of Richmond, and a poem on Liberty addressed to George Lyttelton, ostensibly take the place of a formal dedication of the volumes, and they deal with themes which may be described as the author's main themes throughout the *Miscellanies*.

Fielding's verses are smooth and even elegant sometimes, but the poetry is not of a high order, and the same ideas repeated in different language in about half a dozen poems in the beginning of the first volume of the *Miscellanies* are apt to pall on the reader. As one wades through these pieces, however, one occasionally comes across lively lines, particularly in the poems addressed to Sir Robert Walpole in which Fielding playfully dwells upon and exaggerates his distresses. The love poems of his youth addressed to Celia, a number of which are included in this collection, have nothing remarkable in them, and occasionally the lover's conceits are fantastic enough. In one of them, for example, he tells his lady-love that Walpole for a tender pat from her would have left his place and become her cat, and Pulteney who "raged" for freedom would have sung confined within her cage.

One of the longest poems in the *Miscellanies* is a revised version of that modernization, to which we have already referred, of part of Juvenal's *Sixth Satire*. In this poem Fielding seems to have tried his hand at burlesque for the first time in his life. The earlier composition was now considerably enlarged as the references to Mrs.

Clive, Mrs. Woffington, Theophilus Cibber, and Richardson's *Pamela* indicate. The other poems in the volume hardly deserve any special notice. There are some complimentary verses addressed to young ladies, one or two descriptive pieces, a couple of songs, and a number of rather trite epigrams.

Among the prose compositions in this volume of the *Miscellanies*, perhaps the most notable both for the matter and the vigour and grace of the style is his essay *On Conversation* of which the title is somewhat equivocal as Fielding's main theme in the essay is good breeding. But as he does elsewhere in his writings, he uses the word conversation in the more general sense. He defines good breeding as the art of pleasing in conversation and declares that it is expressed in two different ways, in our actions and our words. The greater part of the essay is devoted to an exposition of his ideal of the conduct of a true gentleman both in private and in public life; and in expatiating on his high ideal he gives expression to some of the strongest antipathies ingrained in his nature—those against the snobbishness of people belonging to the fashionable world and against the beau and the fine lady in particular whom he describes as "the disgracers of the human species."

In the concluding portion of his essay Fielding deals with the art of conversation in the more usual sense of the word, or as he describes it, "good breeding with respect to our words," and his remarks are as sensible as they are practical, particularly his observations on the use of raillery in conversation. The conclusion at which he arrives is that the only raillery which is consistent with good breeding is a gentle animadversion on some foible, which, while it raises a laugh in the rest of the company, does not put the person rallied out of countenance, or expose him to shame and contempt.

Fielding's second essay in the *Miscellanies, On the Knowledge of the Characters of Men*, has much of the vigour of style and soundness of reasoning of the first. This essay is characteristic of the man as it reveals to us the great aversion that his honest and open nature felt against hypocrisy and affectation. He begins with the statement that the greatest part of mankind appear disguised under false vizors and habits which make the whole world a vast masquerade, and his main business in the essay is to instruct the man with the open disposition how to penetrate to the real man behind the glavering smile, the austere countenance or "the sour morose, ill natured censorious sanctity." He admits that nature imprints sufficient marks on the countenance to inform an accurate and discerning eye, but the actions of men are the justest interpreters of their thoughts and the truest standards by which we may judge them. "Trace the man," he says towards the end of the essay, "proposed to your trust into his private family and nearest intimacies. See whether he hath acted the part of a good son, brother, husband, father, friend, master, servant, etc. If he hath discharged these duties well your confidence will have a good foundation."

Fielding's mood in his next essay in the *Miscellanies* was the same which inspired him to write the most formidable of his satires, *The History of Jonathan Wild*. In *The Champion* he had occasionally shown what a great master of irony he was and in this essay *On Nothing* he exhibits the same skill in the use of this literary weapon. He gravely explains with a skilful if somewhat pedantic juggling with words, which have a powerful but very

genial undercurrent of irony in them, what nothing is,
how many various kinds of it there are and how great its
"dignity" is. His satire ranges over a fairly extensive
field, and has for its objectives a great variety of characters, from the man "bedaubed with lace or with title"
who has nothing in him, or the man who feels nothing
when he has the motions of the spirit in him, to the author
who means nothing when he writes his book. Perhaps
one of the concluding sentences in the essay would fur-
nish the best example of Fielding's happy use of irony.
"Seeing that it is really the end," he says in speaking of
the dignity and importance of Nothing, "of all those
things which are supported with so much pomp and
solemnity, and looked on with such respect and esteem,
surely it becomes a wise man to regard Nothing with the
utmost awe and adoration; to pursue it with all his parts
and pains; and to sacrifice to it his ease, his innocence,
and his present happiness. To which noble pursuit we
have this great incitement, that we may assure ourselves
of never being cheated or deceived in the end proposed."

The other prose pieces in the first volume of the *Miscellanies* are of little importance. In *The Philosophical
Transactions for the year* 1742-3 Fielding parodies some
scientific papers which had been contributed to the Royal
Society by a well-known Swiss naturalist of the time named Trembley, though Fielding's real butt in this skit was
the usurer Peter Walter, the original of Peter Pounce in
Joseph Andrews, whose avarice is very effectively ridiculed in the account that Petrus Gualterus, "a man well
known in the learned world," gives of the ways of the ter-
restrial chrysipi which so closely attach themselves to
one's hand that they can by no means be severed or made

to quit their hold even by the joint and indefatigable labour of several men.

Fielding's essay *On the Remedy of Affliction for the Loss of our Friends* seems to have had its origin in the death of his daughter Charlotte about whom he speaks with such deep feeling in his *Journey from this World to the Next* and to whose death he also refers in this essay. The reflections that it contains have little originality in them, and the soundness of some of Fielding's observations is open to question, as for example when he recommends frequent reflections on the certainty of the loss of our friends as a preparation for affliction and deprecates what he calls the perverseness of our natures in cherishing the words, looks, and other loved memories of a friend we have lost.

In the last two pieces in this volume Fielding deals with classical themes, but his work does not exhibit any special excellence. *The Dialogue between Alexander the Great and Diogenes the Cynic*, the idea of which was obviously suggested by Lucian, is rather a tame affair which hardly contains anything more than the traditional and oft-repeated sentiments ascribed to these great men. The other piece, *An Interlude between Jupiter, Juno, Apollo, and Mercury*, is more interesting and has more of the humour and lightness of touch that Fielding exhibits in his best work. He intended this to be the introduction to a comedy to be called *Jupiter's Descent on Earth*. But the fate of a previous dramatic venture that he had made in the same direction in his farce *Eurydice* apparently dissuaded him from proceeding further with his burlesque of other stories of classical mythology.

"The glory of the *Miscellanies*," to use the words of one of the American biographers of Fielding, is to be found in the second and third volumes which contain *The Journey from this World to the Next* and *The History of the Life of Jonathan Wild the Great*.   The unfinished *Journey* with which the second volume opens seems to have been begun before *Joseph Andrews*, but Fielding, who had already handled the Lucianic theme in his *Author's Farce* and in one of his best contributions to *The Champion*, turned aside for a time from his third and most ambitious effort to deal with a favourite subject in order to write his first great novel. The illness of his wife and his other troubles then intervened and he had little inclination afterwards to finish a narrative which was very well begun.

He had endeavoured to give a new interest to a somewhat overworked theme by introducing a variation into his narrative in the shape of an account of the transmigrations of the soul of Julian the Apostate. But this variation did not achieve its purpose in the end as Fielding made the mistake of dwelling too long on the new theme.

In spite of its drawbacks, however, the *Journey* is good reading on the whole. When he decided to publish it, Fielding made a clever attempt to atone for the fragmentary state of his work and to disarm the reader's objection to it as such by writing an interesting introduction to his account of the journey which contains the ingenious story of a supposed discovery by him in the shop of Mr. Robert Powney, stationer, of a hundred pages of a "huge folio" which had originally contained the whole narrative.

The Journey from this World to the Next begins with a slight variation of the time-honoured description, one of the best examples of which is to be found in Lucian's *Voyage to the Lower World*. Instead of Charon ferry-

ing across the river the souls that Hermes has in his
charge, in Fielding's narrative we have a stage coach
"compounded" of immaterial substances, "spiritual"
horses and a coachman who is "a very thin piece of immaterial substance." This unsubstantial coach starts
from Warwick Lane and it carries seven spirits as passengers. Fielding, "well read in stage coaches," gives us
a very lively account of what happened during the first
stage of this interesting journey in the course of which
the characters of the phantom passengers are revealed to
us in very vivid and humorous touches in the narrative.
The coach halts at the City of Diseases and at the Palace
of Death, and from the account that is given of the first
one realizes that Fielding was thinking of some of the
haunts of vice in London, notably the Covent Garden
district. His ingenuity and powers of description are seen
at great advantage in his account of the novel punishment
of Lord Scrape, the miser, in the spirit world, in his picture of the Palace of Death and its inmates, as also in his
excellent account of the wheel of Fortune and of the
drawing of their lots by souls journeying to the earth.

The best, though not the most original, chapters in the
Journey, however, are those in which Fielding describes
the proceedings at the gate of Elysium and his experiences in the abode of the blest. Minos, "the celebrated judge," examines the spirits waiting for admission at
the gates of Elysium, and the judgments that he pronounces are most interesting as they give us a good insight into Fielding's code of morality. Minos declares
that no man(!) is allowed to enter the gates of Elysium
without charity, and the first spirit that seeks admission
is turned away in spite of the fact that he had been very
liberal to an hospital. So is the second who had constantly

frequented his church, had been a rigid observer of fast days and shown great animosity to vice in others; whereas another spirit who had been driven by necessity to the robbery of eighteenpence for which he had been hanged is admitted by Minos because the unfortunate wretch had been a very tender husband and a kind father and had ruined himself by being bail for his friend. The spirit of a dramatist, again, is admitted into Elysium because he had once lent the whole profits of a benefit night to a friend and by that means had saved him and his family from starvation.

The two following chapters in the *Journey* in which the author describes his experiences in Elysium are even more interesting. In the first of these he tells us how he meets some of the most celebrated men of the past in the Elysian fields. He notices Homer with Madame Dacier on his lap listening to a concert at which the chief performers are Orpheus and Sappho. He goes up to the great Greek bard and asks him the same question that the traveller in Lucian's *True History* asks about the place of his birth, and Homer replies that he is unable to enlighten him. Virgil then comes up to our traveller and he has Addison "under his arm" who, apparently, was not a *persona grata* with Fielding, judging by the picture given of the essayist in this chapter of the *Journey*. A far more congenial spirit, that of Dick Steele, is next introduced, and he is described as soothing the ruffled spirits of Addison by his fulsome flattery which is graciously accepted.

Shakespeare appears on the scene next listening to a heated discussion between the actors Betterton and Booth about "the placing of an accent" in that celebrated line in Othello:

"Put out the light, and then put out the light."

L

The disputants wrangle with much heat, and the spirits standing by join in the dispute. In the end it is decided to refer the matter to the writer of the line whose reply is characteristic. "Faith, gentlemen," the great dramatist says, "it is so long since I wrote the line, I have forgot my meaning. This I know, could I have dreamt so much nonsense would have been talked and writ about it, I would have blotted it out of my works; for I am sure, if any of these be my meaning, it doth me very little honour."

In the next chapter the author describes how some of the best-known characters in the greatest books of the world come up to pay their respects to "the several bards the recorders of their actions." Homer is saluted by Achilles and Ulysses, Virgil by Æneas and Julius Cæsar, Milton by Adam, and Shakespeare by several characters, "amongst whom Henry V made a very distinguishing appearance"; and while our traveller's eyes are fixed on Henry V, a very small spirit who introduces himself as Thomas Thumb shakes him by the hand. This chapter closes with an account of the author's interviews with Cromwell, Alexander the Great, and Livy.

The subsequent chapters in the *Journey* are inferior to the earlier ones. With the exception of the last, which relates the story of Anne Boleyn's life, they are all devoted to accounts of the numerous transmigrations of the soul of Julian the Apostate. The story of these transmigrations is drawn out to excessive length, and the author himself was tired of it before he reached the end. Some of the accounts of the earthly existences of Julian's soul, however, are interesting, and Fielding's gifts for satire are exhibited to great advantage in them.

Apart from some of his plays, Fielding's *Journey from this World to the Next* is perhaps the least original of all his writings. One of his favourite Greek authors was Lucian, and Baker's catalogue of the novelist's books which were sold after his death shows that he had more than half-a-dozen editions of Lucian's works in Greek, Latin, English, and French. In his *Author's Farce* and in one of his essays in *The Champion* to which we have already referred he had laid one of Lucian's *Dialogues of the Dead*, the tenth, under contribution, and some of the expressions that occur in the celebrated auction scene in *The Historical Register* seem to indicate that Fielding had Lucian's *Sale of Creeds* in his mind when he composed that scene. In writing *The Journey from this World to the Next* he made even larger demands on Lucian, though, as we have pointed out already, he contributed enough from his own genius to the narrative by way of innovation and variation to make the work something more than an adaptation. The best part of the narrative, however, was written under the inspiration that he had received from Lucian. The chapter on the judgments of Minos, for example, was obviously suggested to him by what he had read in Lucian's *Voyage to the Lower World* of the examination of the spirits by Rhadamanthus as they reach Hades; and the two chapters in which we have the account of the author's interviews with the spirits of the great men of the world seem to have been likewise suggested by Lucian's account in *The True History* of the great men that his hero saw in the Island of the Blest.

But Lucian was not the only author to whom Fielding was indebted for some of his ideas in *The Journey from this World to the Next*. There are certain resemblances between Fielding's narrative and some of the Sueños or Visions of Quevedo whom Fielding mentions in *Tom*

Jones[1] which point to the fact that he was acquainted with the Spanish writer's best known and most characteristic work. Quevedo's Sueños were translated into English by Sir Roger L'Estrange in 1667, and in 1703 an adaptation of them was made by Ellis Wynne and named *Visions of the Sleeping Bard*, which was very popular in Wales for a long time.

One of the most notable features of the second vision of Quevedo, the "Sueño de la Muerte," is the attack that the Spanish writer makes on the medical profession. Quevedo begins his account of his second vision by describing a procession of physicians each of whom had in his right hand "a staff *à la mode* which he carried rather for countenance than correction." After these come a long train of mountebank apothecaries. Quevedo then proceeds to ridicule the practice of using long and uncouth words in prescriptions, and with delightful humour remarks that were not the very names of their medicines sufficient to frighten away any distemper it is to be feared the remedy would prove worse than the disease.

In *The Journey from this World to the Next* we have the same satire against the medical profession though, of course, this in itself does not prove that Fielding was indebted to Quevedo. The satire against the pretensions of so-called physicians and against the quackery practised in the name of medicine is a very notable feature of the literature of the sixteenth, seventeenth, and eighteenth centuries. In the picaresque literature of Spain, the novels of Le Sage, Sorel, Scarron, or Furetière, and the English imitations of the Spanish and French picaresque fiction the physician and the apothecary are the constant butts of the novelist's satire. Fielding had made

[1] *Tom Jones*, Book VII, Chap. VIII.

the physician the object of his satire more than once in his plays. In *The Champion* he had condemned the pretensions of the medical faculty in strong language, and in *Joseph Andrews* his picture of the surgeon who attends on the wounded Joseph is far from being an attractive one. But it would be hardly safe to suggest that in making these attacks on the medical profession he had taken his cue from any individual writer.

In the satire that he indulges in against the profession in his *Journey from this World to the Next*, however, there is such a close resemblance to the same satire in Quevedo's *Vision of Death and her Empire* that one is tempted to believe that Fielding was indebted to the Spanish writer for some of his ideas. The formal, grave gentlemen in tie-wigs whom the author of the *Journey* meets in the City of Diseases are very like the physicians that Quevedo describes. In place of the staff that each physician carries "rather for countenance than correction" in Quevedo's picture, Fielding's doctors carry amber-headed canes as "insignia or tickets denoting their office." Like Quevedo, Fielding also laughs at the prescriptions of doctors and the long names given to drugs, and he follows up his satire against physicians by ridiculing the practices of apothecaries. In Fielding's *Journey*, again, there is a description, very closely resembling one in Quevedo, of two roads, one "all craggy with rocks, full of boggy grounds and everywhere beset with briars," the way to greatness, and the other, "the most delightful imaginable, leading through the most verdant meadows, painted and perfumed with all kinds of beautiful flowers," the road to goodness, and this, taken with the other resemblances noted above, certainly establishes the fact of his indebtedness to the Spanish writer.

But though Fielding's debt to Lucian and Quevedo is a considerable one, *The Journey from this World to the Next* is far from being a mere adaptation. The humour of the work is Fielding's own, genial and piquant; the finest descriptive passages in it are original, and the accounts of the great men that are given in the course of the narrative are with one or two exceptions Fielding's own work altogether. And one admirer of Fielding at least, M. Kauffmann, who translated this fragment into French, found in the story of the transmigrations of Julian's soul not only a "production vraiment originale, n'est pas indigne de l'auteur de *Tom Jones*," but also the most important part of the narrative, for he called his translation *Julien l'Apostat, ou Voyage dans l'autre monde*.

The *Journey* has one other special claim to our attention. It contains a number of interesting autobiographical references. In his introduction to the fragment, for example, he refers with a delightful *naïveté* to his straitened circumstances, and in the course of the narrative he speaks with deep feeling of the beloved daughter whom he had lost. The most interesting personal touch in the narrative, however, is to be found in the chapter in which he describes the judgments of Minos. One of these refers to himself.

"The judge," he says in describing it, "then addressed himself to me, who little expected to pass this fiery trial. I confessed I had indulged myself very freely with wine and women in my youth, but had never done an injury to any man living, nor avoided an opportunity of doing good; that I pretended to very little virtue more than general philanthropy and private friendship. I was proceeding, when Minos bid me enter the gate, and not indulge myself in trumpeting forth my virtues."

This declaration has been taken very seriously by some biographers of the novelist who were only too willing to believe the vilest calumnies against him, and these people have triumphantly quoted this passage as incontrovertible evidence of the excesses of Fielding's early life.

The most notable of all the compositions that Fielding gave to the world in the *Miscellanies* of 1743 is contained in the third volume which is entirely devoted to the greatest and sternest of all his satires. The spirit of satire dominates the narrative in *The History of the Life of Mr. Jonathan Wild the Great* to such an extent that some critics of Fielding's works have hesitated to call it a novel. Fielding knew at the time he gave his book to the world that the story itself, even with the embellishments that he had given to it, would not arouse his reader's interest sufficiently. Jonathan Wild had figured in too many narratives already. From the year 1725 in which he met his fate at Tyburn till Fielding's satire appeared numerous accounts of the so called Great Man's life had been given to the world in books, pamphlets, and newspaper articles. Some of these, like *The Life and Glorious Actions of the Most Heroic and Magnanimous Jonathan Wilde*, which appeared soon after the great criminal's execution, paid little attention to the actual facts of his life, but frankly traded on the interest that had been aroused and regaled the public with the most sensational stories. Other accounts like those contained in *The Newgate Calendar* or in the pamphlets ascribed to Defoe, to whom Fielding probably refers when he speaks in his Preface to the *Miscellanies* of the "excellent historian" of Jonathan Wild, were supposed to be based on authentic papers and records, and these narratives were certainly more reliable as actual histories of the man's career.

From the time that these narratives first began to appear almost immediately after Wild's execution pamphlets and newspaper articles containing satiric comments in the mock-heroic strain on the "Great Man's" career and exploits were also published by some writers. In the same year in which Wild was executed two articles appeared in *Mist's Weekly Journal* for June 12 and June 19, and these contain some excellent satiric comments on Wild's career and character. The writer of these articles speaks of Wild's greatness in much the same tone of mock admiration that Fielding does in his satire, and the opinion was expressed some years ago by a contributor to *Notes and Queries* that these articles were written by Fielding and they contain the germ of his more elaborate satire in *The Life of Jonathan Wild*.[1] Mr. J. Paul de Castro made a careful comparison of these articles with Fielding's *Life of Jonathan Wild* some time ago, but he came to the conclusion that they were not written by Fielding. And the reasons that he has advanced in support of his view are fairly convincing.[2]

The earliest reference to Jonathan Wild that we have in the writings of Fielding is to be found in an article he contributed to *The Champion* of the 4th March, 1740, in which he makes the following observations:

"Reputation often courts those who regard her least. Actions have sometimes been attended with fame which were undertaken in defiance of it. Jonathan Wyld himself had for many years no small share of it in the kingdom."

These words seem to form the nucleus of the elaborate and fierce satire in *The History of Jonathan Wild*, and it is

---

[1] *Notes and Queries*, 11 S. II, Oct. 1, 1910, pp. 261-3.
[2] *Notes and Queries*, 12 S. II, Dec. 2, 1916, p. 442.

fairly safe to assume that the book was written after the date of this article in *The Champion*. Thomas Keightley, however, in a postscript to his articles on the "Life and Writings of Henry Fielding" in *Fraser's Magazine* for January and February, 1858, expresses the view that if his hypothesis about the underlying political satire in *Jonathan Wild* is correct, then the book was probably written in the heat of Fielding's indignation at the Licensing Act, and it would probably never have seen the light had the author not been pressed for materials to make up his *Miscellanies*.[1]

Though there is no evidence to prove that Keightley was wrong in his conjecture, the cursory reference to Wild in *The Champion* and the language of the paragraphs in Fielding's Preface to the *Miscellanies* in which he speaks of his satire seem to point to a later date. And the probability is that it was planned and begun, though not "substantially finished" perhaps, as Edmund Gosse suggests,[2] before *Joseph Andrews* was published in February, 1742.

The simile in the fourteenth chapter of the first book of his satire, in which Fielding compares Wild's advance to "greatness" to a traveller's progress over the hills near Bath, the Bath simile as it has been called, was "made," we are told, in that watering place. We know that Fielding visited Bath in 1742, as the lines addressed to Miss H—— and in the first volume of the *Miscellanies* are described as "written extempore in the Pump Room, 1742." These clues seem to point to the fact that parts of *Jonathan Wild* were written in 1742 in Bath to which

[1] *Fraser's Magazine*, June, 1858, p. 763.
[2] *The Works of Henry Fielding*, edited by Edmund Gosse, Archibald Constable, 1898, Introduction, p. xx.

place Fielding evidently paid a short visit after he had published *Joseph Andrews*. Or if Edmund Gosse's conjecture be correct, the Bath simile as well as the short letter of Peter Pounce in the second book of *Jonathan Wild* were later additions made to the satire when Fielding revised it for publication in 1743. Some recent writers, however, who have given their attention to this subject, contend that *Jonathan Wild* was begun after *Joseph Andrews* had been published and that Fielding worked at it continuously without interruption, as his greatest satire shows all the signs of having been written under the sway of one governing emotion.

And this brings us to the question which has proved, as Keightley says, a perfect crux to the critics, and on this question various opinions have been expressed. Some have contended that *Jonathan Wild* is a political satire in which Fielding denounces the gross corruption of public life in his day and the chief objective of his satire is Walpole. Others are unable to subscribe to this view though they acknowledge that an underlying political meaning is discernible in certain parts of the satire.

Fielding himself speaks at considerable length in his Preface to the *Miscellanies* about his aim and purpose in writing *The History of Jonathan Wild*. He tells his reader that he does not intend "to enter the lists" against writers who have compiled authentic histories of Wild's life, and he emphatically denies that he has portrayed any particular individual of his time in his book. "Roguery, and not a rogue," he says, "is my subject; and as I have been so far from endeavouring to particularize any individual, that I have with my utmost art avoided it; so will any such application be unfair in my reader, especially if he knows much of the great world, since he must be acquainted, I believe, with more than one on whom he can fix the resemblance."

If we go no further than the statements that he makes in his Preface to the *Miscellanies* we must conclude that *Jonathan Wild* is a kind of moral allegory in which Fielding makes a relentless and very effective exposure of the deformity of vice. In his declaration of his aim and purpose in writing *Jonathan Wild* we have some explanation of the particular severity of his denunciation of the vices and frailties of the great which is such a noticeable feature of his writings. Not only is it a moral anomaly which rouses the highest indignation in him that the same frailties and vices should be attended with luxury and honour in one place and with misery and infamy in another; but there is a very serious mistake which men often make when they are dazzled by the "glare of riches" or the "awe of title," and they must be cautioned against this. They give to the so-called great the homage which is due only to the good or to the great and good. In his book he intends to reveal in its true colours the greatness which is totally devoid of goodness, a "bombast greatness" as he describes it. And he declares at the outset that such exposure is necessary because "pride, ostentation, insolence, cruelty, and every kind of villainy are often construed into true greatness of mind."

Villainy, therefore, is the principal object of his satire throughout *The Life of Jonathan Wild*, and the book, as Austin Dobson says, is "a model of sustained and sleepless irony." Indeed Fielding's enthusiasm for righteousness aroused such indignation in him that his terrible irony oppresses the reader. In *Jonathan Wild* there is little of the novelist's characteristic geniality or his usual compassion for the frailties of hard pressed humanity.

What humour there is in the book is almost invariably grim. Coleridge after reading *Jonathan Wild* declared that its irony exceeded anything in *Gulliver's Travels* or *A Tale of a Tub*. It has certainly all the hardness and relentlessness of Swift's satire and more than one critic of Fielding's book has found his sustained irony, magnificent as it is, rather fatiguing. Scott declared that he could not understand "what Fielding proposed to himself by a picture of complete vice, unrelieved by anything of human feeling, and never, by any accident even, deviating into virtue."[1]

But it is by no means certain that *Jonathan Wild* is only or even mainly a moral satire. It is true that Fielding disclaims the idea that he had any particular individual in his mind when he wrote his satire; but the very passage in which his disclaimer is made concludes with the remark that he knows that his reader is acquainted with more than one person "on whom he can fix the resemblance to his hero."[2] Some parts of *Jonathan Wild*, like the chapter on hats, for example, in the second book, or the eleventh chapter in the third, in which he compares his hero to the master of a puppet-show who "dances and moves everything but keeps himself wisely out of sight," have undoubtedly an underlying political meaning. Again, when one reads the account given towards the end of the book of the factions in Newgate, one finds it difficult to resist the conclusion that Fielding had Walpole's fall from power in his mind when he described Roger Johnson's discomfiture and the loss of his influence over the prisoners in Newgate. The words "great man" that he uses so often in his satire which are printed

[1] Scott, *Lives of the Novelists*: "Fielding."
[2] Preface to the *Miscellanies*.

in capital letters in the version of *Jonathan Wild* published in the *Miscellanies* were almost invariably used in this
way by the pamphleteers and other writers of the Opposition to refer to Walpole. Some of the ideas and the
imagery as well as many of the actual expressions which
are the distinctive features of Fielding's attacks on Walpole in *The Champion* and *The Vernoniad* recur constantly
in *Jonathan Wild*.

In the "advertisement" from the publisher to the
reader, written apparently by Fielding himself, which was
prefixed to the revised edition of *Jonathan Wild* published in 1754, the disclaimer made in the Preface to the *Miscellanies* is repeated, but the language of this second disclaimer makes one suspicious that Fielding is laughing
in his sleeve at his reader's perplexity about the real drift
of his satire, and it is significant that he concludes the advertisement by drawing his reader's particular attention
to the chapter describing the Newgate factions in which
the political allusions are unmistakable. The fact of the
matter seems to be that in *Jonathan Wild* Fielding was
more indebted to *The Beggar's Opera* than he was willing
to disclose. The trend of the satire in both the works and
the occurrence of such names as Bagshot and Straddle
in *Jonathan Wild* establish beyond the possibility of
doubt the fact of Fielding's indebtedness to Gay.

Among the critics and biographers of Fielding, Keightley seems to have been the first to suggest that there is an
underlying political satire in *Jonathan Wild*, and he expressed the opinion that from fear of consequences Fielding so veiled the real meaning of the satire that it is hardly
discoverable without a key. Keightley endeavour to find
this key and he made the suggestion that the unusual
terms "prigs" and "priggism" which Fielding so often

uses stand for Whigs and Whiggism; that Jonathan
Wild is Sir Robert Walpole, and the political satire com-
mences at the place where Fielding speaks of the forma-
tion of Wild's gang.[1] In the postscript to his articles on
Fielding to which we have already referred he adds that
in revising his earlier satire for publication in the *Miscellanies* Fielding probably made some additions to it and
altered it considerably to obscure the political meaning
underlying the satire. To this one must add that when
Fielding published his revised version of *Jonathan Wild*
in 1754 he made other significant alterations. Among
other changes that he made in the later version of the
satire he omitted the chapter on proverbs in the second
book, the twelfth in the earlier version, the underlying
political meaning of which was unmistakable; and
throughout the narrative he substituted the word "states-
man" for the "prime minister" of the earlier version.
These and a few other minor changes of the same nature
certainly suggest that Fielding was endeavouring to obscure the underlying political meaning of his satire as
much as possible, if not to eliminate it altogether.

Keightley's interpretation of this meaning is as satisfactory as any that has been offered; only, Keightley's
words seem to imply that *Jonathan Wild* was a carefully
prepared allegory with a continuous undercurrent of
political meaning. It is doubtful if political satire was the
only end that Fielding had in view when he first wrote the
story, though he was glad enough to take advantage of the
opportunities that offered as he progressed with his story
to satirize the political abuses of his time and to suggest
parallels between characters in his story and some of the
foremost politicians of his day. That Fielding had Walpole

[1] *Fraser's Magazine*, February, 1858, p. 213.

in his mind when he first sketched the character of Jonathan Wild is more than probable. He gives special prominence to certain features in Wild's character which must have been interpreted by many of his readers as satiric references to some of Walpole's notorious frailties as a public man. For example, the reader of the novel in those days could not have found it difficult to understand what the real drift of the satire was when Fielding described Wild's skill in organizing his gang and in exercising control over it from behind the scenes, his adroitness in pocketing most of the booty taken by his instruments or his impudence and utter heartlessness. Again, some events in Walpole's life seem to be reflected in the story of Wild's career as Fielding relates it. Walpole's differences with his colleagues, for example, seem to be portrayed in the account given in the story of Wild's quarrels with Blueskin and Fireblood; and the scandals of Walpole's private life seem to have their reflection in the picture given in the course of the satire of Wild's infidelity and the unchastity of Laetitia his wife. But probably the most striking indication of the fact that Fielding originally had Walpole in his mind when he portrayed Wild is to be found in the second chapter in the book in which he burlesques William Musgrave's *Brief and True History of Robert Walpole and His Family* by tracing the genealogy of Wild. In naming the grandfather of Jonathan he momentarily confuses the hero of his story with the objective of his satire.

To the suggestion made by Keightley and others that through the greater part of the narrative Wild can be more or less identified with Walpole quite a number of objections have been made. It has been contended, for example, that the satire is directed more against the unscrupulous conqueror than the politician, a contention that will hardly bear close examination. Again, it has been pointed out that in the chapter describing the factions in Newgate it is Roger Johnson and not Wild who is to be identified with Walpole. Keightley himself makes this identification and remarks that such changes are not unusual in political satires.[1] Indeed this confusion in the underlying political meaning seems to have been deliberately introduced into the satire by Fielding to obscure his allusions for the sake of safety. Or the chapter in question may have been an afterthought and it may have been inserted, as Keightley suggests, by Fielding to mark his disgust at the conduct of Walpole's successors.

The prigs, according to Keightley, stand for the Whigs, and here Keightley seems to have gone astray in his interpretation. A number of passages in *Jonathan Wild* clearly indicate that the prigs belong to more than one political party, and Whitwell Elwin seems to be nearer the truth when he suggests that the prigs are placemen and place-hunters and the debtors in Newgate are the people or taxpayers.[2]

Whatever the underlying political meaning may be in certain parts of the narrative in *Jonathan Wild*, it seems to be fairly obvious from the language he uses in his Preface to the *Miscellanies* and the changes that he made in the later version of his book that he was anxious, as time went on and his animosity to Walpole grew less, to relegate the political meaning of his satire more and more to the background. He therefore placed all the emphasis he could on the moral underlying his satire which certainly

[1] *Fraser's Magazine*, February, 1858, p. 213.
[2] Whitwell Elwin, *Some XVIII Century Men of Letters*, Vol. II, "Fielding," p. 118.

had a general rather than a merely political application and which had been uppermost in his mind all along.

The most striking feature of *Jonathan Wild* is, as has been pointed out by critics again and again, its formidable and pervading irony. This irony, however "sleepless" and fierce as it is throughout the book, is not altogether unrelieved by anything of human feeling, as Scott pronounced it to be. Indeed, Scott's criticism was ill-considered and was evidently based on an imperfect knowledge of the book. It is curious that the relief from the withering irony of *Jonathan Wild* for which Scott looked in vain but which Fielding had taken special care to provide, as he tells us when he introduces Heartfree into the story, has been looked upon as a blemish which destroys the "unity" of the satire.[1]

The plot in *Jonathan Wild* is carefully constructed, and Fielding introduced the story of the betrayal of the Heartfrees into his narrative in order to give a new interest to it. As we have pointed out before, numerous histories of the life of Jonathan Wild had already appeared, and Fielding realized that he must introduce something new into his story to arouse the interest of his reader. There are many features in the story of the betrayal of the Heartfrees that show that Fielding had bestowed much thought on this part of the narrative. The objection that has been made to it on the ground that it disturbs the unity of the satire is hypercritical. While the delineation in the characters of the Heartfrees of that which is good in human nature relieves the strain of the pervading irony of the book, the story of the betrayal adds considerably to the poignancy of the satire. If there was any error of judg-

[1] *The Works of Henry Fielding*, edited by G. H. Maynadier, Vol. X, Introduction, p. xx.

M

ment at all, it consisted not in the introduction of the story into the main narrative but in drawing it out to a somewhat disproportionate length towards the end, where Fielding gives us the narrative of Mrs. Heartfree's adventures.

In dwelling upon certain aspects of his hero's career Fielding was quite content to adhere to some of the known facts of Wild's life because some of these facts served the purposes of his satire very well indeed. He introduced Blueskin or Blake, one of Wild's instruments who afterwards revolted from his authority and made an unsuccessful attempt on his life, into his story and only slightly altered the actual facts of Wild's treachery towards him and of his apprehension. And in describing the closing stages of his hero's career he was content to reproduce the known facts with little variation or embellishment. But apart from this adherence to what may be called historical facts, which after all make up only a small part of the history, Fielding took it upon himself, as he tells us in his Preface to the *Miscellanies*, to describe such actions that his hero "might have performed or would or should have performed than what he really did."

This declaration as well as the repudiation made in the same Preface of any design to write an authentic history would justify us in placing Wild in the same category with Fielding's other characters in the novels, though we must not overlook the fact that he reproduces the lineaments of his original more faithfully in this portrait than in others. Fielding endeavoured to portray the absolute villain in Wild and he was inexorable in his determination to expose the full deformity of vice. Writers of fiction have often portrayed criminals whose villainy has been relieved by redeeming features, and these features,

as we know, have often aroused considerable sympathy
and even admiration for the criminal. We can imagine
how successful Fielding's portrait of a generous highwayman or gamester would have been. But, as he had
done once before in the course of his dramatic career,
when he had portrayed Mr. and Mrs. Modern, Fielding
set out to make his protagonist thoroughly odious, and
he accomplished his object by richly endowing Wild with
those qualities which of all others were most repugnant
to him, hypocrisy, selfishness, and insatiable avarice.
Wild's "greatness" is to be measured by the extent of
these endowments and not so much by the magnitude of
his crimes or the subtlety of his methods.

As a psychological study of a villain Fielding's Jonathan Wild is inferior only to Iago, and the greatness of
Fielding's achievement lies mainly in the truth of the portrait. In a work such as he had undertaken there was a
special danger that the spirit of satire within him and his
indignation at prosperous villainy might make him lose
sight of the facts of life. In describing Wild's devious
ways of doing business, however, Fielding took special
care not to allow his imagination to run away with him.
His hero's mentality, abnormal as it is, is the mentality of
a criminal that one meets with in real life and his motives
of action are quite intelligible. A very characteristic Fielding touch in the portrait which heightens its realism is to
be found in the so-called flaws in Wild's intelligence
which enable inferior beings like Count La Ruse and
Molly Straddle to overreach him.

The other character in the book that arouses the
reader's whole-hearted repugnance is "the chaste Laetitia." It has been very well remarked that she is a woman
whom any "hero" may acknowledge as his better half

without being unduly derogatory to himself. As in his portrait of his hero, Fielding was determined to make his picture altogether a revolting one, and this is unusual as Fielding rarely made his women of easy virtue absolutely repulsive. There is nothing in "the fair Laetitia," however, to relieve the terrible sordidness and depravity of her character.

The other characters in the story need not detain us very long. The more prominent among the instruments of Wild, criminals like Bagshot, Fireblood, or Blueskin, are cast in the same mould. We have the usual type of the criminal, a coward at heart who undertakes certain enterprises because they promise considerable booty and are not attended by anything more than the ordinary risks. In La Ruse, however, Fielding portrays a different type of criminal, the gentleman thief and swindler, with an attractive person and insinuating manners. Snap the bailiff has been described by a critic as the most disagreeable person in the story,[1] but it is difficult to understand why he should be singled out for this particular honour. Nor is it easy to agree with Professor Saintsbury when he describes Heartfree as "a kind of idiot."[2] The good jeweller's faith in the friend of his schooldays, from whom he had hitherto received no injuries that he knew of, is no disparagement to his intelligence.

In pointing out the imperfections of *Jonathan Wild* the majority of Fielding's critics have exhibited themselves to little advantage and have more or less contradicted each other. Some have found the sustained irony of the book oppressive, while others have objected to the

[1]"Fielding's *Jonathan Wild*," by G. T. Bispham in *Eighteenth Century Literature*, an Oxford Miscellany.
[2]*The Temple Fielding*, Introduction, p. xvii.

relief that Fielding sought to provide through the story of the Heartfrees, and described it as an irrelevant and lengthy digression. The picture of villainy given in the book is admitted to be a fairly comprehensive one, and the need of such a picture in a satire like Fielding's is tacitly recognized, and yet some have recoiled from the mass of disagreeable matter they have found in the book. Frederick Lawrence, one of Fielding's biographers, writes in rather an exaggerated strain of "the revolting villainies and unrelieved depravities which the book unfolds to the general reader." [1] After all, in the choice of his subject and his hero and in the very explicit statement of his aim and purpose in writing the book he had given fair warning to his reader what to expect. The withering irony which castigates vice and villainy practically in every page in the book certainly exonerates Fielding from any blame that he might have incurred in other circumstances by dwelling too long and too exclusively on scenes of vice. And so far as the ugliness of his pictures or the licence and suggestiveness of amorous and vicious scenes and episodes are concerned Fielding is very far from being as guilty as some of his predecessors and contemporaries were.

Some modern readers of the book have felt that the satire would have appealed to a far larger circle of readers than it has actually done if it had a little more of Fielding's characteristic humour in it to relieve the strain of the irony. For with all due deference to Murphy who found such "seasonings of humour" in the book that he had little doubt it would be "a very high entertainment to all," the grim pleasantry that the satirist constantly indulges in can hardly be called humour. When the reader has an occasional taste of Fielding's genial humour, as for ex-

[1]Frederick Lawrence, *Life of Henry Fielding*, p. 189.

ample in the picture that is given of the disturbance of the harmony of Wild's countenance when he discovers how he has been relieved of his ill-gotten gains by Molly Straddle, or in the account that we have towards the end of the book of the Newgate ordinary's preference for punch because it is nowhere spoken against in the Scripture, he finds it very refreshing indeed.

CHAPTER VII

POLITICAL JOURNALISM

FOR more than two years after the publication of the *Miscellanies* Fielding gave nothing to the world worthy of his genius. This inactivity was not due altogether to the serious troubles that overtook him at this time. It was the result as much of disappointment as anything else. The *Miscellanies* had been a considerable financial success undoubtedly; but they do not seem to have added much to his reputation as a man of letters. *The Journey from this World to the Next* and *The History of Jonathan Wild* had apparently made little impression on the public, judging by the absence of appreciative references to them in the letters and diaries of contemporaries. The newspapers and magazines practically ignored them or only made an occasional contemptuous reference, as *Old England* did, for example, when it launched its violent tirade against Fielding.[1]

This neglect, added to the many disappointments that he had met with in the course of his chequered literary career, had left him rather sore, and his bitterness was aggravated by his many troubles. Indeed, the year 1744 was one of the unhappiest in his life. His financial resources were at a very low ebb and to this great trouble were added many others, the lingering illness of his wife, for example, his own loss of health or his gloomy prospects in his profession.

Apparently the only literary effort that he made in this

[1] *Old England*, March 3, 1748.

year of trouble was a preface that he wrote for the second edition of his sister Sarah's novel, *David Simple*. This book had been ascribed to him by the public, and in justice to his sister as well as to himself in view of the undertaking that he had given to the public that he would not publish anything anonymously, he felt it to be his duty to disclaim the authorship of the book. And as for some time people had been ascribing all kinds of writing to him, "half the scurrility, bawdy, treason, and blasphemy," as he bitterly complained, "that these last years have produced," he was glad to make use of the opportunity that this preface to his sister's novel gave him of protesting against the free use of his name. He was particularly indignant because the mischievous pamphlet, the *Causidicade*, in which one " Porcupinus Pelagius" wantonly ridiculed some of the most eminent members of the legal profession under the pretext of protesting against the appointment of William Murray, afterwards Lord Mansfield, as Solicitor-General, had been ascribed to him.

In the autumn of 1744 the cup of his sorrows seemed to be full. His wife, who had been ill for some time, died at Bath, and Murphy tells us that the death of Charlotte Fielding for whom he cherished a love that was the ruling passion of his life, brought on the novelist "such a vehemence of grief that his friends began to think him in danger of losing his reason."[1]

We have few direct references to Charlotte Fielding in the writings of the novelist. But when he does speak of her, as for example, in his essay *On the Remedy of Affliction for the Loss of our Friends* or in *Tom Jones*, his words breathe an unusual tenderness; and all readers of Field-

[1]Arthur Murphy, *An Essay on the Life and Genius of Henry Fielding*.

ing's novels are aware that his finest pictures of women were inspired by his great love and admiration for his first wife.

Shortly after the death of his wife Fielding took a house in Old Boswell Court near the Inns where he seems to have lived for some time. But very little is known of his life or activities at this time. He seems to have made special efforts to succeed in his profession, but success seemed to be as far off as ever.

The memorable events of the year 1745 brought Fielding prominently before the public once again. The Jacobite rising which the government made light of at first soon gave it cause for anxiety. The victory of the Highlanders at Preston Pans on the 21st of September was only a prelude to other surprising successes that were to follow in quick succession to bring home to the country the extent of the danger that threatened. As events were to prove, sympathy with the Jacobite cause was far from being widespread in England. But this was not known to the government at the time that Charles gained his first victory. On the other hand, the lack of enthusiasm among the people for the House of Hanover was very evident, and the government realized that special efforts must be made to rouse the people out of their lethargy to rally to the support of the existing "establishment," or at any rate to prevent them from drifting into sympathy with the Jacobite cause.

Fielding came forward at this juncture to help the government to educate public opinion and to do propaganda work on behalf of the government. It is probable that some member of the government, his school friend Lyttelton perhaps, who at this time was one of the Lords of the Treasury, approached him to enlist his services.

But this is mere conjecture and it is as likely as not that Fielding, who had a good deal of experience in political journalism, resolved of his own accord to emulate Addison's example in *The Freeholder* with an eye, perhaps, to some reward in the shape of a post or a pension from the government, though it would be a mistake to lay too much stress on his interested motives. His antipathy to the Jacobite was a deep-rooted one and he threw himself into the campaign against the Jacobites with great goodwill and enthusiasm which required little stimulation from any prospect of reward.

He seems to have opened his campaign with a political pamphlet named *A Serious Address to the People of Great Britain*, which appeared in October.[1] In the same month he published another pamphlet against the Jacobites written in a lighter vein and named *A Dialogue between the Devil, the Pope, and the Pretender*.[2] Both these pamphlets were published anonymously. The *Serious Address* is a powerful appeal made in dignified and eloquent language for united action in the face of the common danger. The *Dialogue* is an ingenious skit, and in some places its humour, sinister as it is, is piquant enough. But Fielding is inclined to be much too abusive and intemperate in his satire and exhibits more intolerance than he usually does in his polemical writings.

These pamphlets were only the preliminaries to an elaborate campaign against the Jacobites which was destined to absorb Fielding's varied literary gifts almost wholly for three years. As the Jacobite menace assumed serious proportions Fielding decided to help the government by editing a weekly political paper. This was named *The True Patriot and the History of Our Own Times*, and

[1] *The Gentleman's Magazine*, October, 1745.   [2] *Ibid.*

the first number of the journal appeared on the 5th of November. It was a double sheet printed for M. Cooper at the Globe in Paternoster Row and it appeared every Tuesday. Though Smollett afterwards asserted that Fielding had been in the pay of the government, and some of the latter's enemies in the newspaper world bestowed such titles as "pensioned scribbler" and "press informer" on him, he does not appear to have received any financial support from the government though, of course, his activities were approved, and he evidently had access to more reliable information than the "authors" of the majority of the other papers had.

The main object of the paper was to discredit the Jacobite cause, or as Fielding himself stated it, "to alarm his fellow subjects with the dangers which the Rebellion threatened to their religion and liberties, indeed to everything valuable which they possessed"[1]; and in the thirty-three numbers of the paper that were issued this aim was kept constantly in view. Like other newspapers of the time, *The True Patriot* furnished under different headings the foreign and domestic news of the time, the latter consisting mainly of the latest information about the developments in the North. The characteristic feature of the paper, however, was the part called the "Apocrypha" which was "a curious collection of certain true and important 'We hears' from the newspapers," and in this as well as in an occasional "Apocryphal History of the Rebellion" Fielding commented, with many a brilliant sally of wit, somewhat after the manner of *Punch* at the present time, on items of news of all kinds appearing in the contemporary newspapers.

[1] *The True Patriot*, No. 33, June 17, 1746 (from extract in *The London Magazine* for June, 1746, p. 298).

On the whole, so far as the interest of the average leading article is concerned, *The True Patriot* is an improvement on *The Champion*. Fielding entered on his enterprise
with the avowed intention of attaining a higher level of
excellence than that of the other papers of his time, and in
the first number of his paper he referred contemptuously
to them, describing them as altogether devoid of truth
and good sense. This indiscriminate condemnation was
not only tactless but unfair, and it exasperated his enemies
who retaliated by making violent personal attacks on him.

The assumption of superiority was, however, substantiated by his performance. Fielding's leading articles
in *The True Patriot* have much to recommend them.
Though in the face of the tirades that he indulges in
against the Jacobites and the Roman Catholics the reader
is inclined to smile at the claim that he makes more than
once to moderation in his dealings with all parties, there
is much sound reasoning and political wisdom in his papers. His arguments are generally forcible and his case
clearly stated. One of the most attractive features of his
leading articles is their variety. Sometimes his tone is
altogether serious, and he makes earnest appeals to his
readers to serve the best interests of their country and to
defend it against its enemies. Occasionally he takes recourse to a genial and very effective irony to rouse the
people to a sense of their duty. The humour, again, of
some of the papers in which he ridicules the Jacobites, as
for example, the papers which contain letters from J.R.
to His Royal High—s Charles P—of W—s[1], and from
a Jacobite father to his son at Oxford,[2] is as delightful as
it is effective.

[1] *The True Patriot*, No. 12, January 21, 1746.
[2] *The True Patriot*, No. 24, April 15, 1746.

But the best numbers of *The True Patriot* are those in which Fielding tries to forecast the immediate conse-quences of the success of the Jacobite rising[1] and gives his readers the benefit of Parson Adams' reflections on the crisis. Adams is supposed to address two very charac-teristic letters[2] to the editor of the paper, and in the second of these which contains an account of the out-rageous conduct of a "member of the society of *bowes*" we have Fielding's humour at its best.

Though *The True Patriot* had its origin in the Jacobite rising of 1745 and propaganda work against the Jaco-bites was the main, if not the only, item on its programme, its leading articles were not always political. Occasionally Fielding dealt with other matters in which he was in-terested, a subject like imprisonment for debt,[3] for ex-ample, or the odium or contempt brought on certain pro-fessions by the incompetence or misconduct of certain members belonging to them.[4] Again, he sometimes in-dulged in the satiric or humorous vein to ridicule, after the manner of the elder essayists, some of the foibles and follies of the world of fashion. He laughs, for example, with much good humour at the vagaries of "the Town" in damning plays,[5] and ridicules the extravagance of hoop petticoats[6] in very much the same strain as Addison had done in *The Spectator*.

In the numbers of *The True Patriot* that appeared after the first week in March, 1746, one notices symptoms of relaxing energy in the "author" of the paper. The lead-

[1] *The True Patriot*, No. 3, November 19, 1745, and No. 10, January 7, 1746.
[2] *The True Patriot*, No. 7, December 17, 1745, and No. 13, January 28, 1746.
[3] *The True Patriot*, No. 5, December 3, 1745.
[4] *The True Patriot*, No. 14, February 4, 1746.
[5] *The True Patriot*, No. 18, February 25 to March 4, 1746.
[6] *The True Patriot*, No. 15, February 11, 1746.

ing articles after this date are not as good as the previous
ones, and they deal with topics of general interest rather
than with the immediate concerns of the moment. More
than one of these leading articles evidently did not come
from the pen of Fielding. The "Apocrypha" also disappeared from the paper about this time. All these symptoms point to the fact that Fielding was busy elsewhere.
Perhaps the demands of his profession made it impossible for him to devote all the time and energy to his paper
that he had hitherto given to it. The last number of the
paper, the thirty-third, which was dated June 17, and from
which an extract appears in *The London Magazine* for
June, 1746, contains the author's farewell to his reader,
in the course of which he explains that as "the rebellion
is now brought to a happy conclusion by the victorious
arms of his Royal Highness the Duke of Cumberland, it
is a proper time for this paper which was entirely occasioned by the rebellion to cease with it."

During the rest of the year 1746 Fielding published
nothing of any importance. A pamphlet named *The
Female Husband* has been ascribed to him because it is
included in one of Millar's lists of his works.[1] But the
style of the pamphlet, a copy of which is in the British
Museum, does not point to Fielding as the author of it;
and though it is true that the novelist's literary activities
had ranged over an extensive field, yet one is inclined to
believe that he was above writing a pamphlet on a subject
like that of *The Female Husband.*

In *The Gentleman's Magazine* for February, 1747, in
the list of books and pamphlets published during the
month occurs the name of a work, *Ovid's Art of Love*

---

[1] Professor W. L. Cross in his *History of Henry Fielding*, Vol. II, p. 52,
mentions this list as appearing on a flyleaf of Sarah Fielding's *Lives of Cleopatra and Octavia*, second edition, 1758.

Adapted to the Present Times, which Millar includes in his lists of Fielding's works that appear in the advertisement pages in the 1754 edition of *Jonathan Wild* and the 1758 edition of Sarah Fielding's *Lives of Cleopatra and Octavia*. Only one copy of this edition of the adaptation is known.[1] A reprint of it was made in Dublin in 1759 with the title, *The Lover's Assistant or New Year's Gift, Being a New Art of Love, Adapted to the Present Times*; and this work, a copy of which is in the British Museum, is described on the title page as a translation from the Latin made by "the Late Ingenious Henry Fielding of Facetious Memory."

This paraphrase of part of the first book of Ovid's *Ars Amatoria* resembles Fielding's earlier " modernization" of part of Juvenal's *Sixth Satire* which appeared in the *Miscellanies* of 1743. In both the books the original Latin and the English paraphrase are printed side by side on opposite pages and in both the text is accompanied by notes which contain many bright sallies of wit. The paraphrase of Ovid is introduced by a preface in which, in very much the same language as in *Tom Jones*, the assurance is given to the reader that it contains "nothing capable of offending the nicest ear." These features of the book and a further resemblance to the earlier "modernization" of Juvenal in the transformations of classic characters and environment that are attempted on a larger scale in the later work seem to point to Fielding being its author. And the evidence of the style confirms this.

Fielding's next literary effort about which we have certain knowledge consisted of a preface and some letters

[1] This was until recently in the possession of Mr. L. Rice-Oxley of Keble College, Oxford. It was sold to Messrs. Quaritch at an auction sale held by Hodgson & Co. in December, 1926.

which he contributed to his sister Sarah's *Familiar Letters Between the Principal Characters in "David Simple" and Some Others*. This rather dull book, for the idea of which Sarah Fielding was evidently indebted to Richardson, was published by subscription in April, 1747.[1] Fielding contributed the last five letters in the volume to the collection, as a note introducing these letters, written evidently by Sarah, informs the reader. In this note Sarah makes her protest against "the imputation of much scurrility and nonsense" to her brother.

The preface to *The Familiar Letters* does not contain much that is of special interest or value. In view of the success of *Pamela* it is somewhat surprising to find Fielding venturing on the statement that no one will contend that the epistolary style is in general the most proper to a novelist. But of course he relied on his reservation for the soundness of the statement. In this preface he also expresses the opinion that a knowledge of human nature is not gained by living in the hurry of the world, but true genius is able to make a vast progress in this knowledge with the help of a little "conversation." He pays a glowing tribute to Lyttelton and is lavish in his praise of his sister's book, likening it to a glass "by which young ladies may dress out their minds, and adorn themselves with more becoming, as well as more lasting graces, than the dancing-master, the mantua-maker, or the milliner can give them." Of the five letters that he contributed to his sister's volume, the first only, which gives a graphic picture of the state of the country, is really noteworthy.

For some months after the publication of his sister's book Fielding seems to have published nothing of greater importance than an occasional political pamphlet. A

[1]*The Gentleman's Magazine*, April, 1747, p. 204.

book named *A Compleat and Authentick History of the Rise,
Progress, and Extinction of the Late Rebellion*, published in
April, has been ascribed to him mainly because the narrative is based on the accounts of the rebellion that had appeared in *The True Patriot*. But the evidence of the style
of this history and its general tone do not point to Fielding as the author of it, and the reasons that Professor
W. L. Cross has advanced in support of his view that
Fielding purposely disguised his hand when writing the
book are not very convincing.[1]

In June[2] appeared an electioneering pamphlet named
*A Dialogue between a Gentleman of London, Agent for two
Court Candidates, and an Honest Alderman of the Country
Party* which is declared to be the work of the "author" of
The Jacobite's Journal in *A Proper Answer to a Late Scurrilous Libel*.[3] The *Dialogue* is far from being a lively one and
and is drawn out to excessive length. Its most noteworthy
feature is its spirited defence of the government. Fielding zealously advocates the Whig cause and upholds the
existing "establishment" with arguments that are as forcible as they are comprehensive.

Meanwhile, he had taken a step which was bound to
give rise to much sarcastic comment. Fielding's earlier
biographers have nothing to say about his second marriage to his wife's maid, Mary Daniel or Macdaniel, which
event took place on the 27th of November, 1747. But his
contemporaries were far from being as reticent as his first
biographers were after his death. Smollett, for example,
made an ill-natured reference to this marriage in the
course of his attack on Lyttelton in the first edition of
Peregrine Pickle. And Lady Mary Montagu's remark,

[1] W. L. Cross, *The History of Henry Fielding*, Vol. II, p. 56.
[2] *The Gentleman's Magazine*, June, 1747.
[3] Footnote, p. 28.

N

made some years afterwards, that Fielding's natural spirits gave him rapture with his cookmaid[1], was a kind of comment that was to be expected in the circum-stances. Soon after his marriage he took rooms in Twick-enham where he seems to have lived for a year in a house in Back Lane, and it was from here that his son William was baptized on the 24th of February, 1748.

It was not long after his second marriage that Field-ing made his presence felt in the political world once again by starting another political paper which he ironic-ally named *The Jacobite's Journal.* Jacobite feeling and sentiment, as Scott points out in his *Life of Fielding*, had been effectually crushed on the field of Culloden; but Fielding in his zeal for the existing "establishment," which was not altogether disinterested perhaps, still pro-fessed to apprehend danger from what he made out to be a recrudescence of Jacobitism in the winter of 1747. And this apprehension was not absolutely without foundation when one takes into account the fact that the country had formidable external enemies with whom she had been struggling for some years and one of whom at least had professed much sympathy with the Jacobite cause.

The first number of Fielding's new political paper came out on the 5th of December, 1747. With the excep-tion of a striking but somewhat enigmatic woodcut which adorned the first page of the journal and which has been ascribed to Hogarth, its appearance in other respects was very much like that of its predecessor, though the con-tents were not so varied or interesting. As he had done in *The Champion,* Fielding now assumed a pseudonym, John Trottplaid, the first part of the name being borrowed

[1]*Lady Mary Montagu's Letters and Works,* edited by Lord Wharncliffe, 1861, Vol. II, p. 282.

from a former contributor to *The Craftsman* and the extra syllable added at the end because it indicated the party to which the "author" professed to belong.

The Jacobite's Journal was issued every Saturday and its principal contents were the usual ones of the newspapers of the time. There was a certain amount of humorous comment on the news items of the day, but the columns of foreign and home intelligence in the paper were not as full of bright sallies of wit as the columns of *The True Patriot* had been, and until Fielding hit upon the happy idea of inserting the proceedings of "John Trottplaid's Court of Criticism" in his paper it was less entertaining on the whole than its predecessor had been.

Fielding ushered in his new journalistic venture in very much the same way as he had done *The True Patriot*. He began by making contemptuous references to the other newspapers of the time. A journalist's talents, he declared in the first number of his paper, must be very indifferent if he is not capable of shining among a set of such dark planets, and in the concluding paragraph of his first leading article he singled out *The London Evening Post*, *Old England*, and *The Westminster Journal* for special abuse. His adversaries who were thus attacked were neither very slow nor very scrupulous and honest in the settlement of their account with him.

The journal, as the engraving on its first page proclaimed, professed to be an organ of the Jacobite party, and Fielding assuming the guise of a Jacobite declared his aim and purpose with characteristic irony. "In this dress," he says in the first number of the paper, "I intend to lash not only the m——stry but every man who hath any p——ce or p——ns——n from the g——v——rnm——nt or who is intrusted with any degree of power or trust under it, let his rank be never so high, his f——rt——ne never so great or his ch——r——ct——r never so good." His real aim, of course, was to pursue the Jacobites relentlessly with ridicule, "to laugh men," as he said afterwards, "out of their follies, and to make them ashamed of owning or acting by principles no less inconsistent with common sense than detrimental to the society."[1]

After some time, however, Fielding found it necessary to drop the mask of irony that he had put on at the beginning. He did this in the seventeenth number of his paper and explained to his readers that the campaign which he had undertaken was too momentous to be fought with the weapons of irony and ridicule alone. Moreover, he had found that his irony was apt to be misunderstood.

Altogether, forty-nine numbers of *The Jacobite's Journal* were issued before the paper ceased to appear. The leading articles in it, with one or two exceptions perhaps, are all from the pen of Fielding, and they are mostly political essays or letters from correspondents dealing with political subjects. These political essays have little of the variety that is such an attractive feature of the articles in *The True Patriot*. A good number among them are devoted to so-called expositions of the Jacobite creed and to accounts of the supposed ramifications of the party. Fielding enunciates what he calls the principal Jacobite tenets and makes very pertinent comments on them.[2] He speaks of the "esoteric" and the "exoteric" mysteries of Jacobitism. The former he describes as shared alike by men and women Jacobites. Of the exoteric mysteries, that is to say, those that are outward and visible, he says that drinking belongs principally to the men and fighting to the women,

[1] *The Jacobite's Journal*, No. 17, March 26, 1748.
[2] *The Jacobite's Journal*, No. 3, December 19, 1747, and No. 5, January 2, 1748.

and these mysteries, we are told, "have a right to the most ancient organization and are indeed no other than the famous Orgia of old celebrated in honour of the god Bacchus."[1]

But the pursuit of the Jacobite party with ridicule and contempt was not the whole programme of the journal. Fielding also constituted himself the champion of the government's policy and undertook to defend it against its critics. The only matter in regard to which he felt disposed to criticize the ministry was its delay in making peace. The eulogy on the ministry contained in the pamphlet named *A Dialogue between a Gentleman of London and an Honest Alderman of the Country Party* was cordially endorsed in *The Jacobite's Journal*.[2] When the preliminaries of peace were signed, and later on when the peace itself was concluded, *The Jacobite's Journal* was lavish in its praise of the ministry and denounced in strong language the opposition papers for "roaring forth loudly against the peace" and insinuating that the ministry had been bullied into the acceptance of dishonourable terms by the address and threats of France.[3]

But Fielding did not take up the cudgels to defend only the policy of the ministry. He fought the battles of individual ministers also. He espoused the cause of Thomas Winnington who not long after his death was represented as a Jacobite in a pamphlet which professed to be an autobiography.[4] Fielding replied to this not only in his journal but also in a pamphlet named *A Proper Answer to a late Scurrilous Libel entitled, An Apology for the*

[1] *The Jacobite's Journal*, No. 2, December 12, 1747, and No. 6, January 9, 1748.
[2] *The Jacobite's Journal*, No. 10, February 6, 1748.
[3] *The Jacobite's Journal*, No. 47, October 22, 1748.
[4] *An Apology for the Conduct of a late celebrated second-rate Minister.*

Conduct of a late celebrated second-rate Minister. In *The Jacobite's Journal*, again, Fielding was particularly warm in his defence of Lyttelton who as the supposed author of *A Letter to the Tories* in which the Walpole administration had been severely arraigned had come in for much abuse in Horace Walpole's *Letters to the Whigs*.[1]

These controversies, however, were mild ones compared to his encounters with the journalists of the time who in the end were to prove more than a match for him because they were utterly unscrupulous. It could hardly be expected that they would take lying down the fresh provocation that Fielding had given to them when he had started *The Jacobite's Journal*. As a matter of fact, soon after Fielding embarked on his new journalistic venture he was assailed by enemies who were as furious as they were unscrupulous in their attacks on him. The use of invective was lavish on both sides, but it is very much to the credit of Fielding that unlike his adversaries he never dragged the private affairs of his adversaries into the controversies in order to humiliate them. This is the outstanding feature of his conduct in all the controversies in which he was engaged during his whole life. His enemies, however, chief among whom was "Porcupinus Pelagius" who had signalized himself as the author of the *Causidicade* and other satires on which John Trottplaid in his "Court of Criticism" pronounced the censure they richly deserved, felt no hesitation in making the most violent personal attacks on him, grossly exaggerating his frailties and raking up for embellishment and misrepresentation whatever was open to criticism in Fielding's past life.[2]

[1] *The Jacobite's Journal*, No. 18, April 2, 1748.
[2] *Old England*, March 5, 1748. For other attacks on him see *Old England*, April 23 and 30, June 25 and November 12, 1748. Also *The London Evening Post*, March 12-15, 15-17, 29-31, April 7-9, July 28-30. These attacks continued for a long time in both these papers.

Fielding replied to these attacks with a great deal of spirit and ingenuity though, as we have pointed out before, he was incapable of indulging in personalities in the way his adversaries did. This placed him at a disadvantage and he seems to have felt that such replies as he could give to the violent and utterly unscrupulous attacks made on his character were rather futile. He complained bitterly of the treatment that he had received and declared that a heavier load of scandal had been put on him than ever fell to the share of any single man. "Several writers," he says in one of the papers in which he makes this complaint, "were no sooner possessed of my name than they attempted to blacken it with every kind of reproach; pursued me into private life, even to my boyish years; where they have given me almost every vice in human nature."[1]

Though Fielding was far more preoccupied with politics in *The Jacobite's Journal* than he had been in *The True Patriot*, yet in some numbers of the former he found room for non-political subjects. He went out of his way in one of his earlier contributions to the journal to commend the first two volumes of Richardson's *Clarissa Harlowe* which had been published in the same month in which *The Jacobite's Journal* had come into existence. The praise given to Richardson's masterpiece was as ungrudging as it was sincere. Indeed, the warmth of it tempts one to believe that Fielding was trying to make amends for his past behaviour to his rival. "Such simplicity, such manners," he says in the course of a letter supposed to be addressed by a correspondent to his paper, "such deep penetration into nature; such power to raise and alarm the passions, few writers either ancient or modern have been possessed of. My affections are so strongly engaged, and my fears

[1] *The Jacobite's Journal*, No. 20, April 16, 1748.

are so raised, by what I have already read, that I cannot express my eagerness to see the rest."[1]

But besides commending books like Richardson's *Clarissa Harlowe* or Thomson's *Castle of Indolence* Fielding also dealt with some social problems of the day in his paper. Among other matters that engaged his attention was the condition of the Highlands of Scotland, and he put forward an elaborate scheme suggesting improvements.[2] Again, in two other numbers of his paper[3] he made John Trottplaid hold forth at considerable length in his "Court of Criticism" on the need for making some effective provision for the relief of the widows and children of poor clergymen, a cause he advocated more than once in his later life.

To the modern reader the most interesting part of *The Jacobite's Journal* would perhaps be the paragraphs in some numbers of the paper that are devoted to reports of the proceedings in John Trottplaid's "Court of Criticism." Fielding had made some use of this device before when he reported the proceedings of Captain Hercules Vinegar's Court of Censorial Enquiry in *The Champion*; but the idea, excellent as it was, was not developed sufficiently in the earlier paper. Fielding now revived it, and from the seventh to the thirty-fourth number of *The Jacobite's Journal* with only a few interruptions he enlivened his paper with very humorous accounts of the proceedings in John Trottplaid's "Court of Criticism" which was set up "for the well ordering and inspecting all matters any wise concerning the Republic of Literature."[4] His experience as a lawyer and his skill in burlesquing legal phraseology en-

[1] *The Jacobite's Journal*, No. 5, January 2, 1748.
[2] *The Jacobite's Journal*, No. 16, March 19, 1748.
[3] *The Jacobite's Journal*, No. 31, July 2, 1748. and No. 32, July 9, 1748.
[4] *The Jacobite's Journal*, No. 6, January 9, 1748.

abled him to write excellent accounts of these proceedings. The cases brought up to the court and the applications made therein were as various as they were interesting. His implacable enemy "Porcupine Pillage" was brought before "the Censor of Great Britain" more than once, and the Court passed the sentence of contempt on the author of the *Causidicade* and other satires, and committed him to the Bridewell of Billingsgate and the pillory of *The Jacobite's Journal*. The writer of a letter to the journal commending *Clarissa* received the thanks of the Court. Thomson's *Castle of Indolence* was declared to be "a noble allegorical poem which truly breathes the spirit of that author which it professes to imitate."[1] And the other judgments that were pronounced were equally sound.

But the Court's jurisdiction was not confined to authors and their activities alone. Mr. Garrick received the thanks of the Court "for his great improvement of theatrical entertainments."[2] Mr. Rich was "admonished for suffering private characters to be ridiculed by mimicry and buffoonery on the stage,"[3] and "Samuel Fut of the parish of St. Giles's, Labourer" was indicted for "mauling and hacking" people in a certain part called their character.[4] These and other judgments pronounced by Mr. John Trottplaid make the accounts of the proceedings of the "Court of Criticism" very interesting reading indeed.

According to an announcement in *The Jacobite's Journal* of the 23rd July, 1748, the "Court of Criticism" suspended its sittings for a time because the Grub Street writers

[1] *The Jacobite's Journal*, No. 27, June 4, 1748.
[2] *The Jacobite's Journal*, No. 10, February 6, 1748.
[3] *The Jacobite's Journal*, No. 10, February 6, 1748.
[4] *The Jacobite's Journal*, No. 22, April 30, 1748.

were supposed to be away in the country working in the fields. From this date the proceedings of the Court cease to be reported in the paper, and about the same time its news items begin to be printed with little of the customary comment. These indications point to a dwindling interest in the paper on the part of its editor who apparently had not much time to devote to it. Perhaps he was busy attending the Western Circuit.

Late in autumn in 1748 Fielding felt that as he had "palliated the evil" of Jacobitism, and as the party was no longer a danger to the country there was hardly any justification for the continued existence of the paper. The last number of *The Jacobite's Journal* appeared on the 5th of November, 1748, and Mr. John Trottplaid made his exit "compassionately advising his antagonists," as *The Gentleman's Magazine* described it, "to submit to the powers that be, if for no other reason, because those powers will most certainly be, in defiance of all which the courts of Rome and Hell can devise against them."[1]

[1] *The Gentleman's Magazine*, November, 1748, p. 515.

CHAPTER VIII

THE MASTERPIECE

IT was not long after *The Jacobite's Journal* had ceased to appear that Fielding was appointed a magistrate for the city and liberties of Westminster, the only reward that his friend Lyttelton was able to obtain for him from a government which, as Keightley points out, was lavishing its favours on men who deserved them much less than Fielding did. The office was far from being an honourable one as the nickname given to it, "trading justice," indicates significantly enough. And this bad odour that belonged to it was inevitable, as the custom of augmenting by questionable practices the income of the office which was derived wholly from fees had become established by a kind of corrupt tradition. Fielding's commission which was afterwards extended to the whole county of Middlesex is dated the 25th of October, 1748, and he seems to have commenced his duties in the month of December.

He had held office only a few months when his greatest work was published. The question, when Fielding commenced writing *Tom Jones*, is a difficult one to answer. In 1744 when he wrote his Preface to his sister's novel, *David Simple*, the thought of writing *Tom Jones* had not evidently entered his mind, as he speaks in that Preface of abandoning the thorny paths of literature in order to devote himself to law. In dedicating *Tom Jones* to Lyttelton he declares that it was his friend who first suggested the idea of the novel to him, and he tells his reader that it cost him the labour of some years of his life.

It has been conjectured from the slight historical background that Fielding gave to his story, in one part of which we are taken back to the last months of the year 1745, that he commenced his novel soon after the sensational events of these months had happened. This is an accord with what the novelist says in his dedication of *Tom Jones* about many years having passed since the idea of the novel was first suggested to him. Moreover, an occasional correspondence of thought in some of the earlier chapters in *Tom Jones* with some of Fielding's utterances in *The True Patriot* seems to lend support to the view that *Tom Jones* was begun early in the year 1746. The novelist's receipt for the six hundred pounds that Millar originally paid for *Tom Jones*, to which a hundred pounds were added afterwards, appears to have been signed before the novel was quite ready for the press. This document is dated the 11th of June, 1748. More than eight months were to elapse before the novel could be published, and a considerable part of this time seems to have been taken up by Fielding in giving the finishing touches to his work—in writing the introductory chapters to the different books, in adding a few notes and, of course, in revision. The story seems to have been substantially finished by the end of the year 1747. Of this we have evidence in the following statement made in a letter which the Rev. Thomas Birch wrote to John, the fifth Earl of Orrery, on the 19th of January, 1748. "Mr. Fielding," Birch says, "is printing three volumes of adventures under the title of The Foundling. Mr. Littleton, who has read the manuscript, commends the performance to me as an excellent one, and abounding with strong and lively painting of characters, and a very copious and happy invention in the conduct of the story."[1]

But in regard to this matter of the time that the novelist took to write *Tom Jones*, as well as the other question as to where *Tom Jones* was written, the biographers of Fielding have to content themselves with conjectures only. The novelist tells us practically nothing as to where *Tom Jones* was written. The only clue that we have, if it can be called a clue at all, is the mention of a "little parlour" in the first chapter of the thirteenth book of the novel which contains one of his famous invocations. And the only contemporary of the novelist who gives us any further information on the subject is the Rev. Richard Graves, the author of *The Spiritual Quixote*, who in his *Trifling Anecdotes of the late Ralph Allen, Esq.*[2], tells his reader that Fielding lived at the village of Twerton or Tiverton about a mile and a half from Bath while he was writing *Tom Jones*, and that he dined almost daily at Prior Park, Ralph Allen's palatial residence. Evidently Graves refers to visits that Fielding paid to the neighbourhood of Bath during the three years from 1746 to 1748, in search of health perhaps. The greater part of the novel was probably written in the house in Old Boswell Court which he took on the death of his first wife, and in those rooms in Back Lane, Twickenham, in which he lived for more than a year after his marriage to Mary Daniel.

The History of Tom Jones, a Foundling, was published by

[1] *The Orrery Papers*, edited by the Countess of Cork and Orrery, London, 1903, Vol. II, p. 14.
[2] The "Trifling Anecdotes of the late Ralph Allen, Esq." are to be found in the third part of Graves' book called *The Triflers*, published in 1806. In a note appended to the first page of the "Trifling Anecdotes" Graves says: "In what I am going to relate in these few anecdotes, I do not pretend to great accuracy, but they are what were generally known and related as facts fifty years ago when I first came to reside in the vicinity of Bath."

Andrew Millar on the 28th of February, 1749, in six volumes 12mo. The public of whom Edmund Gosse speaks so contemptuously, who had gone into raptures over Richardson's sentimentality and had been inclined hitherto to treat Fielding with a "ladylike disdain," seem to have done some justice to the novel on its first appearance, if an unusual demand for it may be looked upon as a sign of appreciation. Almost simultaneously with the appearance of the novel Millar found it necessary to announce that "as it was impossible to get sets bound fast enough to answer the demand for them, such gentlemen and ladies as pleased might have them sewed in blue paper and boards at the price of 16s. a set." This evidently was not a bookseller's "puff." The demand for the book was an exceptional and unexpected one. Of this we have further evidence in the appearance of the second edition of the novel in less than two months after the first. A Dublin edition also appeared simultaneously with the second London edition of *Tom Jones*. In France M. de la Place undertook a translation, or rather the preparation of an abridged version of *Tom Jones* soon after the appearance of the second edition of the novel in England.

For this demand for the book some of Fielding's friends, and particularly Lyttelton, were responsible to some extent. The novelist had apparently read over the manuscript of *Tom Jones* to some of his friends, among whom were Lyttelton and Pitt,[1] and we have the authority of Fielding's implacable enemy, *Old England*, for the statement that Lyttelton had "run up and down the town

[1]Miss G. M. Godden in her *Memoir of Fielding* (p. 179) prints an extract from a letter written by a descendant of Sanderson Miller, at whose house, Radway, in Warwickshire, Fielding is believed to have read his manuscript. George Harris in his *Life of Lord Chancellor Hardwicke*, vol. II, pp. 456-7, also refers to this as a "tradition."

and made visits and written letters" to commend *Tom
Jones* to the public.¹ And this is confirmed by what the
Rev. Thomas Birch tells the Earl of Orrery about *Tom
Jones* in the letter from which we have already quoted.

When we turn to the earliest expressions of contemporary opinion on the novel we find that on the whole they
were favourable. Of this we have evidence in the complaint of the most determined of the detractors of the
novel, one "Orbilius," author of *An Examen of the History
of Tom Jones*, that too much notice had been taken of the
performance as an inimitable one.² In the same month in
which *Tom Jones* appeared *The London Magazine* devoted
its opening pages to a favourable review of the book,
extolling its morality and its skilfully constructed plot.
The Gentleman's Magazine which had more or less ignored Fielding in the past did not offer the hospitality of its
pages to any review of the novel until more than a year
had passed after its publication, when it printed a "literary
article from Paris" reviewing M. de la Place's version of
the novel.³ *The Gentleman's Magazine* for August, 1749,
however, contains some good laudatory verses on *Tom
Jones* written by a man named Thomas Cawthorn. *The
Monthly Review* addressed a seasonable and richly
deserved rebuke to "Orbilius," one of that tribe of
journalists who were determined to carry on their feud
with Fielding by reviling him for everything he did.
"Aretine" in *Old England*, for example, vented his spleen
on "the Justice" by denouncing his "motley history
of bastardism, fornication, and adultery" as "highly
prejudicial to the cause of religion in several parts of

¹*Old England*, May 27, 1749.
²*An Examen of the History of Tom Jones, a Foundling.   In Two Letters to
a Friend*, London, 1750, p. 118.
³*The Gentleman's Magazine*, March, 1750.

it."[1] But this kind of invective came only from Fielding's known and implacable enemies.

The expressions of opinion on the novel in the letters and other literary remains of well-known contemporaries are also generally favourable, though adverse criticism is by no means rare. Richardson who was obsessed with the idea that Fielding had entered deliberately into rivalry with him—and in this curiously enough one of Fielding's latest critics agrees with him[2]—exhibited all the pettiness of his nature whenever any of his friends or correspondents attempted to do justice to the merits of *Tom Jones*. When, for example, Minerva and Astraea, the charming and clever daughters of Aaron Hill, wrote to him praising Fielding's novel, he could not contain himself but launched out into a violent tirade against his rival which is one of the most absurd performances imaginable. As his letter preserved in the Forster Collection at South Kensington shows, he was not ashamed to vent his spleen by pronouncing judgment on the book because he had heard it condemned by "several judicious friends" and was discouraged from reading it, though it is evident from his familiarity with the main incidents and characters of the story that his want of first-hand knowledge of the book was an absurd pretence. This and his ill-concealed delight whenever he came across any indications of hostility to *Tom Jones* prove that the enthusiastic praise that Fielding had given to *Clarissa Harlowe* in *The Jacobite's Journal* had not placated him in the least. He was utterly incapable of doing justice to Fielding.

Apart from Dr. Johnson, who, as Hannah More tells us in a letter written in 1780 to her sister, pronounced

[1] *Old England*, May 27, 1749.
[2] Aurélien Digeon, *Les Romans de Fielding*, Chap. IV.

Tom Jones to be a vicious book and scolded Hannah because she had alluded to a passage in it,[1] there were few even in Richardson's own circle who agreed with him in utter condemnation of the novel, though many discerning and altogether fair-minded readers deplored its "bizarreries" and pronounced its hero a sorry scoundrel.

On the other hand, the number of imitations of *Tom Jones* that were published within a few years of its appearance[2] shows that the novel was popular, though it would be rather hazardous to suggest that Fielding's contemporaries fully realized the greatness of his achievement. One or two among his most discerning readers were even inclined to prefer *Joseph Andrews* to *Tom Jones*. Lady Mary Montagu, for example, expresses this preference in one of her letters[3] though she appears afterwards to have altered her opinion, as Lady Louisa Stuart tells us that her grandmother admired *Tom Jones* above all the other writings of her cousin and wrote the words "ne plus ultra" on her copy of the novel.[4] Lady Luxborough, Bolingbroke's sister, writing to the poet Shenstone on the 23rd of March, 1749, expresses her opinion on the first four volumes of *Tom Jones* that she

[1] *Memoirs of the Life of Mrs. Hannah More*, by William Roberts, Esq., 1836, vol. I, p. 143.

[2] Among the contemporary imitations the most notable were the anonymous *History of Charlotte Summers, the Fortunate Parish Girl*, Dr. John Hill's *Adventures of Mr. Loveill*, and William Chaigneau's *History of Jack Connor*. Francis Coventry's *Pompey the Little* can hardly be described as an imitation of *Tom Jones*, though the novel contains unmistakable evidence of the influence of Fielding.

[3] Letter to the Countess of Bute. October 1, N.S. 1749. *The Letters and Works of Lady Mary Montagu*, edited by Lord Wharncliffe, third edition, 1861, Vol. II, p. 185.

[4] *The Letters and Works of Lady Mary Montagu*, edited by Lord Wharncliffe, 1861, Introductory Anecdotes, p. 107.

O

has read, and seems inclined to prefer the earlier novel to the masterpiece.[1]

A preference like this appears surprising when one considers what an epoch-making advance there is in Fielding's art in *Tom Jones*. Almost all his great qualities appear at their best in this novel, and succeeding generations of Fielding's readers have felt no hesitation whatsoever in pronouncing it to be his masterpiece. The knowledge of life that he exhibits in *Tom Jones* is comprehensive, and true to the promise that he has made at the commencement of the novel he shows us as much of the "prodigious variety" of life as it is possible for an author to deal with.

Neither in *Joseph Andrews* nor in *Jonathan Wild* had he done this. He had not attempted to do it. In his Preface to *Joseph Andrews* he asks his reader more than once to remember that the ridiculous only fell within his province in that novel. And in *Jonathan Wild* the exigencies of his satire made it imperative that he should confine himself almost exclusively to one aspect of life.

The most striking proof of the fact that Fielding had attained to the full maturity of his powers when he wrote *Tom Jones* is to be found in the wonderful originality of the novel. In the portrayal of character and the construction of his plot Fielding now depended almost entirely on himself, on his own powers of observation and knowledge of the world. In *Joseph Andrews*, as we have noticed already, his debt to other novelists was not altogether a negligible one. In *Jonathan Wild* he had been content to base his satire and build his story on what had already been chronicled of Wild's exploits, and had portrayed certain personages as they had actually played their parts

[1] *The Letters of Lady Luxborough to William Shenstone*, London, 1775, p. 89

in the drama of the thief-taker's life. In *Tom Jones*, however, Fielding's indebtedness to other writers is so small that it scarcely deserves any mention. The plot is his own entirely, the episodes and adventures that he relates owe little to the writings of others, and the characters are more original than they are in any other great English novel. And this originality appears all the more marvellous when we consider the range and magnitude of the story, the wealth of characters in it and the variety of episode and adventure that characterizes it.

His achievement is no less remarkable in the mastery that he displays over the technique of his art. So much admiration has been expressed for the plot of *Tom Jones* that some critics of Fielding have felt it to be their duty to call attention to some of the defects in it. Austin Dobson speaks deprecatingly of Coleridge's "over-quoted and somewhat antiquated dictum" by which *Tom Jones* is grouped with *The Alchemist* and *Œdipus Tyrannus* as one of the three most perfect plots in the world, which certainly places *Tom Jones* on too high a pedestal. But the imperfections that Dobson and others have enumerated are far from being serious ones. The digression introduced into the main narrative by the story of the Man of the Hill, for which Fielding could quote many a precedent in the work of the great masters of the art of fiction, has been made the most of as a blemish because there are so few serious ones to be found in the plot.

The other defects are so slight as to be hardly noticeable. It has been remarked that in the course of the narrative money is lost and found very conveniently to meet the exigencies of the plot without any attention being paid to probability. This is hardly a just comment if it refers to the loss of the five hundred pounds which Jones received as a parting gift from Allworthy, or to that of Sophia's pocket book which is found afterwards by a beggar.[1] And though Fielding, perhaps because he was of an improvident nature himself, was not very careful as a rule to provide his characters with sufficient funds when they set out on their peregrinations, yet Sophia's ability to defray the expenses of her journey and to reward chambermaids and postboys liberally for their services, even after she has sent sixteen guineas to Tom and lost her hundred pound note, need not be looked upon as a miracle after all.

There are, however, a few inadvertencies in the story which Fielding never corrected. His attention was not drawn to them as they had escaped the notice of the contemporary critics who had made adverse comments on the novel. These slips were more or less inevitable in a work of the size of *Tom Jones*. Indeed, when one takes into account the extensive ramifications of the plot of the novel one marvels at the immunity from any serious inconsistency that characterizes it. But this, of course, is not his strongest claim to the admiration of his reader so far as the development of the action in his novel is concerned. His marvellous skill in the handling of an elaborate plot, for which Scott among others expressed great admiration more than once in his writings, is exhibited in the way in which he preserves the secret of Tom's birth, keeps within its proper dimensions the story of his hero's early life and steadily enhances the reader's interest in the main action till it reaches its very effective climax. And

[1] "Orbilius" in his *Examen of the History of Tom Jones* says, "The adventure of the beggarman is certainly one of the most surprising incidents in this marvellous history. That he should find the individual gilt pocket book of Sophia; that he should not be able to read; nor find any of his own fraternity or a publican that could; that therefore he could not gut it of the 100*l* note ; all these tend to advance the marvellous; but scarce any the probable." P. 82.

throughout the novel Fielding never obtrudes for a moment the mechanism of his plot on his reader's notice.

But the maturity of Fielding's powers is exhibited in many other features of *Tom Jones* besides the construction of its great plot. And the most noteworthy of these other features is the splendid gallery of portraits that he presents to his readers in the novel. It is an extensive gallery, and the portraits are as varied as they are magnificent. Few English novels contain such a wonderful variety of original characters.

It is true that in his first novel he had given to the world a character to which we have no parallel in the novelist's masterpiece. Parson Adams is one of those products of creative genius that stand alone, and Fielding never created any character quite as great as this even when he had come to the fullness of his powers. In *Tom Jones*, again, Fielding seems momentarily to lose sight of the realities of life in portraying one or two of his characters. In Squire Allworthy, for example, "excellent compound of Lyttelton and Allen" as he is, we have one of those models of passionless perfection that one occasionally comes across in the pages of Scott. This is the one character in his novels in which he has idealized too much. The portrait would have been more interesting and lifelike if the novelist had exhibited something more in the shape of frailty or idiosyncrasy in him than that lack of insight into the characters of men which makes him so unsuspicious of the designs of the Blifils.

Again, Fielding's extreme hatred of hypocrisy betrayed him into the other extreme in his portrait of the villain. Like his great disciples in the next century he pursued his villain to infamy with a relentlessness which is somewhat fatiguing. The hypocrisy of Blifil had become an obsession with the novelist, and this oppresses the reader. Moreover, there is a certain lack of verisimilitude in the portrait of the villain, as some of Fielding's critics have pointed out. The precocity of the boy hypocrite is extraordinary, and the novelist certainly places too great a strain on the limits of probability in the accounts that he gives us of the boy's schemes to further his own interests in life.

For this lack of verisimilitude in the portraits of Blifil and Allworthy there is ample compensation in the magnificent realism of the other characters in the novel. Of Fielding's hero it is sufficient to say here that the novelist was much more anxious to make and keep him human than to arouse the reader's admiration for him. At the same time it would be a mistake to suggest that Fielding did not expect his reader to feel any admiration for Tom Jones. His own admiration cannot be mistaken, and he tells us plainly enough that Jones had much of the hero in his composition.[1] He endows him generously with that which is attractive—a handsome person, some generosity, and a great deal of good humour. But these and certain other good qualities that may be placed to his credit hardly atone for the serious blemishes in his character, and Fielding's attitude to these blemishes has made many an admirer of the novel take strong exception to his hero.

It would seem that after the joke that he had indulged in at the expense of Richardson by creating his immaculate Joseph and the picture of unrelieved villainy that he had given in *Jonathan Wild*, Fielding felt that in justice to his own genius which was essentially realistic he must

[1] *Tom Jones*, Book VII, Chap. XII.

give to the world a full-length portrait of an ordinary mor-
tal such as one meets with every day, in whom "foibles
and vices tend to become more glaring objects from the
virtues which contrast them and show their deformity."
And in *Tom Jones* he records it as his carefully considered
opinion that no good purpose is served by introducing
characters of angelic perfection or diabolical depravity
into any work of fiction.[1] But as the character of Tom
Jones will be discussed again when we deal with the
question of the morality of the novel we shall leave
Fielding's hero for the present and pass on to some other
characters in the novel, pausing only for a moment to
consider why Fielding made his hero illegitimate.

This question has never been satisfactorily answered.
The calumny that emanated from Richardson that in
Tom Jones Fielding's hero " is made a natural child because his own first wife was such"[2] was one of the meanest blows that he aimed at his rival, and no evidence has
ever been brought forward to substantiate his statement.
The majority of Fielding's critics and biographers who
have given any attention to this subject content themselves with the remark that uncertainty of birth has been
the constant theme of dramatists and writers of fiction
from time immemorial. Scott is one of the few who go
deeper into the matter, and he points out that there could
have been no adequate motive for keeping his hero's
birth a secret from a reasonable and compassionate man
like Allworthy if in Fielding's story Mrs. Blifil had been
privately married to the father of Tom Jones.[3] This explanation, good as it is, leaves out of account the fact that

[1] *Tom Jones*, Book X, chap. I.
[2] Letter to Mrs. Donnellan, *The Correspondence of S. Richardson*, edited
by Mrs. Barbauld, Vol. IV, p. 59.
[3] Scott's *Lives of the Novelists:* "Fielding".

Fielding was determined to make his portrait of Mrs.
Blifil as interesting and realistic as possible, and in the
matter of Tom's birth as in other features in his story he
carried his realism further than other writers would have
ventured to do.

In the magnificent realism of his portrait of Squire
Western, Fielding more than compensated for that lack of
verisimilitude that his critics have noticed in his portrait
of Allworthy. He had always excelled in the portrayal of
certain types of character, notably the country gentleman
of his time. His portraits of country squires in the
plays and in *Joseph Andrews* bear witness to this. And
these rudimentary sketches of the country squire that are
found in his earlier work, in Squire Badger or Sir Thomas
Loveland, for example, in *Don Quixote in England*, or
the country squire in *Joseph Andrews* in whose house
Adams is "roasted," are brought to perfection in the
most realistic and interesting portrait of the country
squire that has ever been painted. It is a great tribute to
Fielding's realism that no critic has ever suggested that
the picture is a caricature, though the novelist has exhibited much that is bizarre in Squire Western's "foaming
impulses," his outrageous coarseness, his violent Tory
prejudices and a host of other frailties too numerous to
mention. The only feature in the portrait which critics
have felt inclined to cavil at is the lack of courage that
Western displays when he is struck by Lord Fellamar's
friend. Scott finds in this episode a stumbling-block to a
whole-hearted admiration for the portrait and suggests
that the passage describing the incident is an interpola-
tion.[1] And yet in spite of what Scott says one cannot help
thinking that the feeling of being overwhelmed or cowed

[1] Scott's *Lives of the Novelists:* "Fielding".

that comes over him at a critical moment is neither an indelible stain on his courage nor altogether unnatural.

Fielding's heroine in the novel, for whom he felt an admiration which he declared a little too enthusiastically perhaps, is undoubtedly one of his most beautiful characters. There is no dearth of great portraits of good and beautiful women in English fiction and drama ; but it is scarcely an exaggeration to say that Fielding's heroine takes a very high position among the finest women portrayed by the dramatist and the writer of fiction. Schiller was of opinion that Shakespeare's Juliet and Fielding's Sophia Western are altogether superior to the most beautiful feminine portraits of antiquity.[1]

The purity of Sophia's nature and the delicacy of her feeling which cannot be contaminated by all the coarseness of her brutal father, her tenderness which never degenerates into mawkish sentimentality, the dignity born of her innocence and purity which appears at its best when she is confronted with brutality and licence of speech and something much worse, and a remarkable charm of personality and manner which wins the hearts of all who come in contact with her—these are only a few of the graces of the character of Sophia Western.

But Fielding's heroine has not received the unquestioning homage of all readers of the novel. Mrs. Barbauld expressed the view that "her behaviour will scarcely satisfy one who has conceived high ideas of the delicacy of the female character."[2] Byron considered her too emphatic,[3] and some other critics of the novelist have disapproved of her conduct in leaving her father's house. And yet if

[1]Schiller's *Briefe*, edited by Fritz Jonas, Vol. IV, p. 355.
[2]*The British Novelists*, Vol. XVIII, Preface by Mrs. Barbauld, p. xiv.
[3]*Don Juan*, Canto XIII, cx.

she had sacrificed her lover to her father's will these
critics would probably have pitied her as a weak, insipid,
and silly creature. As it is, in spite of her opposition to her
father's will, Thackeray is full of compassion for her as a
"fond, foolish, palpitating little creature."

But it is not possible to do justice to all the characters
in *Tom Jones* within the compass of a book like this, which
endeavours to make a survey of the whole of Fielding's
achievement as a literary man. One can only name some
among them though practically all the principal characters in the novel deserve special study. Allworthy's erring
sister Bridget, "so discreet in her conduct that her prudence was as much on the guard as if she had all the snares
to apprehend which were ever laid for her whole sex";
the two women servants, Deborah Wilkins and Mrs.
Honour, not so piquantly portrayed perhaps as Mrs.
Slipslop, and yet inimitable in their own way; that incom-
parable pair, Square and Thwackum, with so little that is
good in them because, as Fielding would have us believe,
one neglected religion and the other virtue in the composition of their several systems, and both utterly disre-
garded all natural goodness of heart; poor Partridge,
"master of much pleasantry and humour," and in spite
of all his frailties, one of the best-natured fellows in the
world, so much the victim of circumstances and yet doing his best under them as the husband of a terrible wife,
as a schoolmaster, barber, surgeon, friend and mentor to
the hero, and rewarded in the end by the latter with a pension of £50, and by the novelist with the hand of Molly
Seagrim! Worthy Parson Supple, remarkable for his
taciturnity at the dinner table, "though his mouth was
never shut at it," and his unique vocabulary ; the masculine Mrs. Western with her fondness for politics, her

knowledge of "manners, customs, ceremonies, and fashions," her erudition and her contempt for her brother's country ways and Jacobite leanings; the old Man of the Hill whom some readers have found such a stumbling-block to their enjoyment of the story; Mrs. Waters, the Jenny Jones of better days, another victim of circumstances, skilled in "amorous parleys," and destined after an extremely chequered career to find rest and respectability in the arms of poor Parson Supple; Ensign Northerton with his whole-hearted aversion to "Homo and Corderius," with his language so sumptuously larded with oaths, and his agility of foot and hand; pretty Mrs. Fitzpatrick the runaway wife, so elusive and such an adept in the discreet management of her "affairs"; the well-meaning, garrulous Mrs. Miller, one of the few good landladies that Fielding has portrayed, her pretty daughter and that gay young spark, her lodger Nightingale; and much more striking than these, and a somewhat unusual character delineated with masterly strokes and as realistic as Fielding's finest portrait work in the novel, the imperious Lady Bellaston in whom Fielding's satire against the vices of the fashionable world finds its culmination—in these and many others, men and women belonging to all ranks in society, from the noble lord and his minion to the puppet-show man, gipsy, or ostler at an inn, Fielding gives his reader a true and sufficient account of the "prodigious variety" that is to be found in life.

And from what we know of the varied experiences of his life and the special qualities of his genius we can conclude that if any novelist was qualified to give a complete picture of life, Fielding was that novelist. He was a gentleman by birth and possessed personal, first-hand knowledge of "that higher order of mortals which is not to be seen, like all the rest of the human species, for nothing, in the streets, shops and coffee-houses." So far as his pictures of "high life" were concerned he had no need, like Richardson, to evolve his figures and details entirely out of his own imagination. Again, the geniality of his temperament and his contempt for snobbishness enabled him to ride roughshod over social barriers in a way that few people of his rank and position have been able to do. The many vicissitudes of his life threw him among all sorts and conditions of men. As his friend the pedantic James Harris has observed in his *Philological Enquiries*, his "pictures of human kind" would neither have been so various nor so natural if his life had not been spent in a "promiscuous intercourse with persons of all ranks." Some of the anecdotes of his life that have come down to us show how much he was at home with humble folk. He was of an open and free nature, and as the late Sir Walter Raleigh says of Shakespeare, the tradition of geniality clings to his name like a faded perfume.

Among the other qualities noticeable in Fielding, in which he greatly resembles Shakespeare are his magnanimity and large-hearted sympathy with the weaknesses and follies of men. In this he presents a great contrast to some of the best-known literary men of his age. He had seen much of the seamy side of life and had come closely in contact with that which is evil and repulsive in man. He knew from his long experience of the ways of the *beau monde* how many ugly things are covered by the superficial gloss of fashion. He realized only too well that what we call nature is more often than not a brood of secret passions, malicious and vulgar, which surge within us, ill covered by the cloak of decency under which we try to hide them. "Son art et son plaisir," says M. Taine, "comme celui de Molière, consistent à lever un coin du manteau."[1]

And yet all his knowledge of the evil in man had not embittered him into the misanthrope. It is true that his mind had gathered a certain amount of coarseness, but it had not been poisoned. He always preserved his faith in the reality of good impulses and the existence of good and unselfish men in this world. What a contrast he presents to Swift in this! He had his strong and deep-rooted antipathies, but there was nothing sinister or malignant in his general attitude towards mankind. He did not, like Swift, travesty the facts of human life in order to gratify a morbid taste for that which is repulsive in man. "His morality," says Leslie Stephen, "is at the superior antipodes from the cynicism of a Wycherley, and far superior to the prurient sentimentalism of Sterne or the hot-pressed priggishness of Richardson, or even the reckless Bohemianism of Smollett."[2]

One conspicuous feature of Fielding's satire is that it is only in exceptional cases that it makes its objects absolutely contemptible and odious. His wholesome laughter is a very sure safeguard against any constant and recurring tendencies in this direction. Even when he is ridiculing the weaknesses and evils that are most repugnant to him, he does not allow the spirit of bitterness to take possession of him. There is something in the serenity and imperturbable good humour of the man that constantly reminds one of Shakespeare.

Hypocrisy is one of the few weaknesses of human nature which has the power to move him to bitter satire. And yet it is hardly fair to suggest that he is unjust when

[1]H. Taine, *Histoire de la littérature anglaise*, Livre III, Chap. **VI**.
[2]Leslie Stephen, *Hours in a Library*, Third Series, "Fielding's Novels."

he deals with this grievous fault in man. When we study his portrait of young Blifil we cannot with any show of justice describe his scorn of the evil he pictures as excessive or overdone.

When he deals with other infirmities of human nature, as for example, pride of birth, prudery, or want of charity, his satire, unsparing and severe as it is, is altogether free from anything that may be described as sinister or malignant. Even when the follies and weaknesses of men and women arouse much repugnance in him, he can laugh very heartily indeed. In the portrait of Parson Supple, for example, in which he satirizes many of the frailties that he had condemned severely in *The Champion*, how happily the satire is blended with wholesome and kindly laughter! The same spirit of fun lightens up his portrait of Mrs. Western, a type of character which, like the prude, aroused a strong antipathy in him. Exquisite little touches like the following are of the very essence of the spirit of good humour. In the course of her long lecture to Sophia on the subject of matrimony, Mrs. Western says,

"Argue with me, child! I do not indeed expect it. I should have seen the world to very little purpose truly, if I am to argue with one of your years. I have taken this trouble, in order to instruct you. The ancient philosophers, such as Socrates, Alcibiades, and others, did not use to argue with their scholars. You are to consider me, child, as Socrates, not asking your opinion, but only informing you of mine."[1]

There is a refreshing geniality in his laughter when he ridicules the extravagances of Square and Thwackum, or describes with inimitable raciness and good humour the quick changes of attitude in his landlords and landladies

[1] *Tom Jones*, Book VII, Chap. III.

when they find out their mistakes about the rank and position of their guests, or pictures the effect produced on susceptible hearts by the wiles of charmers like Mrs. Waters.

But it is hardly fair to his genius to try and pick out particular examples to illustrate the kindliness of his laughter and the magnanimity of his temper. His novels overflow with them. Stern and grave satire is an exceptional thing with him. As M. Taine says, "Celui aime la nature tout expansive et abondante chasse loin de lui, comme des ennemis, la solennité, la tristesse et la pruderie des puritains."[1]

But this very magnanimity of temper betrayed him into an amount of tolerance of the weaknesses and vices of men and women which is hard to reconcile with the highest ideals of morality. Many of his critics from the time of Richardson onwards have contended that the novelist's own ways of life had blunted the delicacy of his moral sense to such an extent as to make it incapable of seeing in its true colours much that was ugly and evil in human character and conduct. But in this, as in the other charge brought against him, of being coarse and licentious in his descriptions and humour, the tendency of the majority of the novelist's critics has been to exaggerate his offence. With a few exceptions his biographers have been notoriously unfair to him, making him out to be a roystering Bohemian and losing sight altogether of the greater and nobler Fielding, the hard working law student who struggled so heroically to escape from the mire of Grub Street and to provide a comfortable home for the wife he loved so much; Fielding the magistrate who made such a noble effort to redeem the office to which he was

[1] H. Taine, *Histoire de la littérature anglaise*, Livre III, Chap. VI.

appointed from the discredit into which it had fallen
through the malpractices of fee-hunting predecessors;
Fielding the philanthropist whose humane and practical
zeal in seeking remedies for the evils of society makes
him so unique among his contemporaries.

But the charge, pressed too far as it has been, is not
altogether a baseless one. One of the chief impressions of
Fielding's ideas of morality that the reader of his works
carries away with him is that the novelist is continually
making an appeal on behalf of nature. When the "natural
temper or bent of affections," to use the phrases of
Shaftesbury, in a man who is born with good and generous instincts is perverse and tends to lead him astray, the
novelist is inclined to adopt an apologetic attitude and
seldom goes to the length of pronouncing denunciation
without reservation. The lapses of which his heroes in
Tom Jones and *Amelia* are guilty are treated much too
lightly by the novelist. Not only in his great novels but
also in his other works he is a constant advocate of the
claim that has been made by so many great men in the
histories of whose lives we have little of that close contact
with vice which is so apt to be fatal to the delicacy of our
moral sense: the claim that the frailties of the man of
noble and generous instincts should be treated with less
severity than those of others.

This appeal on behalf of what were to him the cardinal
virtues of human nature is made repeatedly in his novels
in the striking contrasts that he presents to us between
the generous and mean nature, between those who can
make sacrifices for others and those who are incapable of
them, between the postilion who takes off his great coat
to give it to Joseph and the passengers in the stage coach
who indulge in pleasantries, between a Parson Adams

and a Parson Trulliber, a Jones and a Blifil, an Amelia and a Betty Harris. But while the reader of Fielding's works realizes how much weight this appeal carries with it—and Fielding's way of making it is very effective indeed—he yet feels that if forbearance and sympathy with serious lapses are carried too far they would lead to a very equivocal code of morality.

But we must not conclude from this that Fielding deliberately refuses to recognize the fact that lapses are wrong in themselves. He makes the claim continually in his novels that he is writing in the interests of virtue. And it would be unfair to him to suggest that he had no right to make the claim. He certainly is capable of portraying virtue in attractive colours and, as Leslie Stephen points out, he is incapable of the solecism which Richardson commits in substantially preaching that virtue means standing out for a higher price.[1]

When we examine his conception of the "goodness" on which he places such a high value and in consideration for which he is prepared to look upon blemishes with compassion, we find that his standards, on the whole, are unimpeachable. His good man is the man of generous instincts, full of warmth of heart, thoroughly unselfish, altogether above meanness and cruelty, frank and sincere, true to himself and to others. Such a nature has often a simplicity in it which makes it the victim of the craft and deceit of designing men. And in the best examples of goodness that Fielding has given us, in Parson Adams, for example, or in Squire Allworthy or Dr. Harrison, unselfishness and a charitable disposition are among the chief beauties of character.

His readers and critics, however, have been very much

[1]Leslie Stephen, *Hours in a Library*, Third Series, "Fielding's Novels."

P

divided in their opinion as to the thoroughness of his denunciation of certain vices and particularly of the vice of
immorality; and this difference of opinion has sprung
mainly from the different lights in which they have view-
ed Fielding's hero, Tom Jones. Some admirers of the
novelist, though their number is not very large, have no
hesitation in pronouncing Fielding to be an effective and
sound moralist. "Tom Jones," says Murphy, "will at all
times be a fine lesson to young men of good tendencies to
virtue who yet suffer the impetuosity of their passions to
lead them astray."[1] Another critic, Thomas Keightley,
writing on the same subject nearly a century afterwards,
declares that he could not find any vices in Jones. "Vice is
a habit," Keightley says, "and he had no vicious habit.
He did not drink, swear, cheat, game, oppress, malign,
etc."[2] And he endeavours to apologize for Jones' affairs
with women and deprecates the criticism that describes
Fielding's hero as a degraded wretch.

In the same ranks of the defenders of the morality of
Tom Jones are to be found critics like Coleridge and
Lamb. The former rightly emphasizes the fact that Tom
Jones does not profess to be an exemplar of conduct, and
he admits that judged by the moral standards of his day
Fielding's hero stands thoroughly condemned. But he
would have us remember that with the change in manners
from generation to generation moral standards also
undergo some change, and he is so far from admitting
that the morality of the novel is a questionable one that he
asserts that no "young man who consulted his heart and
conscience only, without adverting to what the world

[1]Arthur Murphy, "An Essay on the Life and Genius of Henry Fielding,
Esq.," prefixed to the *Works of Henry Fielding*, edited by Murphy, 1762.
[2]*Fraser's Magazine*, February, 1858, p. 215, "On the Life and Writings
of Henry Fielding."

would say, could rise from the perusal of Fielding's *Tom Jones*, *Joseph Andrews*, or *Amelia* without feeling himself a better man."[1] And Charles Lamb's remark about one cordial honest laugh of a Tom Jones absolutely clearing the atmosphere that was reeking with the breathings of the hypocrite Blifil is well known.[2] Among the more modern critics of Fielding those who have considered the question remind us that the novelist never intended to portray a model young man in Tom Jones.

Against these defences we have the unhesitating and in many cases the strong condemnation pronounced by others. Much of this hostile criticism, that of "Orbilius" in his *Examen of the History of Tom Jones*, for example, or Richardson's triumphant characterization of Fielding's hero as a "kept fellow, the lowest of all fellows," was prompted by a personal animus against the novelist. And yet some of the bolts shot by these enemies found their mark. "Orbilius" hit the novelist rather hard when he numbered *Tom Jones* among books that "paint modern vices as if they were peccadilloes, and by that means endeavour to overthrow the boundaries of virtue and vice."[3] In France the Council of State issued an *arrêt* against *Tom Jones* as an immoral book and *The Gentleman's Magazine* for March, 1750, informs us that French ladies were shocked by Tom's breaches of faith to Sophia.

To Dr. Johnson's unfavourable opinion of the morality of the novel we have already referred. His editor and biographer, Sir John Hawkins, fully shared his views. In his

[1] Coleridge, *Literary Remains*, collected and edited by Henry Nelson Coleridge, London, 1836, Vol. II, p. 374.

[2] "Genius and Character of Hogarth." *The Works of Charles Lamb*, edited by Lucas, Vol. I, p. 83.

[3] *An Examen of the History of Tom Jones. In Two Letters to a Friend.* London, 1750, p. 73.

Life of Johnson Hawkins says, "His morality, in respect
that it resolves virtue into good affections, in contradic-
tion to moral obligation and a sense of duty, is that of
Lord Shaftesbury vulgarized, and is a system of excellent
use in palliating the vices most injurious to society. He
was the inventor of that cant-phrase, goodness of heart,
which is every day used as a substitute for probity, and
means little more than the virtue of a horse or a dog; in
short, he has done more towards corrupting the rising
generation than any writer we know of." Byron speaks of
Tom Jones as an "accomplished blackguard."[1] And in
spite of the facts to which attention has recently been
drawn that Thackeray was inclined to be obsessed with
the calumnies current against Fielding nearly as much as
Johnson and some others were, and that Thackeray's later
verdict on the morality of *Tom Jones* was entirely different from the one he had pronounced earlier, few present-
day readers of Fielding's novel will be inclined to quarrel
with our novelist's greatest disciple for the opinion that
he expressed in the course of his fifth lecture on the English Humorists of the Eighteenth Century that there is
an error in art and ethics in *Tom Jones*.

It is not, however, the appearance of many imperfections in the character of his hero that causes all the dissatisfaction in the reader of *Tom Jones*. One constantly
wishes as one reads Fielding's masterpiece that the novelist had not dragged his hero through as much degradation as he has done. He might have spared his reader the
last depth of degradation in Jones, his liaison with Lady
Bellaston, though even that ugly episode in Jones' career
has found its apologists. And it is hard to agree with
Coleridge when he says that a single paragraph "more

[1] *Don Juan*, Canto XIII. cx.

fully and forcibly unfolding Tom Jones's sense of self-degradation on the discovery of the true character of the relation in which he had stood to Lady Bellaston, and his awakened feeling of the dignity and manliness of chastity would have removed in great measure any just objection."[1]

But while we criticize the novelist for the want of true delicacy of feeling that he displays and wish that he had cast some of his characters in other moulds, we cannot deny that his incursions into the sordid and unlovely regions of life are attended by a distinct gain of realism to his art. A great deal of the success that he attained in picturing real life is to be attributed to this unhesitating and frank portrayal of frailties in his characters. The study of character in Mrs. Blifil would be a poor thing if we leave out the most serious of her frailties. The picture of life given in the novel would be an infinitely poorer one if Lady Bellaston did not appear in it at all. It is difficult to imagine a more effective anti-climax to poor Square's "rule of right and the eternal fitness of things" than the discovery of the man in Molly Seagrim's garret. We cannot for a moment deny that Fielding has achieved a triumph of realism in his portrait of Squire Western, and the least reflection will convince us that this wonderful realism is attained by the exhibition of many frailties in him.

There is a tendency among some critics of Fielding to describe his realism as the realism of coarseness only, as if the novelist was incapable of perceiving and describing that which is refined and beautiful in human nature. That "independent" and eccentric critic, Emanuel

---

[1]Coleridge, *Literary Remains*, collected and edited by Henry Nelson Coleridge, London, 1836, Vol. II, p. 375.

Green, in the course of an estimate of the novelist's genius made some years ago, expresses an opinion which many of the readers of Fielding's novels have held, judging by the drift of their remarks. "Realism," Green says, "may be made charming in its atmosphere, its reality, its romance—the healthy admiration of healthy minded people. But unfortunately it is apt to run wild, is difficult to limit and may be unpleasant, and often, as with Fielding, may become the realism of foulness."[1]

This idea about the most striking feature of Fielding's work as a novelist has not originated wholly from the occasional "bizarreries" that are to be found in his writings. The majority of his critics and biographers until recent years have deplored the absence of true delicacy of feeling in him and have ascribed it to the supposed Bohemian ways of his life. As we have pointed out before, these critics and biographers, taking their cue from the slanders that were so sedulously propagated during the novelist's lifetime and from an occasional utterance of a contemporary who may have been referring to a particular period of his life, have been notoriously unfair to Fielding.

The charge of " continued lowness'" was brought against him in the first instance because he had given an importance in his novels to men and women belonging to the humbler ranks in society which had never been done before. But the criticism which tried to make out that the majority of the characters in his novels belong to these ranks is so manifestly inept that it deserves no comment. If, however, the words be taken to apply to the kinds of adventure that loom so largely in his narratives, it must be acknowledged that the criticism is not absolutely un-

[1] Emanuel Green, *Henry Fielding, His Works: An Independent Criticism.* London, 1909.

fair though the word "low," so fashionable in Fielding's days, is hardly an appropriate one to describe the incidents that make his stories what they are. The adventures that his characters meet with on the road or in taverns are as a rule lively and boisterous. Fielding finds great delight in describing fights in which the combatants, male and female, use all kinds of weapons, crabtree cudgels, pans full of hogs' blood, skulls and bones picked up from new dug graves, and lay about them with great gusto and effect. An American admirer of the novelist ingeniously suggests that Fielding indulged in these descriptions of tavern brawls to quicken the movement of the action in his story and to show the inherent pugnacity of human nature.[1]

But these special features of his work instead of becoming a source of weakness or cause of imperfection strengthen his claim to be considered a great portrayer of life. "Some literary critics," says the late Sir Walter Raleigh, "with a taste for subdued tones in art, have found some of Fielding's loudest notes too strident for enfeebled ears, but not to the great musician can the whole range of the orchestra, not to the great painter can the strongest contrast of colours, profitably be denied."[2]

[1] Henry Harper, *The Genius of Henry Fielding*.
[2] Raleigh, *The English Novel*.

CHAPTER IX

AMELIA

THE years of Fielding's official life as a magistrate on the Middlesex Bench and in the justice room in Bow Street were notable for the greatest achievements of his life. He not only won his greatest triumphs in the literary world during this period, but revealed the nobility of his character in a way in which it had not been revealed before. The generations that have succeeded Fielding's own have more or less contented themselves by paying their tribute of admiration only to the masterpieces of fiction that he has given to the world. But there is another side to the greatness of the man of which we get a glimpse in the humanitarian and reforming activities of the last years of his life. And the record of these years so full of noble endeavour is all the more glorious because it is the record of a man broken in health.

More than one contemporary of his refers to his growing infirmities at this time as a just punishment for his sins. Hurd, for example, writing to the Rev. Mr. Balguy on the 19th of March, 1751, describes him as "a poor, emaciated, worn-out rake." The poet Edward Moore on whose behalf Fielding had warmly interested himself to bespeak a favour of Lyttelton speaks of him in very much the same strain. Perhaps these good people were not calumniating him altogether. Even if we concede that there was some justification for such remarks as these, we cannot help recognizing that Fielding endeavoured heroically during the last years of his life to atone for whatever he had done amiss in the days gone by.

His legal attainments and his conscientiousness in the discharge of his duties soon earned him esteem and honour. Within six months of his appointment as magistrate he was elected Chairman of the Sessions at Hicks' Hall, an honour which was conferred on him again and again. On the 29th of June, 1749, he delivered a charge to the Middlesex Grand Jury which the justices of the peace for the city and liberties of Westminster considered so "learned, ingenious, excellent, and useful" that it was published by order of the court.

The Charge is not only remarkable for the knowledge of law that it exhibits but it deserves the attention of the lay reader because it is an excellent example of Fielding's prose style at its best, vigorous, graceful, and lucid. Fielding begins with an eloquent eulogy on the system of trial by jury, describing it as a very sure safeguard of the liberties of the people. He then defines the function of the grand as distinguished from the petty jury. The most significant part of the Charge, however, is that in which he speaks of the state of society and public morals in his day, and he denounces in strong language the universal "fury after licentious and luxurious pleasures." This denunciation is pronounced not only on gaming houses, dancing halls, and houses of ill fame, but the excess of his zeal betrays Fielding into something of the severity of the renegade when he pronounces judgment on the theatres. Some of his enemies, of course, did not fail to make the most of this opportunity. "Aretine" in *Old England* parodied the justice's Charge and with bitter sarcasm pointed to a moral.[1]

But Fielding's efficiency as a magistrate was not prov-

[1]Extract from *Old England*, August 5, 1749, quoted in *The Gentleman's Magazine* for August, 1749.

ed on the Bench only. He devoted himself to the task of battling with the forces of disorder and of preventing crime with a remarkable energy which rose superior to his growing physical infirmities. The references that are made in the newspapers and magazines of the day to his work as a magistrate show that he did not spare himself in examining at all hours men and women charged with offences, and that he brought a humanity, common sense and patience to his work which, added to his knowledge of the law and his sterling honesty, must have made him one of the best magistrates of the time.

The prompt measures that he took to deal with the serious situation that developed early in July, 1749, when a mob of rioters broke into houses of ill fame in the Strand and committed other excesses, show that he was a man of action who could be relied on in an emergency. It was in the course of these riots that a young man named Bosavern Penlez had been taken into custody with a bundle of linen in his possession. The conviction and execution of this man, who had evidently taken part in the attacks made on the disorderly houses, aroused considerable feeling among the public, which found expression in some of the periodicals and in one or two pamphlets. Fielding endeavoured to educate public opinion in this matter by issuing *A True State of the Case of Bosavern Penlez* and this was published in November, 1749.[1] This pamphlet, which is a long one, begins with a vindication of the Riot Act, places before the public the evidence that was sworn before him during his examination of the nine men who had been arrested, and concludes with a defence of the conviction of Penlez. The legal issues of the case are ably debated and the arguments of the sympathizers of Pen-

[1] *The London Magazine*, November, 1749.

lez sufficiently refuted. "When by our excellent Constitution," he says towards the end of the pamphlet, "the greatest subject, no, not even the King himself, can without a lawful trial and conviction divest the meanest man of his property, deprive him of his liberty or attack him in his person; shall we suffer a licentious rabble to be accuser, judge, jury, and executioner?" There is evidence in the support that his views met with in the pages of *The Gentleman's* and *London Magazines* that the pamphlet largely fulfilled its purpose.

But Fielding did not content himself with the work of assisting in the administration of justice in the metropolis and of redeeming the office of the Westminster magistrate from much of that odium that clung to it so persistently. More than any other official of his time, perhaps, he realized the importance of preventive measures in the struggle against crime which had assumed such serious proportions at this time that it threatened to destroy all sense of security among the people. Although highway robbery was in no sense a peculiar product of the lawlessness that characterized the earlier half of the eighteenth century, it seems to have assumed alarming and unprecedented proportions at this time; and it is significant that some of the most noted criminals that England has ever known, men like Jack Sheppard, Jonathan Wild, and Dick Turpin, flourished during the first half of the eighteenth century. "It is shocking to think," writes Horace Walpole in 1752, "what a shambles this country is grown. Seventeen were executed this morning after having murdered the turnkey on Friday night, and almost forced open Newgate. One is forced to travel, even at noon, as if one was going to battle."[1] The impunity with

[1] Letter to Horace Mann, *The Letters of Horace Walpole*, edited by Mrs. Paget Toynbee. Vol. III, p. 88.

which outrages were committed in the streets of London is scarcely believable. The newspapers of the time are full of accounts of the most daring crimes committed openly in public places and often in broad daylight. The highwayman and the footpad felt no hesitation in adding the crime of murder to that of robbery because they knew that it would not alter their punishment, as the law made both capital. The Mayor and Aldermen of London in 1744 presented a petition to the King complaining that "diverse confederacies of great numbers of evil disposed persons armed with bludgeons, pistols and cutlasses, and other dangerous weapons infest not only the private lanes and passages, but likewise the public streets and places of usual concourse and commit most daring outrages upon the persons of your Majesty's most good subjects . . . and these are frequently perpetrated at such times as were heretofore deemed hours of security."[1]

The guardians of the safety of the public, the watchmen and constables, were hardly of any use against these gangs of criminals. They were as a rule aged and infirm people, altogether unfit for the work entrusted to them; and even when they were physically fit, they were so corrupt and sometimes so much afraid of the criminal that the latter openly defied them. Fielding gives us graphic pictures of these guardians of law and order in *The Coffee-House Politician* and in a well-known chapter in *Amelia*, and we have every reason to believe that his pictures were true to life.

In these circumstances it is not at all surprising that crime should be rampant in the metropolis to an extent almost unprecedented. And it was to a struggle with this epidemic of lawlessness and crime that Fielding devoted

[1] Andrews, *Eighteenth Century*, p. 230.

the greater part of his energies during the closing years of his life. He had not served as magistrate for more than six months before he realized that the existing laws were inadequate to deal with the magnitude of the evil. In July, 1749, he prepared a draft of a Bill for the Better Preventing Street Robberies, which, as we learn from an extant letter of his to Lord Hardwicke, the Lord Chancellor, was submitted to that high official for consideration. This draft bill, all trace of which has been lost, apparently did not find favour with the authorities. But undeterred by this Fielding vigorously continued his campaign against crime and did his best to improve the efficiency of the force of constables and watchmen with which London was so poorly provided.

In January, 1751,[1] he published a remarkable treatise named *An Enquiry Into the Causes of the Late Increase of Robbers* in which he traces the evil to its root, the increasing demoralization of the people. The masterly analysis that he makes of the causes that had led to this demoralization and the firm grasp that he has of every detail of his subject show how closely he had studied the problem and how well equipped he was to deal with it.

As in his Charge to the Grand Jury at the Westminster Sessions, in the *Enquiry* Fielding denounces the inordinate hankering of the working classes for amusement and draws the attention of his reader to the waste of money and time resulting therefrom, this being "indeed a certain method to fill the streets with beggars and the gaols with debtors and thieves." In speaking of drunkenness, "a second consequence of luxury among the vulgar," he vividly portrays the evils of gin drinking, to which his friend Hogarth also drew the attention of the public

[1] *The Gentleman's Magazine*, January, 1751.

shortly afterwards in a more effective manner. Gaming is another cause of demoralization that he names, and he points out that though the law is sufficient to deal with the evil, its prevalence must be attributed to a lamentable slackness in prosecuting the keepers of gaming houses. In dwelling upon the miserable condition of the poor, another notable cause of crime, Fielding pronounces a scathing condemnation on the houses of correction.

The later sections of the *Enquiry* deal with the more direct causes that encourage robbery, and Fielding lays special emphasis on the facilities that London afforded to criminals to escape with their booty and to dispose of it to advantage. He shows the defects of the Act of Parliament Concerning Vagrants and gives his readers a vivid description of the houses in which vagrants and incipient criminals found accommodation. The last section of the *Enquiry* is a notable one. In nothing is Fielding more in advance of his age than in his denunciation of the conduct and frequency of public executions. "The day appointed by law for the thief's shame," he says, "is the day of glory in his own opinion. His procession to Tyburn, and his last moments there, are all triumphant; attended with the compassion of the meek and tender-hearted, and with the applause, admiration, and envy of all the bold and hardened. His behaviour in his present condition, not the crimes, how atrocious soever, which brought him to it, are the subject of contemplation. And if he hath sense enough to temper his boldness with any degree of decency, his death is spoken of by many with honour, by most with pity, and by all with approbation."

This protest against public executions was unheeded at the time, and legislators took nearly a century to provide the swift, solemn, and private executions that he advocated in place of the brutal "Tyburn holiday" celebrated every six weeks for the benefit of the Georgian mob.

His *Enquiry*, however, produced some good effect. A month after its publication a Parliamentary Committee was appointed "to revise and consider the laws in being which relate to felonies and other offences against the peace." In April, 1751, it was resolved that a Bill should be brought into Parliament on the resolution of this Committee appointed to consider criminal legislation. In the month of March, 1752, an Act " for the better preventng Thefts and Robberies and for regulating Places of Public Entertainment and punishing of Persons keeping Disorderly Houses" received the royal assent.

In the midst of these activities Fielding found time to write another great work of fiction, and this is all the more remarkable because the state of his health at this time was far from being satisfactory. No information whatever can be obtained from the references to Fielding in the writings of his contemporaries as to when *Amelia* was begun, and the novelist himself does not give us any satisfactory clue that would help us to find out how long he had worked on the novel. The second chapter in *Amelia* which contains a scathing indictment of the administration of justice "within the liberty of Westminster" was obviously written by a man who had intimate personal knowledge of the evil that is the subject of his satire. And this knowledge could only have come to him after he had served for some time as a magistrate, to which office, as we have seen, he was appointed at the end of the year 1748.

Though the novel contains nothing in the shape of inconsistency that could be definitely ascribed to haste, yet it is evident that Fielding did not give as much time to the composition of *Amelia* as he had done to *Tom Jones*. His last novel is shorter than his masterpiece, the number of characters that make their appearance in it is smaller, and with the exception of a brief and rather perfunctory "exordium" in the first chapter the novel does not contain any introductory chapters to its different books. And yet it would be hazardous to conclude, as Professor Wilbur L. Cross does,[1] that the novel was begun after the publication of the *Enquiry Into the Causes of the Late Increase of Robbers* in January, 1751. This would give barely a year to the composition, revision, and publication of *Amelia*. It is more than doubtful if Fielding, busy as he was at this time with his magisterial duties and in indifferent health, would be able to write a novel of the size of *Amelia* in such a short time, even if we allow him more facility in composition in 1751 than he had when he wrote *Tom Jones*.

Fielding's last novel was published on the 18th of December, 1751,[2] in four 12mo volumes. Andrew Millar who, according to Scott, had paid £1,000 for the copyright had misgivings about its sale, but he very successfully bluffed the booksellers into buying up the first impression of the novel by refusing to deliver it to the trade on the usual terms of discount. As in the case of *Tom Jones*, the aid of the "puffing" advertisement had also been invoked, and Millar had announced that though he had requisitioned the services of four presses "to satisfy the earnest demand of the public" for the volumes, yet he had found it impossible to get them bound in time.[3]

These measures were the more necessary, perhaps, be-

---

[1] *The History of Henry Fielding*, Vol. II, p. 311.
[2] *The Whitehall Evening Post*, December 17-19, 1751.
[3] *The General Advertiser*, December 2, 1751.

cause apparently Fielding's influential friends who had exerted themselves to ensure the success of *Tom Jones* were not able to do the same when *Amelia* was about to be published. And so far as the sale of the first impression was concerned Millar's tactics were entirely successful. We have the evidence of Dr. Johnson to corroborate this. The good doctor declared that *Amelia* was perhaps the only book which being printed off betimes one morning, a new "edition" was called for before night.[1] Millar's ruse with the booksellers succeeded because *Tom Jones* had made Fielding's name great among the novelists of the day. But it was soon apparent that *Amelia* was far from being the popular favourite.

The reviews of the novel in the more important periodicals of the time were not unfavourable on the whole. *The London Magazine*, which published an elaborate summary of the novel, described it as amusing and its characters "well kept up." But it also dwelt at some length on certain imperfections which Fielding's enemies made the most of in running down the novel. It pointed out what it described as a "glaring anachronism" in the novelist's description of Booth and his wife, who had been married before the siege of Gibraltar in 1727, as still young when they go to the masquerade at Ranelagh, where masquerades were not introduced till the middle of the century; and it called attention to the state of the heroine's nose which "had been beat all to pieces" and which, the reviewer declared, should have been "set to rights by the help of some eminent surgeon."[2]

The Monthly Review gave more unqualified praise to the novelist, commending his morality, his boldness in at-

[1] *Johnsonian Miscellanies*, edited by G. B. Hill, 1897, Vol. I, p. 297.
[2] *The London Magazine*, December, 1751.

Q

tempting to give the history of persons already married, and his skill in making such a history palatable to the reader. The only feature of the novel, according to *The Monthly Review*, which stood in need of an apology was the "lowness" of its characters.[1] *The Gentleman's Magazine* for March, 1752, printed a letter from "Criticulus" which warmly commended "the noble reflections on the follies and vices of human nature" contained in the novel and its excellent character sketches. "Criticulus" was severe on the novelist for the "anachronism" to which *The London Magazine* had drawn attention, but he deprecated the harsh criticism of the nose of Fielding's fair heroine. Indeed, this circumstance of the heroine's "noselessness," as it has been facetiously described, was responsible to a very great extent for the misfortunes of the novel, and Dr. Johnson was not guilty of much exaggeration when he declared that the "vile broken nose never cured ruined the sale" of the book.[2]

Fielding's mistake in the first edition of the novel in not taking sufficient care to make it clear to his reader that the accident that had caused the injury to his heroine's nose had not really impaired her beauty gave an excellent handle to his many enemies who indulged in witticisms which more than one contemporary of the novelist rightly characterized as "low."

But these were not the only imperfections of the novel that provoked hostile criticism. The novelist had also given offence by trying to advertise through the medium of his novel a business enterprise, the Universal Register Office, a kind of agency for houses and servants, which he and his brother had set up. Moreover, apart from her

[1] *The Monthly Review*, December, 1751.
[2] *Johnsonian Miscellanies*, edited by G. B. Hill, 1897, Vol. I, p. 297.

physical shortcoming Fielding's heroine came in for a
good deal of adverse criticism, and this also from readers
who had little or no bias against Fielding. His hero likewise gave much offence to many readers; and though
Richardson, carried away by his rancour against Fielding, was constantly betrayed, as we have seen, into a travesty of actual facts, there was just a shade of truth in his
remark that "Captain Booth had done Fielding's business."[1]

In addition to Johnson's and Richardson's statements
about the failure of *Amelia*, and the persistent and triumphant obituaries of Mrs. Amelia Booth that Fielding's
enemies among the journalists delighted in printing in
their papers, we have the evidence of readers like Mrs.
Delany and "the learned Mrs. Carter" who had hitherto
shown little bias against Fielding. The latter writing to
her friend Miss Talbot says, "Methinks I long to engage
you on the side of this poor unfortunate book, which I am
told the fine folks are unanimous in pronouncing to be
very sad stuff."[2]

Though he was quite used to hostile criticism by this
time, Fielding was nevertheless very much distressed at
the reception that his novel had met with. He realized
that he had been guilty of a serious oversight in not remedying the deficiency of his heroine, and in the third number of his last paper, *The Covent Garden Journal*, he inserted a paragraph, half jocose, half serious, in which he declared that the violent hurt in Amelia's nose had been so
absolutely cured that scarcely a scar was left. In two later
issues of the same paper, the seventh and the eighth, he

[1]Letter to Mrs. Donnellan. *The Correspondence of S. Richardson*, edited by
Mrs. Barbauld, Vol. IV, p. 59.
[2]*A Series of Letters Between Mrs. Elizabeth Carter and Miss Catherine
Talbot*, London, 1809, Vol. II, p. 71.

placed *Amelia* at the bar of the Court of Censorial Enquiry which "Sir Alexander Drawcansir" of *The Covent Garden Journal* had "erected," and after stating the principal charges that his detractors had brought against his book, namely, that the novel was "a heap of sad stuff, dullness, and nonsense," that the characters were low and foolish, and that Amelia in particular was not only a fool and a milksop but a beauty without a nose, he declared that though "his child" was not entirely free from faults, she did not deserve the rancour with which she had been pursued by the public. And when he revised his novel for a new edition, he tried his best to remedy those defects which had enabled his detractors to make out a real case against him. He omitted all the references to the Universal Register Office that the first edition of the novel had contained, and in regard to the nose of his heroine which had been "beat all to pieces" by the overturning of a chaise, he endeavoured to remove the handle that he had given to his readers to enable them to laugh at the expense of his heroine by inserting two sentences in two different places in the novel in which he emphasized the fact that his heroine's nose was well proportioned even after the accident had happened, and that the scar which was all that the accident had left behind it rather added to her beauty.[1]

In spite of these and a number of other changes of minor importance that he introduced into his novel, *Amelia* never seems to have made much headway in the good opinion of the novelist's contemporaries. It was more unfortunate from the time of its birth than the other novels of Fielding and its greatest misfortune was that its imperfections which, after all, were far from being as serious as

[1] *Amelia*, IV, vii, and XI, i.

the novelist's detractors represented them to be, completely overshadowed its merits, so far at any rate as contemporary readers were concerned. It was certainly a case of the voice of the detractor—and Fielding in the course of his chequered literary career had arrayed too many of them against him—prevailing against any claim that the work may have advanced on its own merits.

And yet though the merits of Fielding's last novel are great and his complaint quite legitimate that it was treated with a rancour it did not deserve, the verdict of posterity that has assigned to *Amelia* a place much below *Tom Jones* is not an unjust one. *Amelia* has not the vigour and buoyancy of the masterpiece or of *Joseph Andrews*. There is a very conspicuous want in it of characters possessing the *joie de vivre* of Adams, Squire Western, or Tom Jones, which makes the atmosphere of Fielding's earlier novels such a joyous one. In place of the buoyant personality of Parson Adams in *Joseph Andrews* we have Dr. Harrison in *Amelia*. Partridge gives place to the more matter-of-fact and more serious Sergeant Atkinson. Tom Jones and Captain Booth are very different from each other in their outlook on life and their capacity for enjoyment. And Fielding's last novel contains no characters like Mrs. Slipslop, Mrs. Honour, or young Nightingale.

This was inevitable. Fielding's growing infirmities, the close proximity to crime and wretchedness to which his office relegated him, and the time that had passed since *Tom Jones* was written, for we must remember that Fielding had taken some years to write that novel, and the comparatively close proximity of the dates of publication of the two novels makes the interval between them appear shorter than it actually was—all these had helped to make Fielding's outlook on life different from what it had been before. There was a certain amount of sadness in the retrospective wisdom that had come to him with increasing years and this was bound to be reflected in his work.

The outstanding feature of Fielding's last novel is the spirit of retrospection that lies behind the story. Though it would be a mistake to read the actual facts of Fielding's life in the history of the married life of Captain Booth, it is nevertheless true that when he wrote *Amelia* Fielding's own experiences in life were present in his mind to a far greater extent than they had been when he had written his other novels.

More than one contemporary of the novelist speaking from personal knowledge of him identified Captain Booth and Amelia with Fielding and his first wife. Richardson who never missed an opportunity of vilifying his rival by reading or pretending to read in almost all the stories of dissipation and riotous living that occur in Fielding's novels faithful records of the profligate's abandoned ways of life identified him with Booth, and his wife Charlotte with Amelia "even to her noselessness."[1] Lady Mary Montagu without any spite against her cousin did the same,[2] and these identifications seem to have been generally accepted in Fielding's day.

Though the novelist nowhere specifically declares that his first wife was the original of Amelia, the identification made by his contemporaries and insisted on by the majority of his biographers has never been questioned. Lady Louisa Stuart tells us in her Introductory Anecdotes to Lord Wharncliffe's edition of *Lady Mary Montagu's Letters and Works* that she had heard her mother, Lady Bute,

[1]Letter to Mrs. Donnellan, February 22, 1752, *The Correspondence of S. Richardson*, edited by Mrs. Barbauld, Vol. IV, p. 61.
[2]*The Letters and Works of Lady Mary Wortley Montagu*, edited by her grandson, Lord Wharncliffe, London, 1861, Vol. II, p. 279.

say that "even the glowing language he knew how to employ did not do more than justice to the amiable qualities of the original." And from what little is known of Charlotte Fielding it is evident that Amelia resembled her even more than Sophia Western did. Many circumstances in Amelia's life history as related in the novel, for example, her living with her widowed mother and sister at the time Booth courted her, her mother's bequest of the bulk of her property to her and the chequered course of her married life, leave little room for doubt that Fielding's beautiful and devoted first wife was the original of the heroine of his last novel.

But it would be hazardous to carry the identifications any further than this, though one is greatly tempted to read something of the history of Fielding's own life in Booth's experiences. For example, the handsome young Booth "not quite of the most delicate make" with his prominent nose and his broad shoulders seems to be young Fielding himself, though probably the actual events leading up to Booth's marriage as related in the novel are very different from what had happened at the time of Fielding's own first marriage. We ought not to find it difficult to understand the novelist's desire to cover the facts with elaborate embroidery of fiction even to the extent of introducing the somewhat superfluous and improbable episode of the hero's attempt to gain access to his ladylove in a hamper. And so far as some of the other events in Booth's life are concerned, in which the novelist's biographers and critics have endeavoured to find a record of his own experiences in life, his failure as a gentleman farmer, for example, or the vicissitudes of his married life in Spring Gardens, it is very far from certain that they are wholly or even mainly autobiographical.

There is a good deal in the character and circumstances in the life of Captain Booth that seems to point to the fact that Fielding was thinking more of his father than of himself when he portrayed his hero. His father like Booth was a military man, had been on active service, had tried his hand at farming and failed, was constantly in financial difficulties into which he was led as much by a fatal propensity for gambling as by his spendthrift ways of life. The novelist himself, whatever his other weaknesses may have been, was not a gamester. Nor have we any evidence at all to prove that he was unfaithful as a husband, though some of his biographers have not hesitated to insinuate this.

The fact seems to be that while the memory of his first wife was constantly present with him as he was writing his last novel and this memory inspired him to portray one of his finest women, for his hero and other characters in the novel Fielding did not depend solely or even mainly on particular living originals; and so far as the story of Captain Booth's life is concerned, he allowed himself full liberty, of course, to weave fiction into fact as the exigencies of his plot demanded it, though there was more of fact in the web than there was in *Tom Jones* or *Joseph Andrews*. It is not easy to escape this conviction if one reads the novel carefully and compares the main events in the story with the known facts of Fielding's life.

It is futile, however, to try to find out where fact ends and fiction begins in any part of the story. They are consciously and deliberately blended together by the novelist. But though we are unable to separate them, we cannot at the same time fail to notice that as Fielding wove the experiences of his own life into the web of his story the reflective mood tended to predominate in him more and more as it was bound to do. As a consequence of this we find little of the exuberance and joy of life of *Joseph Andrews* and *Tom Jones* in *Amelia*.

But this spirit of retrospection in the novelist reflected in his work is not the only feature of *Amelia* that distinguishes it from Fielding's earlier work. The graver mood of the novelist in *Amelia* threatened to banish altogether from the last novel that wonderful humour that largely makes the earlier novels what they are. It is significant that *Amelia* begins with descriptions of scenes that are more or less tragic. And as the story progresses we have little of that kind of adventure on the road or in inns that enlivens the narrative so wonderfully in his earlier works and gives the novelist such excellent openings for his magnificent mock heroic descriptions and similes. We have hardly any account in *Amelia* of the kind of "battle" that Fielding describes so constantly and with such gusto in *Joseph Andrews* and *Tom Jones*, in which all kinds of weapons from the crabtree cudgel to the pan full of hog's blood are wielded with such good will and which leave so little bitterness or material damage behind them. And when Fielding paints his humorous portraits in *Amelia* there is little, except in the case of the portrait of Colonel Bath or that of the author who is so dexterous with his proposals, of the old genial and exuberant laughter at the eccentricities and frailities of men and women. And even Colonel Bath and the author do not enliven the story in the way that Fielding's humorous characters in the earlier novels do.

But though the novelist's outlook on life now is very different from what it had been before, and in the reformatory zeal that characterizes the last years of his life he gives much more attention to the abuses and evils of his time in his last novel than he had ever done before, *Amelia* is very far from being a dull book. There was some danger, as *The Monthly Review* had pointed out, that the novelist's defiance of established custom in venturing to give the history of two persons already married, might result in an uninteresting tale hardly worth telling. But Fielding's performance gave the lie to this fear, and whatever other imperfections may be found in the novel, the story on the whole is quite as interesting as it is in Fielding's earlier novels. And though one is inclined to be impatient with the narratives into which some of the novelist's characters launch out, particularly with the long narratives of Miss Matthews and Booth at the beginning, this error of judgment, if error it can be called, does not result in the paralysis of the action.

It is true that in the construction of the plot of *Amelia* Fielding made use of materials that he had already used in plays like *The Temple Beau*, *The Coffee-House Politician*, and most of all in *The Modern Husband*. He had already portrayed the good and the bad justice, the aristocratic roué and his minion, the virtuous wife and the erring husband whom she reclaims. But we must remember that when Fielding wrote *Amelia*, a novel dealing with some of the themes of these plays and particularly with the main theme of *The Modern Husband* was more or less a new experiment in the art of fiction. Besides, the dramatic presentment of them had obviously been unsatisfying. And as the years that had passed since he had written the plays had brought a riper knowledge of the world to Fielding, he must have felt that he had much to add to what he had said before. One is inclined to believe that he turned to these themes again not because his originality was exhausted but because he found in them exactly the

kind of material that he could build up into a great story.
Moreover, we must not forget that at the time he wrote
Amelia he had less leisure to devote to his literary labours
than he had when he had written *Tom Jones*.

Fielding's story, again, loses none of its interest because there is a marked tendency in the novelist to expose
and hold up to condemnation some of the most flagrant
evils of his time. His reforming zeal never outruns the
discretion and sure instinct of the novelist, and in this he
gives us a signal proof of his mastery over his art. It is remarkable that those very chapters in *Amelia* in which he
portrays the evils and corruption of his time are among
the most interesting in the novel. The criticism that suggests that Fielding's didactic purpose in the novel seems
at times to cloud the fine perception of the artist is far
from being just. His arraignment of the venality and
corruption in the administration of justice in his day is
pitiless and thorough, but the reader would be hypercritical who would suggest that the account given in the
novel of the activities of Justice Thrasher and his lieu-
tenants is a mere excrescence which adds nothing to the
interest of the main story. The prison scene in one of the
earlier chapters in the novel, the story of Booth's unsuccessful efforts to secure a commission, the pictures that
are given in the book of widespread corruption and of the
prevalence of the practice of "touching," these and other
didactic features of the novel do not detract in the least
from the interest of the story, or act as clogs to its progress.

If *Amelia* compares unfavourably with *Tom Jones* in
one respect much more conspicuously than in others, it is
in its want of that masculine vigour which Fielding exhibits so abundantly in his earlier work. There is a singular irony in the fact of Fielding exhibiting something of

that sentimentality that he had despised so much in Richardson at one time. Some of the tender scenes in *Amelia* are apt to pall on the reader because they recur too often. And though it would be a mistake to suggest that Fielding was lacking in the power of portraying real pathos, seeing that one of the most pathetic scenes in eighteenth century fiction—that well-known one in *Amelia* which describes the heroine waiting with her historic little supper for the appearance of her husband—was written by him, yet one cannot help feeling that Fielding's hero and heroine are a little too lachrymose, his hero particularly, who over and above the copious and rather unnecessary tears that he sheds on other occasions, allows more than one torrent to gush from his eyes as he relates to Miss Matthews how he had won his lady-love.

But in spite of this and the weakness of his character it would be a mistake to describe Fielding's hero as contemptible. As a soldier his conduct was unimpeachable, and the novelist is careful to point out that he was of "the most untainted honesty", and had been a dutiful son and an affectionate brother. These and some other good features in his character, as for example, his good humour or his sincere repentance for his errors, do not, however, go very far to atone for his deficiencies, and it is difficult to endorse Thackeray's preference of Booth to Tom Jones. The pity not unmixed with a certain amount of antipathy that he inspires is due more to the absence of generous instincts in him than to the weakness of his character. For with the exception of the incident related at the commencement of the story, his coming to the assistance of a man who was making an unequal fight against odds, there is hardly an episode in the story that proves the existence of generous instincts in him. Even Keightley, stout apologist for Fielding's heroes as he is, is unable to make out a case for him, and one is inclined to question the justice of the claim that has been advanced by Thackeray and supported by a fair admirer of the character that Booth's adoration of his wife gives him a title to our regard.

The harsh criticism that was levelled at Fielding's heroine by many contemporary critics has not been endorsed by posterity. The libels against her intelligence have been sufficiently refuted, and Fielding's readers in the generations that have succeeded his own have done justice to the splendid picture of wifely devotion that he gave to the world in his last novel. Her beauty, the charm of her personality, and the many virtues of her character are paraded a little too ostentatiously perhaps; but this has not lessened very materially the admiration that many a gifted reader of Fielding's novel has felt for his heroine. Nor has it grown less because it has been pointed out more than once that in her the "yielding" qualities of the sex predominate over intellectual strength. While we give our assent to this, we cannot forget that she exhibits in moments of sore trial and tribulation an unusual fortitude in the face of which the charge of weakness brought against her falls altogether to the ground. She is the central figure in the novel on account of her remarkable personality and the wonderful beauty of her character, not through any adventitious circumstances. And the fact that men so different from each other as Johnson and Thackeray have pronounced substantially the same verdict on Fielding's heroine, giving her pre-eminence over all heroines of fiction, ought to have given pause to critics who have expressed the view that Fielding's Bohemian ways of life had made him incapable of portraying all that is most beautiful and noble in the fair sex.

Among Fielding's other characters in the novel the most striking is Colonel Bath or "old honour and dignity" as the younger officers in the army described him. The fire-eater is a character that one comes across constantly in drama and fiction. But the majority of writers who have portrayed him have contented themselves with pictures of the swaggerer or the bully who maintains his reputation as long as he is able to avoid a conflict with a man of real courage and determination. Fielding's *preux chevalier* is very different from the conventional type though he is endowed by the novelist with considerable skill in the trick of the "threatening brow." He is not only "a great dealer in the marvellous and constantly the hero of his own tale," but war and martial exploits are the ordinary topics of his conversation. He tells us himself that the dignity of his nature has always been his reason for drawing his sword.

Apart from these he has his full share, or rather more than his full share, of other singularities. And yet it is remarkable that, multitudinous as they are, they do not make the portrait a caricature. It is saved from being a caricature because the novelist all the time that he dwells on Colonel Bath's singularities also reveals the real man, showing us, as he had set out to do, "a perfect good Christian, except in the articles of fighting and swearing."

In Dr. Harrison, Fielding portrays a clergyman who is very different from Parson Adams, though in the sterling worth of their characters the two men have much in common. Like Adams, Harrison is fearless and outspoken whenever wrong-doing has to be denounced, whether among the high or the low. Like Adams again, he is of a generous and open nature, indefatigable in the performance of his duties and in his acts of charity. But he can be

stern on occasions as his conduct in getting Booth arrested shows. In this he is different from Adams who, apart
from his views on the question of imprisonment for debt,
would have been the last man to take out a writ against
anyone. Moreover, Harrison has not the childlike simplicity of Adams, nor are there any of those immortal eccentricities in him which largely make Fielding's best-
known character what he is. In Adams is reflected the
exuberant geniality of Fielding's youth; in Harrison the
wisdom of his graver middle age.

More than one critic of the novelist has expressed the
view that in *Amelia* Fielding exhibits the same masterly
skill as in *Tom Jones* in the portrayal of his minor characters. It is difficult to agree with this. A few of the minor
characters in *Amelia*, it is true, are as good as those in *Tom
Jones*. In Miss Matthews, Fielding gives us an interesting
study of a woman whose misfortunes have not the power
to make the reader forget her frailties. Mr. Bondum the
bailiff or "officer," as he preferred to style himself, sketched with a few strokes as he is, is vividly portrayed. So is
Justice Thrasher. But some of the other characters in the
novel, in whom we have more or less full-length portraits,
as in the characters of Serjeant Atkinson and his wife, for
example, or Colonel and Mrs. James, do not come up to
the level of the minor characters in *Tom Jones*.

Fielding owed much more to Smollett for his portrait
of Atkinson than for that of Partridge, and the latter is a
far more interesting character than either Atkinson or
Strap in Smollett's *Roderick Random*. Mrs. Atkinson is
not a very convincing character, as the novelist's earlier
picture of the unfortunate and unhappy but entirely lovable young woman is hard to reconcile with the aggressive
bluestocking into which she is transformed. In Colonel

James and his wife we have characters that are true to life, but there is nothing particularly striking in the portraits. Mrs. Ellison apart from the skill and efficiency with which she does her work is hardly interesting enough otherwise. The "noble lord" is handsome and generous to those who minister to his pleasures, but we know very little more about him. The accounts that are given of Captain Trent's methods and the history of his life are interesting enough; but the character, perhaps because the minion of the aristocratic roué has been delineated again and again, does not stand out from the characters of fiction and drama in the same way as the majority of the minor characters in *Tom Jones* do.

CHAPTER X

THE LAST PHASE

SOON after the publication of *Amelia* Fielding made his last venture in journalism. *The Gentleman's Magazine* giving the literary news for the month of January, 1752, refers to the new enterprise in a short paragraph which is typical of Sylvanus Urban's usual attitude to the novelist. " Mr. H—y F—ld—g," the paragraph tells us, "after having failed in *The Champion*, *The True Patriot* and *The Jacobite Journal* has this month made another attempt to establish a newspaper by prefixing an essay and interspersing occasional pieces of humour."

As a matter of fact the new "paper of entertainment by several eminent hands" had been announced to appear as early as November 6, 1751.[1] But evidently Fielding had been busy with *Amelia*, and the first number of *The Covent Garden Journal*, as the new paper was called, did not make its appearance till the 4th of January, 1752.

During the first six months of its career the paper was a bi-weekly, appearing every Tuesday and Saturday ; but afterwards it was converted into a weekly and came out on Saturdays only. In the later announcements of its first appearance[2] there was no mention of the " several eminent hands" spoken of before, and the paper was now declared to be under the direction of "Sir Alexander Drawcansir, Knight," a name which the success of Buck-

---

[1] *The General Advertiser*, October 31, 1751.
[2] *The London Daily Advertiser*, December 18, 1751.

R

ingham's *Rehearsal* had made famous, and which had
already been bestowed on Fielding by Colley Cibber in
his *Apology*.

Though Fielding was the moving spirit in this enterprise and the bulk of the writing for the journal was done
by him, he was evidently assisted in his work by some of
his friends.   The most useful of his assistants were his
clerk, Joshua Brogden, and his friend and "quotation
hunter," the Rev. William Young.   It has been conjectured that Arthur Murphy was also associated with
the others in the work. It appears, however, from the evidence of the style of the great majority of the leading
articles in the journal, which unmistakably points to
Fielding being their author, that to his assistants were
assigned the more mechanical parts of the work, like
the compilation of the news items or the writing of the
reports of the cases heard in Fielding's Court, which were
a regular feature of the paper.

In appearance *The Covent Garden Journal* was very
much like *The True Patriot* and *The Jacobite's Journal*, and
its usual contents were the leading article or letters from
correspondents, the news of the day, domestic and foreign, occasionally enlivened by "variorum" notes, reports
of the cases heard in Fielding's Court, legal notices and
announcements made by the Universal Register Office.

The first four numbers of the paper contained a mock-
heroic "Journal of the Paper War" in which the "author"
gave his readers humorous accounts of his encounters
with the forces of Grub Street and their allies; and when
this journal was discontinued, Fielding revived the idea,
of which he had made such happy use before, of a Court
of Censorial Enquiry "to hear and determine all manner
of causes which in anywise relate to the Republic of

Letters." The proceedings of this Court were reported somewhat irregularly till the twenty-eighth number of the paper and once again in the last.

Fielding seems to have been induced by many considerations to undertake the responsibility of editing a periodical when he had so much other work on his hands and when his health was so bad. The emoluments of his office as magistrate were anything but large, as he tells us in his *Journal of a Voyage to Lisbon*, and he hoped to add to his scanty income by devoting himself to journalism in his spare time. The high price, three pence, that was put on the paper confirms the suspicion that it was as much a business enterprise as anything else. Moreover, as one of the proprietors of the Universal Register Office he seems to have felt the need of a newspaper to help it in its various activities.

But the consideration which seems to have been of the greatest weight in inducing him to embark on this enterprise was that if he had a newspaper of his own he would be able to carry on more effectively the "paper war" against his enemies who were determined to nurse the ancient feud with increasing bitterness.

He set out on his new journalistic adventure by disclaiming any desire to deal with politics or with personal slander and scurrility; but at the same time he entered the fray with great good will and energy, abusing his adversaries and particularly the journalists as a tribe of stupid and infamous scribblers and arrogating superiority to himself and his paper. It was evident from the tone of his first leading article and the "Introduction to a Journal of the present Paper War" that accompanied it that Fielding had come into the newspaper world again to do battle with his enemies. Indeed, it is significant that in those

earlier numbers of his new journal in which he declares
his purpose he has very little to say about any general reformatory programme that he might have had in his mind
or about any desire to raise the existing literary standards
of the newspaper world. We must not, however, leave
these altogether out of the account.

In the earliest numbers of *The Covent Garden Journal*
the controversies into which Fielding had dragged himself and had been dragged by others demanded the greater
share of his attention, though he remained faithful to the
undertaking he had given to the public and refused to be
dragged into politics. Quite early in the career of his new
paper he crossed swords with the notorious and versatile
Dr. John Hill who, as the author of the leading articles
which had been appearing since March, 1751, under the
title, "The Inspector," in *The London Daily Advertiser*,
resented the slur that was put on him when Fielding spoke
contemptuously of the whole tribe of contemporary journalists. But this was by no means Hill's whole grievance
against the "author" of *The Covent Garden Journal*. Fielding had given him further provocation in his "Journal of
the Paper War" "by describing at considerable length his
encounters with "his Lowness the Prince of Billingsgate"
and by taking many liberties with Hill's name. "The
Prince of Billingsgate" replied to these attacks in an
equally abusive strain in *The London Daily Advertiser*.

Another and a much greater contemporary to whom
Fielding gave offence by means of his "Journal of the Paper
War" was Smollett, who evidently was not yet forgiven
for the ill-natured reference to the elder novelist's second
marriage that he had introduced into the first edition of
Peregrine Pickle, though he had tried to make some
amends afterwards by removing the objectionable pas-

sage from the book. But perhaps it was Smollett's well-known and oft-expressed animosity to Lyttelton that drove Fielding to ridicule "Peeragrin Puckle" and "Rodorick Random" and to describe their discomfiture in the paper war which he had declared against the forces of Grub Street. Whatever may have been the cause of the offence that Smollett had given to Fielding in the past, it was the latter who now added fresh fuel to the embers.

Smollett's reply, which took the form of a pamphlet named *A Faithful Narrative of the Base and Inhuman Arts that were lately practised upon the Brain of Habbakkuk Hilding, Justice, Dealer, and Chapman*[1] was characteristic. Taking his cue from Pope's *Narrative of the Frenzy of John Dennis*, the irascible Scotch novelist repaid Fielding for the attentions he had received from him with interest. He painted a lurid picture of "divers extravagancies" which he declared he had observed of late in Fielding's behaviour, and in describing these "extravagancies" he allowed his imagination to run riot quite as much as the brain of his adversary was supposed to have done. He endeavoured to divert his readers and feed his rancour with a very garbled account of the vicissitudes of Fielding's life from which some of the latter's biographers have probably derived many of their ideas about the Bohemian ways of his life. Smollett brought Lyttelton once again into the controversy, abusing him under the name Sir Gosling Scrag, which he had bestowed on him before. Sir Gosling is described as inciting his "zany" Habbakkuk to make war on his foes, to treat them all as "cowards, asses, grubs and vermin," and to let loose "the chief torrent of his gall" against that rascal Peregrine Pickle who had exposed them both to ridicule and shame. Towards

[1]Published January 15, 1752 (*The London Daily Advertiser*, January 15).

the end of the pamphlet Smollett falls foul of Amelia and echoes the parrot cry about her noselessness, making it the occasion for free indulgence in coarse language which indeed is the outstanding feature of the pamphlet. Some of Fielding's other characters come in for their share of abuse, and Smollett also accuses Fielding of having "stolen" his Strap and Miss Williams from *Roderick Random*. The pamphlet ends with an amusing account, which is a kind of burlesque of Fielding's manner in his "Journal of the Paper War," of the rout of a cavalcade at the head of which "Habbakkuk mounted on a jackass" had placed himself.

But if Fielding had to thank himself for some of these attacks made on him, there were numerous others made by journalists and pamphleteers on whom he had made no personal onslaughts. One of the most pertinacious assailants of *The Covent Garden Journal* was Bonnell Thornton, an Oxford man and something of a scholar, whose services seem to have been hired by the promoters of a new Register Office which had been set up as a rival to the one established by Fielding and his brother. Thornton brought out a series of pamphlets by way of parody of Fielding's newspaper, and he called his publication *The Drury Lane Journal*. The paper systematically travestied Fielding's leading articles in *The Covent Garden Journal*, burlesqued its news items, carried on an uninterrupted campaign of vilification against Fielding in the twelve numbers that were published, and endeavoured to turn the tables against him in the paper war. Fielding, however, took little notice of this industrious literary hack.

The fact seems to be that Fielding was beginning to realize that the paper war if it was to be carried on successfully would demand more of his attention than he was prepared to give to it. He also felt, as he tells us in the fifth number of his paper, that the contest would not be a fair one because he knew that the enemy would make use of unfair methods. He therefore made special efforts to extricate himself as best he could from the entanglement of controversy in which he had to some extent involved himself. He was determined not to embroil himself any further, and gave no reply to Smollett's attack on him nor to Bonnell Thornton's ridicule of his paper and vilification of his character in *The Drury Lane Journal*. And in the fourth number of his periodical he made definite overtures for a "firm peace, amity and concord" between Sir Alexander Drawcansir and his enemies.

Having renounced all intention to carry on the paper war Fielding declared more definitely and clearly than he had done before that the aim and purpose of his paper were to "serve the noble interests of religion, virtue and good sense and to restore that true and manly taste which hath within these few years degenerated in these kingdoms." After this he carefully avoided all personal controversies and conducted his paper on very much the same lines that the elder essayists had followed in *The Tatler* and *The Spectator*.

Though many of Fielding's leading articles in *The Covent Garden Journal* are interesting, exhibiting as they do the fullness of knowledge and ripe judgment of his later life, and in a few papers his humour and ingenuity are shown to great advantage, on the whole *The Covent Garden Journal* is heavy reading and Fielding's lay sermons are apt to be tiresome. The "Journal of the Paper War" with which he endeavoured to enliven his periodical when it commenced its career has little of the finished perfection, lightness of touch and raciness of Swift's *Battle of the Books* from which Fielding seems to have derived his main idea. The controversies which occasioned it were not great enough to give it a hold on the popular imagination or an abiding literary interest. And the mock-heroic vein in the journal is somewhat thin and forced. The proceedings of the Court of Censorial Enquiry which Sir Alexander Drawcansir "erected" and which were reported in eight out of the seventy-two numbers of the periodical that were issued are only occasionally enlivened by the caustic wit that is such a great feature of the reports of the examinations and trials in the Courts of Captain Hercules Vinegar or of Justice Trottplaid. The only trial of particular interest in Sir Alexander Drawcansir's Court is that of *Amelia* to which we have already referred, though the remarks made by "the Censor of Great Britain," as Sir Alexander described himself, on Mrs. Charlotte Lennox's *Female Quixote* or Mrs. Haywood's *History of Betsy Thoughtless* are interesting enough to the reader who has any knowledge of the byways of eighteenth century fiction.

In spite of these deficiencies, however, there is a good deal in *The Covent Garden Journal* that is worthy of attention. If in his social satire Fielding goes over the same ground more or less that he had already traversed in some of his plays, in his earlier periodicals and the novels, many of the papers which contain this satire are of great interest nevertheless because they give us his final verdicts on the follies and infirmities of the world of fashion. And in a few papers, those, for example, which contain his comments on the measures adopted by the authorities for the suppression of the social evil, he turns to questions to which he had given little attention before. As regards his papers on the diversions, follies, and weaknesses of

fashionable people, the verdicts that he pronounces are
as severe as his earlier ones. In the second number of the
journal, for example, in which his powers of irony are
seen to great advantage, he pronounces a scathing indictment on the prevailing corruptions of the age, and in
the fourth number he returns to the charge again in an ingenious paper in which he gives his readers a "modern
glossary" of words and makes very caustic comments on
the evils of the age as he explains the meanings of the
words in his glossary. Some of the diversions of the rich
are denounced in other papers, and in one, the liveliest
perhaps of all the numbers of the journal, he exposes very
effectively the enormity of the practice of swearing.[1] The
picture of the beau that is given in this paper is one of the
best that he has painted, and as one reads the paper one
realizes how much more interesting *The Covent Garden
Journal* would have been if Fielding had given his reader
some more portraits of this kind.

But though these papers have much to recommend
them in the attractive vigour of language and the good
sense that characterize them, Fielding's most interesting
contributions to *The Covent Garden Journal* are his articles
on literary subjects. The best of these perhaps is an essay
on reading[2] in which he speaks of the place of wit and
humour in literature and expresses the opinion that
"pleasantry should be made only the vehicle of instruction; but when no moral, no lesson, no instruction, is con-
veyed to the reader, where the whole design of the composition is no more than to make us laugh, the writer
comes very near to the character of a buffoon." He then
proceeds to subject some of the greatest masters "who

[1] *The Covent Garden Journal*, No. 33, April 23, 1752.
[2] *The Covent Garden Journal*, No. 10, February 4, 1752.

have sent their satire laughing into the world" to this test, under which he would hardly have come off unscathed himself, and finds that he can hold in the highest esteem only "the great triumvirate," Lucian, Cervantes, and Swift. To Shakespeare and Molière he gives more measured praise. But two other great humorists, Aristophanes and Rabelais, whose aid he had sought in his famous invocation in *Tom Jones* "to fill his pages with humour"[1], are now proscribed because "their design appears very plainly to have been to ridicule all sobriety, modesty, decency, virtue and religion, out of the world." Another master, whose aid he had invoked before, Marivaux, is now altogether ignored.

The pre-eminence among the humorists that he gives to Lucian is also insisted on in another paper in which he refers to a project, which was never accomplished, of a translation of the works of Lucian in collaboration with his friend Young.[2] He opposes the view that Dryden had advanced that Lucian might be looked upon as an imitator of Aristophanes, and in the same paper he tells us that he has formed his style on that of Lucian. Among the moderns he finds only one writer, Jonathan Swift, who may be described as a worthy imitator of Lucian.

Indeed, in *The Covent Garden Journal* Fielding gives much more attention than he had ever done before to the subject of humour. He devotes a number of papers to it and discusses at considerable length the question of the essential constituents of humour. Some of the views that he expresses appear somewhat startling at first sight; but when he says that "by humour is generally intended a violent impulse of the mind determining it to some one

[1] *Tom Jones*, Book XIII, Chap. I.
[2] *The Covent Garden Journal*, No. 52, June 30, 1752.

particular point" and that "no passion or humour of the mind is absolutely either tragic or comic in itself,"[1] one realizes that he is aiming at a comprehensive definition, the soundness of which is not altogether above suspicion, to include the Elizabethan acceptation of the word. If we keep this in mind, we shall find it less difficult to understand his meaning in that paper in which he speaks of tragical humour,[2] and in another one in which he tells his reader that there is perhaps more wit in the sermons of Dr. South than in the comedies of Congreve.[3]

But these were not the only papers of literary interest that Fielding contributed to the journal. Among his other contributions on literary subjects are an excellent satire on the vagaries of the learned commentators of Shakespeare[4] and some interesting remarks on the unities of the classical drama and the chorus.[5] He also gave his readers some poetry occasionally, and one of the poems that appeared in his journal called "A Plesaunt Balade or Advice to the Fayre Maydens"[6] and described as "written by Dan Jeffry Chaucer" is of special interest because it furnishes the only proof that we have in his writings that he had studied Chaucer, if we are justified in assuming that the poem was written by him. But the assumption is somewhat hazardous, as the conspicuous absence of the name of Chaucer from all his references to the great humorists of the world seems to indicate that either Fielding was not sufficiently acquainted with the father of English poetry or, as seems more probable, he was

[1] *The Covent Garden Journal*, No. 55, July 18, 1752.
[2] *The Covent Garden Journal*, No. 19, March 7, 1752.
[3] *The Covent Garden Journal*, No. 18, March 3, 1752.
[4] *The Covent Garden Journal*, No. 31, April 18, 1752.
[5] *The Covent Garden Journal*, No. 62, September 16, 1752.
[6] *The Covent Garden Journal*, No. 50, June 23, 1752.

not inclined to assign a very high rank to him among the great humorists of the world.

By the middle of the year 1752, after *The Covent Garden Journal* had continued its somewhat chequered career for six months, there are indications that Fielding was beginning to find the work of editing the paper something of a burden. As a matter of fact, *The Covent Garden Journal* had lost some of its most attractive features quite early in its career. The "variorum" notes to the news items in the paper and the reports of the proceedings of the Censorial Court had ceased to appear for some time; and in the fifty-third number we are told that Sir Alexander Drawcansir, who had lately given some hints of an intention to resign his office, had only been prevailed upon by the importunities of the whole town to continue his journal, but henceforward it would appear once a week only.

This it did for five months more. In the last number which appeared on the 25th of November, 1752, Fielding in laying down his pen rather abruptly told his readers that he did so because he had neither inclination nor leisure to continue his journalistic labours. He declared at the same time that he had no intention of holding any further correspondence with the gayer muses for some time.

During the year 1752 besides writing his articles for his journal Fielding found time in spite of his other duties to write a pamphlet of considerable length to help the cause of law and order to which he devoted himself so heroically during the last years of his life. He had pointed out in his paper early in the year that more shocking murders had been committed in England during the preceding twelve months than for many years before.[1] The case

[1] *The Covent Garden Journal*, No. 9, February 1, 1752, and No. 18, March 3, 1752.

of the notorious Miss Mary Blandy who had poisoned her father seems to have determined him to carry out a project which, as he tells us in his dedication of the work to the Bishop of Worcester, he had pondered over for some time and which he had discussed with the bishop.

The *Examples of the Interposition of Providence in the Detection and Punishment of Murder*, as the pamphlet was named, was published on the 13th of April, 1752.[1] It was intended to be a deterrent to the crime which had assumed such alarming proportions, and the advertisements announcing the publication of the pamphlet described it as "very proper to be given to all inferior kind of people and particularly to the youth of both sexes." *The Covent Garden Journal* even went to the length of suggesting that "no family ought to be without this book and it was most particularly calculated for the use of those schools in which children were taught to read."[2]

The pamphlet or book, as Fielding preferred to call it, is rather an interesting one and the writers evidently had given much care and thought to it. On the title page the introduction and conclusion only are declared to be the work of the novelist, and the manly vigour of Fielding's style is seen to great advantage in these parts of the work. As he had already done in *The Covent Garden Journal*, Fielding attributes the prevalence of murder to a general neglect of religion "which hath grown to be a kind of fashion and like other fashions hath gradually descended through all orders." And he solemnly asks his reader to remember that besides "the frequent declarations of God's most bitter wrath against this deadly sin and the fearful and tremendous sentence of eternal punishment

[1]*The General Advertiser*, April 13, 1752.
[2]*The Covent Garden Journal*, No. 30, April 14, 1752.

against it, the Divine providence has been pleased to interpose in a more immediate manner in the detection of this crime than of any other."

He gives thirty-three examples of this interposition of the Divine providence and these are taken from such various sources as Plutarch, Baker's *Chronicle*, Nathaniel Wanley's *Wonders of the Little World*, Henry More's *Immortality of the Soul*, and one or two other books which are altogether forgotten now.

Though Fielding's hand is traceable here and there in these "examples," the compilation of the stories seems to have been entrusted by the novelist to some friend or acquaintance, perhaps to William Young. The stories themselves are selected with care and judgment though occasionally they are a little too full of wonders. But it is hardly fair to cavil at this, as one of Fielding's biographers has done,[1] seeing that Fielding's object in citing these examples was to create as great an impression as possible in the minds of "the inferior kind of people" for whom his book was mainly intended and among whom it was freely distributed.

Apart from the revised version of *Jonathan Wild* that was published in March, 1754, to which we have already referred in a former chapter, the last two works from Fielding's pen that were given to the world before his death were his *Proposal for Making an Effectual Provision for the Poor* and the *Clear State of the Case of Elizabeth Canning*. The former, which is a kind of sequel to his *Enquiry Into the Causes of the Late Increase of Robbers*, was published in January, 1753.[2] It is a carefully written pamphlet of nearly a hundred pages which contain an in-

[1] W. L. Cross, *The History of Henry Fielding*, Vol. II, p. 270.
[2] *The Gentleman's Magazine*, January, 1753.

troduction, a statement of the proposals in different numbered paragraphs, and "arguments in explanation and support of the proposals" at the end. To these is added "a plan of the buildings proposed with proper elevations drawn by an eminent hand."

In his introduction to the proposals Fielding tells his reader that he "has applied himself long and constantly to this subject" and that he "has read over and considered all the laws in any wise relating to the poor with the utmost care and attention; and the conclusion to which he has come is that the laws for relieving the distresses of the poor and for restraining their vices have not answered their purposes," and this, he says, is "the universal voice of the nation."

In the same introduction he makes an earnest appeal on behalf of the poor and points out that their sufferings are less noticed than their misdeeds. "If we were," he says, "to make a progress through the outskirts of this town, and look into the habitations of the poor, we should there behold such pictures of human misery as must move the compassion of every heart that deserves the name of human. What indeed must be his composition who could see whole families in want of every necessary of life, oppressed with cold, nakedness, and filth, and with diseases, the certain consequence of all these; what I say must be his composition who could look into such a scene as this, and be affected only in his nostrils?"

The proposal that he put before the public was for a country workhouse with a house of correction adjoining where men and women to the number of six thousand and even more could be housed, kept under discipline and made to work, instruction being given to them "in the manufactures and mysteries now exercised in the kingdom." In this connection Fielding also suggested measures that might be adopted for the better prevention of vagrancy.

His proposals received little encouragement from the Government, perhaps because the cost of giving effect to them which the novelist estimated at £100,000 was felt to be excessive. Fielding, however, had not taken the matter up as a hobby, nor was he merely speculating as to what might be done. He was intensely earnest in his desire to see the amelioration of the conditions which made the life of the poor such a great hardship in these days. And we know from the evidence of his contemporaries that he was not content merely with drawing up paper schemes. He was always most willing and eager to lend his helping hand to the work of improving existing conditions, and his intimate knowledge of the slums of eighteenth-century London could only have been acquired by constant visits to the localities in which life presented the tragic spectacle that he describes more than once in his writings.

Fielding's last pamphlet, *A Clear State of the Case of Elizabeth Canning*, was published in March, 1753.[1] Like his earlier *True State of the Case of Bosavern Penlez* this was written to vindicate the judicial proceedings in one of the most sensational cases that London had known for some time. Elizabeth Canning, a young domestic servant apparently of good character, had disappeared from her master's house and after nearly a month's absence appeared in a most miserable condition in her mother's house and related rather an improbable story to the effect that she had been kept confined almost without food in the house of a Mrs. Wells in Enfield where she had been

[1] *The London Magazine*, April, 1753, Monthly Catalogue for March, 1753.

robbed of her stays by a gipsy woman named Mary
Squires. Squires and Wells were tried at the Old Bailey
and were both convicted, the gipsy woman receiving the
sentence of death.

The improbability of Elizabeth Canning's story and
the defence of Mary Squires that she was not in London
at the time the crime was alleged to have been committed
gave rise to a storm of controversy in which one of Fielding's most determined enemies in the journalistic world,
Dr. John Hill, took a leading part. The whole course of
the judicial proceedings was challenged and Sir Crisp
Gascoyne, the Lord Mayor of London, forwarded a me-
morial to the King which resulted in Mary Squires being
respited and pardoned. Elizabeth Canning was subse-
quently tried for perjury and convicted.

Fielding had taken some part in the judicial proceedings that had led up to the conviction of Mary Squires
and Mrs. Wells. The information of Elizabeth Canning
had been sworn before him and he had also examined
two women belonging to Mrs. Wells' house. His *Clear
State of the Case of Elizabeth Canning* was a reply to the
adverse comments that had been made in the newspapers
and in pamphlets on the conduct of the whole case.

He declares in the opening pages of his pamphlet that
his object is not merely to satisfy the curiosity of the public. He is anxious "to prevent them from forming a very
rash and possibly a very unjust judgment." He gives a
clear résumé of the whole case, describes fully the part he
had taken in the judicial proceedings, and admits that
Canning's story is "strange, unaccountable and scarcely
credible." But after subjecting the whole evidence
brought forward in the case to a very careful examination
he declares that he is as firmly persuaded as he is of any

S

fact in this world that Mary Squires was guilty. As to his own conduct in this affair he is inclined to believe that it entitled him to the very reverse of censure. But as he has no pretensions to infallibility he admits that he may have been imposed upon. Finally he suggests that since the issues at stake are momentous the best course to follow in the circumstances would be for the Government to authorize some able and entirely unbiased people to scrutinize the case to the bottom and particularly into the alibi defence of Mary Squires.

After the publication of this pamphlet Fielding did not apparently undertake any literary work of importance during the rest of the year. By the middle of the year the state of his health was such that his physicians advised him to go immediately to Bath. But as he was making preparations for the journey he received repeated summons from the Duke of Newcastle who desired to consult him about the measures that could be most effectivly employed to deal with the alarming increase in robberies and murders in London. Fielding undertook to outline a plan of operations which in due course was submitted to the authorities. This plan, of which the main feature was the breaking up of a gang of criminals who were mainly responsible for the prevalence of crime, was carried out with complete success as soon as the necessary funds were placed at the disposal of Fielding.

But the hard work that he had undertaken, particularly that of examining the criminals who were apprehended, and of taking depositions against them, resulted in a complete breakdown in his health and in the winter he went into the country "in a very weak and deplorable condition," as he tells us himself, "with no fewer or less diseases than a jaundice, a dropsy, and an asthma, altogether uniting their forces in the destruction of a body so entirely emaciated that it had lost all its muscular flesh."[1]

He returned to town in February, 1754, and placed himself under the treatment of Dr. Ward whose medicines producing no good results the trocar was used to draw off the accumulations due to the dropsy which by this time had assumed serious proportions. He tried a course of tar water with a little more success; but the disease continued its ravages, and the summer on which he and his friends had placed their hopes proving to be a particularly bad one, he was advised to try the effects of a warmer climate. Lisbon was the place that was finally decided on for a change, and he set out on his journey in search of health on the 26th of June, 1754, accompanied by his wife, his eldest daughter, and Margaret Collier of Salisbury, daughter of Arthur Collier the metaphysician. It was during this journey that he wrote his memorable *Journal of a Voyage to Lisbon*, a work of great biographical as well as literary value. The idea of writing the journal first came into his mind while the ship, the *Queen of Portugal*, which was conveying him to Lisbon was lying off the coast of Deal waiting for a favourable wind. Fielding and his party reached their destination on the 7th of August and the warmer air of the South seems to have wrought a slight improvement in his health at first. But the "complications of his disorders" had made fatal progress and the change of climate only brought a short respite of two months to the novelist. He died in a little villa that he had taken at Junqueira about two miles from Lisbon on the 8th of October, 1754.

Fielding's last great work, *The Journal of a Voyage to Lisbon*, was published after his death by Millar in a duo-

[1]Introduction, *The Journal of a Voyage to Lisbon.*

decimo volume which also contained a fragment of *A Comment on Lord Bolingbroke's Essays*. David Mallet's edition of *Bolingbroke's Works* appeared in March, 1754, and soon after this Fielding seems to have made up his mind to controvert the ideas of the great sceptic. In spite of his broken health he entered on his self-imposed task with remarkable energy, making, as Murphy tells us, "long extracts from the Fathers and the most eminent writers of controversy." His aim was to subject Bolingbroke's opinions to a searching examination and to point out the danger and fallacy of his conclusions. The fragment of the contemplated work that he has left behind him shows that though Fielding was not a theologian he was well qualified by his learning and his remarkable gifts of eloquent and lucid expression for the task he had undertaken. His biographer Lawrence praises the work enthusiastically and suggests that it can challenge a comparison with the best controversial productions of the period.[1]

The Journal of a Voyage to Lisbon, though it can scarcely be described as one of Fielding's masterpieces, is nevertheless a work of exceptional interest. During the year that followed Fielding's death two versions of the journal were published by Millar. As the extracts from the registers of William Strahan the printer made by Mr. R. A. Austen Leigh disclose,[2] the original manuscript of the journal as Fielding had left it was being printed by Strahan for Millar when someone intervened, and a reprint of the book with "extraordinary corrections," which Strahan's registers describe as a second edition, was taken in hand. This was the first published edition of the work and

---

[1] Frederick Lawrence, *The Life of Henry Fielding*, p. 361.
[2] *The Library*, April, 1917, p. 154.

it came out on the 25th of February, 1755.[1] In November Millar seems to have decided to take advantage of the sensation caused by the great earthquake in Lisbon to push the sale of the first impression of the book which had been lying on his hands all this time. The publication of the journal was now advertised again, and this version of the book was issued during the first week in December.[2]

The two versions of the journal contained the same dedication to the public which, after giving an "affecting picture" of the late novelist's trembling hand and emaciated body in order "to open each tender heart and call forth a melting tear," declared that it had been thought proper by the friends of the novelist that the book should come into the hands of the public in the same form in which it had been left by the author. As a matter of fact, however, as the "extraordinary corrections" mentioned in Strahan's register would lead one to expect, the two versions of the journal differed greatly from each other. The earlier version had passed through the hands of an editor, evidently Fielding's brother John, who succeeded him as magistrate in Bow Street; and it was felt that the journal as Fielding had left it contained many statements and expressions of opinion which it would be unwise to communicate to the public. The "editor," therefore, had made a number of excisions from the original text of the journal and manipulated it considerably. The most notable of the alterations consisted of the omission of a number of passages from the book which gave very unfavourable accounts of the captain of the ship and his nephew, a lieutenant in the army, who had come to visit him. Fielding's portrait of Captain Veale (that was the name of the

---

[1] *The Public Advertiser*, February 25, 1755.
[2] *The Whitehall Evening Post*, November 29 to December 2, 1755.

man, though Fielding was careful in suppressing it in the journal) is that of a bully and a swaggerer who tried to pass himself off as a gentleman, a character to which his conduct gave the lie. The "editor" transformed this portrait completely by obliterating all the disfiguring touches from it, and exhibited the character to the readers of the journal as that of a gallant old sea-dog. In the same way the striking picture of the "pretty fellow," the lieutenant, was altogether toned down to the commonplace.

The motives that prompted these changes are obvious. The men whose frailties Fielding had described with such freedom were still alive, and one can understand and make some allowance for the editor's action in making his excisions. He also changed the name of the landlady at Ryde in whose house the travellers had stayed for some time; and at the commencement of the journal a number of sentences in which Fielding referred to the Duke of Newcastle were altered to make them absolutely innocuous.

And yet, shorn as it was of much of its beauty, the book was well received. The periodicals had nothing but praise to give to it. *The Gentleman's Magazine*, which had always been more or less niggardly in commending Fielding's work, remarked that "the captain, the seamen, the landlady and her husband and several other characters were described with that humour in which he is confessed to have excelled every other writer of his age" and the book was very valuable for the instruction it contained.[1] *The Monthly Review* was more patronizing in its attitude, but it described the reflections contained in the book as "worthy of a writer than whom few, if any, have been

[1] *The Gentleman's Magazine*, March, 1755.

more justly celebrated for a thorough insight into human nature."[1] *The London Magazine* also reviewed the journal in an equally appreciative strain.

But some among Fielding's well-known contemporaries were inclined to undervalue it. To Lady Mary Montagu the most edifying part of the journal was "the history of the kitten,"[2] that is to say, the history of its rescue from drowning and its subsequent death from suffocation to which Fielding had given some space in his book. Horace Walpole, again, described "Fielding's Travels" as "an account how his dropsy was treated and teased by an innkeeper's wife in the Isle of Wight."[3]

It is not difficult to understand the attitude of these readers to the last great work of Fielding. Being contemporaries of the novelist they did not find the same interest in the biographical information contained in the book that succeeding generations of Fielding's readers have. And evidently some of those who were inclined to underrate the merits of the journal had read only the abridged and mutilated edition of the work that was first brought out.

Still, the pronouncements of Lady Mary and Horace Walpole reflect little credit on their discernment. The former's opinion, if opinion it can be called at all, scarcely needs any comment. Walpole's criticism is almost equally inept. The book is in no sense a history of the physical infirmities from which Fielding suffered so much during the last years of his life. In his introduction to the journal he refers to his dropsy more than once and describes the

[1] *The Monthly Review*, March, 1755.
[2] *The Letters and Works of Lady Mary Wortley Montagu*, edited by Lord Wharncliffe, 1861. Letter to the Countess of Bute, Vol. II, p. 283.
[3] *The Letters of Horace Walpole*, edited by Mrs. Paget Toynbee. Vol. III, p. 294.

state of his health at some length because these were the
occasion of the voyage. But in giving his account of the
voyage itself Fielding shows little tendency to dwell on
his own sufferings. The journal deals with a great variety
of subjects and one of its most notable features is the vivacity of spirit which lightens up many of its pages; and
this vivacity appears all the more surprising when one
remembers that Fielding's physical sufferings were very
great indeed at the time the journal was written. In describing the circumstances in which the idea had its
origin Fielding tells his reader that some of the most
amusing pages of the journal were "possibly the production of the most disagreeable hours which ever haunt-
ed the author."

The journal is a document of particular interest to the
admirers of Fielding's genius and character, not only because it furnishes valuable information about the events
of the last year of his life, but also because it reveals the
indomitable gallantry of spirit of the man. When he set
out on his journey he knew that his days were numbered
and that he had little chance of seeing his native land
again or those dear ones whom he was leaving behind.
The well-known opening words of the journal make this
clear enough. And yet in spite of this knowledge and the
terrible sufferings caused by his many diseases Fielding
is able to breathe into his last great work a spirit of calm
resignation and even of cheerfulness which is almost
unique in the annals of literature. There are no repinings
or complaints of the ill usage of the world in the journal.
The story of the ravages made by disease is related almost
without comment. And as one reads the narrative of the
incidents that varied the monotony of his last journey in
search of health one realizes that though Fielding's phy-

sical frame is exhausted the spirit of enjoyment of the good and humorous things of life is still there, not much impaired. He speaks of his enjoyment of a hearty meal with a gusto that recalls the Fielding of younger days who, according to Lady Mary Montagu, could forget everything when he was before a venison pasty or over a flask of champagne.[1] In describing the misfortunes that overtook the kitten on board the ship Fielding gives his reader a taste of that infectious gaiety of spirit which finds such magnificent expression in *Joseph Andrews* and *Tom Jones*. Arthur Murphy bears witness to this irrepressible vivacity in Fielding in language that is more picturesque than happy. "In this last sketch," Murphy says, "he puts us in mind of a person under sentence of death jesting on a scaffold."[2]

Like many other statements made by Murphy this does much less than justice to Fielding because it is far from being a good and sufficient description of his humour in the journal. There is little of "jesting" in the book in the ordinary acceptance of the term, though there is much quiet and even grim humour and a good deal of Fielding's characteristic irony. This humour is seen to great advantage in some of the character sketches in the journal, and in these we have abundant evidence that the master's hand has lost none of its cunning.

The portrait of the captain of the ship or "the bashaw," as Fielding effectively describes him, is of special interest, because in this the novelist tries his hand at the description of the sea-faring man for the first time in his life. We have a very vivid picture indeed of Captain Veale as he

[1] *The Letters and Works of Lady Mary Wortley Montagu*, edited by Lord Wharncliffe, 1861, Letter to the Countess of Bute, Vol. II, p. 283.
[2] "An Essay on the Life and Genius of Henry Fielding, Esq.," prefixed to Murphy's edition of Fielding's Works, 1762.

was in real life, with his swaggering ways, his pretensions
to gentility and his efforts at gallantry, though Fielding
is scrupulously just to him and does not ignore the good
that there was in the man. A description like the following
shows that Fielding's eye is as keen as ever in noticing
peculiarities in men and manners, and that his hand is as
skilful as in the days gone by in portraying them with a
very sure instinct for striking effects.

"He was a person," Fielding says after telling us something of Captain Veale's past life, "of a very singular
character. He had taken it into his head that he was a
gentleman, from those very reasons that proved he was
not one; and to show himself a fine gentleman, by a behaviour which seemed to insinuate he had never seen
one. He was, moreover, a man of gallantry; at the age of
seventy he had the finicalness of Sir Courtly Nice, with
the roughness of Surly; and, while he was deaf himself,
had a voice capable of deafening all others."[1]

And in the course of the narrative we have many other
touches that give the portrait its finished individuality,
the captain's fondness for animals, for example, and his
"lamentations" on the death of the kitten, or his fright and
abject servility when "the most distant sound of law"
reaches his ears.

Some of the other portraits in the journal also, that of
the Swiss captain, the "brother bashaw" who visits Captain Veale in his ship; or the picture of the latter's nephew
the lieutenant, full of oaths like Ensign Northerton, but
more harmless, with his pretensions to wit and fashion,
"much too pretty a fellow at his years," and "so very
merry that he laughed at everything he said, and always

[1] These words are quoted from the "unedited" version of the Journal. They
are omitted in the other version.

before he spoke"; and more striking than these, Mrs.
Francis, renamed Mrs. Humphrys in the "edited" version of the journal, the rapacious landlady at Ryde, and
her husband, so like the Tow-wouses of *Joseph Andrews*
—these and one or two others certainly deserve a place in
the splendid portrait galleries of the novels.

And it was singularly appropriate that Fielding should
say his *vale* to his readers in a work like *The Journal of a
Voyage to Lisbon*. We see the most remarkable of all his
gifts perhaps, his powers of humorous portraiture, not
only exhibited in the finished portraits themselves but we
can observe the powers actually at work painting the portraits from living originals. The journal, again, is characteristic of Fielding's genius in the sound views that it
contains on many a subject of great interest. Its greatest
claim to the attention of the admirer of Fielding, however, is that it is the most "human" of all the documents
that the great novelist has left behind him, revealing as it
does the innate magnanimity of character and the magnificent serenity of temper of the man which rise superior
to the lapses that the malice of the detractor had triumph-
ed over or the scruples of the apologist had deprecated.

BIBLIOGRAPHY

THE/MASQUERADE,/A/POEM./INSCRIBED TO/C - - - T H - - D - - G - - R./|/—*Velut ægri somnia, vanæ*/—*Species*— Hor. Art. Poet./||/By LEMUEL GULLIVER,/Poet Laureat to the King of LILLIPUT./|[ornament]||/LONDON,/Printed, and sold by J. ROBERTS, in Warwick-lane;/and A. DODD, at the Peacock, without Temple-bar./MDCCXVIII./| /[Price Six-pence]/

8vo. Title p [i]. Blank p [ii]. Dedication pp [iii-iv]. Text pp [1]-11.

First published Jan. 29, 1728 (*The Craftsman*, Jan. 27.) Published with *The Grub Street Opera*, 1731. In the Bodleian.

Reprinted in the *Miscellaneous Works of Dr. Arbuthnot*, Glasgow, 1750.

Never included in any edition of Fielding's Works.

THE PLAYS

LOVE/IN SEVERAL/MASQUES./A/COMEDY,/As it is
Acted at the/THEATRE-ROYAL,/BY HIS MAJESTY's
Servants.///Written by Mr. *FIELDING*.///*Nec Veneris Phare-
tris macer est, nec Lampade fervet;/Inde faces ardent; veniunt a
Dote Sagittæ.*/Juv. Sat. 6///*LONDON*:/Printed for JOHN
WATTS, at the Printing-Office/in *Wild-Court*, near *Lincoln's-
Inn-Fields*. 1728./[Price 1s. 6d.]

8vo. Title p [i]. Blank p [ii]. Dedication, "To the Right
Honourable the Lady Mary Wortley Mountague," pp [iii-vi].
Preface pp [vii-viii]. Prologue p [ix]. Dramatis Personæ p [x].
Text pp [3]-82. Epilogue [1] p.

In the Bodleian and the British Museum.

Another Edition, Dublin, 1728.

German Translation, Strasburg, 1782.

THE/*TEMPLE* BEAU./A/COMEDY./As it is Acted at the/
THEATRE in *Goodman's-Fields*.///Written by Mr. *FIELD-
ING*.///*Non aliter, quam qui adverso vix Flumine Lembum/
Remigiis subigit.* Virg. Georg./*Indignor quidquam reprehendi, non
quia crassè/Compositum, illepidève putetur, sed quia* Nobis./Hor.
Art. Poet.///[ornament]///*LONDON*:/Printed for J. WATTS,
at the Printing-Office in/*Wild-Court* near *Lincolns-Inn Fields*./
//MDCCXXX.[*Price* 1s. 6d.]

8vo. Title p [i]. Advt p [ii]. Prologue p [iii]. Dramatis
Personæ p [iv]. Text pp [1]-80. Epilogue [1] p. 2 Songs [2]
pp. Advt [1] p.

In the Bodleian and the British Museum.

Another Edition, Dublin, 1730.

German Translation, Mannheim, 1782.

THE/AUTHOR'S FARCE;/AND THE/*Pleasures of the Town.*/As
Acted at the/THEATRE in the *Hay-Market*.///Written by

Scriblerus Secundus./|/—*Quis* iniquæ/*Tam patiens urbis, tam ferreus, ut teneat se?*/Juv. Sat. 1./|||/*LONDON*:|Printed for J. ROBERTS, in *Warwick-Lane.*/||/MDCCXXX. [Price 1s. 6d.]

8vo. Title p [i]. Blank p [ii]. Prologue pp [iii-iv]. 2 Songs pp [v-vi]. Persons in the Farce p [vii]. Persons in the Puppet-Show p [viii]. Text pp [1]-59. Epilogue [4] pp.

In the Bodleian.
Second Edition, London, 1730.
Third Edition, London, 1750.
Another Edition, Dublin 1730.

TOM THUMB./A/TRAGEDY./ As it is Acted at the/ THEATRE/IN THE/*HAY - MARKET.*/| [ornament] /|||/*LON-DON,*/Printed: And Sold by J. ROBERTS in/*Warwick-Lane.* 1730.

8vo. Title p [i]. [ornament] p [ii]. Advt p [iii]. Blank p [iv]. Dramatis Personæ p [v]. Blank p [vi]. Text pp [1]-16.
In the Bodleian.
Second Edition, revised, with Preface, Prologue and Epilogue. London 1730.
Third Edition: London 1730.
Another Edition: Dublin, 1730.

RAPE *upon* RAPE;/OR, THE/JUSTICE/*Caught in his own* TRAP./A/COMEDY./As it is Acted at the/Theatre in the *Hay-Market.*/|/[ornament]/|||/*LONDON*:/Printed for J.WATS, at the Printing-Office in/*Wild-Court* near *Lincolns-Inn Fields.* /||/MDCCXXX./ Price One Shilling and Six Pence.

8vo. Title p [i]. Blank p [ii]. Prologue pp [iii-iv]. Epilogue pp [v-vi]. Advt p [vii]. Dramatis Personæ p [viii]. Text pp [1]-78.
In the Bodleian and the British Museum.

THE/Coffee-House *Politician*;/OR, THE/JUSTICE/*Caught in his own* TRAP./A/COMEDY./As it is Acted at the/Theatre Royal in *Lincoln's-Inn-Fields.*/||/Written by MR. *FIELDING.*

/|[ornament]||/*LONDON*:/ Printed for J. WATTS, at the Printing-Office in/*Wild-Court* near *Lincolns-Inn-Fields*./| /MDCCXXX./Price One Shilling and Six Pence.

8vo. Title p [i]. Blank p [ii]. Prologue pp [iii-iv]. Epilogue pp [v-vi]. Advt p [vii]. Dramatis Personæ p [viii]. Text pp [1]-78.

Title "Rape upon Rape or The Justice Caught in his own Trap" retained on p [1] of the text.

The Epilogue different from that in the first edition of the play.

In the Bodleian and the British Museum.

THE/TRAGEDY/OF/*TRAGEDIES*;/OR THE/LIFE *and* DEATH/OF/TOM THUMB *the Great.*/As it is Acted at the/ THEATRE in the *Hay-Market.*/ With the ANNOTATIONS of/*H. SCRIBLERUS SECUNDUS*.|||/*LONDON*,/Printed; And Sold by *J. Roberts* in *Warwick-Lane.*|||/MDCCXXXI./Price One Shilling.

8vo. Frontispiece, plate by Hogarth. Title p [i]. Blank p [ii]. "H Scriblerus Secundus; His Preface" pp [iii-vii]. Dramatis Personæ p [viii]. Text pp [1]-58.

In the British Museum.

OTHER EDITIONS

LONDON.

1737 (Third Edition). 1751 (Fourth Edition). 1765. 1776. 1780. 1805 (altered by Kane O'Hara). 1806 (Cawthorn's *Minor British Theatre*, Vol 1). 1810? (Fairburn's *Complete Edition*). 1811 (Altered by Kane O'Hara. *The Modern British Drama*, Vol 5). 1815 (Altered by Kane O'Hara. *A Collection of Farces* Selected by Mrs. Inchbald, Vol 6). 1824 (*The British Drama*, Vol 1). 1829 (Cumberland's *British Theatre*, Vol 23). 1830 (With illustrations by G. Cruikshank). 1838 (Thomas's *Burlesque Drama*). 1861(Lacy's *Acting Edition of Plays*). 1884 (*Tom Thumb, a burlesque Opera*, altered from Fielding by Kane

O'Hara. Dicks' *Standard Plays*). 1885 (*Burlesque Plays and Poems*). 1925 (Edited by John Hampden. *Garrick Playbooks*).
DUBLIN.
   1743.
NEW YORK.
   1825 (*Living Plays*, Vol 2). 1914 (*Representative English Dramas from Dryden to Sheridan*).
BERLIN.
   1899.
NEWHAVEN.
   1918 (Edited by James T. Hillhouse).

THE/LETTER-WRITERS:/Or, a New Way to Keep/*A* WIFE *at* HOME./A/FARCE,/In THREE ACTS./As it is Acted at the/THEATRE in the *Hay-Market*./||/Written by *Scriblerus Secundus*./|[ornament]|||/*LONDON*,/Printed; and Sold by *J. Roberts* in *Warwick-Lane*./||/MDCCXXXI./ [Price One Shilling]
   8vo. Title p [i]. Blank p [ii]. Advt p [iii]. Dramatis Personæ p [iv]. Text pp [5]-48.
   In the Bodleian.

OTHER EDITIONS

   LONDON. 1740 and 1750.
   German Translation. Mannheim 1781.

THE/WELSH OPERA:/ OR, THE/*Grey* MARE *the better* HORSE./ As it is Acted at the/NEW THEATRE/IN THE/*HAY-MARKET*./||Written by SCRIBLERUS SECUNDUS,/Author of the *Tragedy of Tragedies*./|||Cobler. *Say, why what d'ye think I say? I say,/All men are married for their Sins,/And that a Batchelor Cobler, is happier than a/Hen-peck'd Prince*./|||*LONDON*:/ Printed for *E. Rayner*, and sold by *H. Cook*, at the/*Hawk*, near *Water-Lane*, and at the *Golden-Ball*, near/*Chancery-Lane*, both in *Fleet Street*./Price One Shilling.

8vo. Half Title p [i]. Blank p [ii]. Title p [iii]. Blank p [iv].
Preface pp i-ii. Introduction pp i-iii. Dramatis Personæ [i] p.
Text pp [i]-39. Advt [i] p.
In the Bodleian.

The GENUINE/Grub=Street/OPERA./As it was intended
to be Acted at the/NEW THEATRE/IN THE/HAY-
MARKET./||/Written by Scriblerus Secundus./|||/Nom. Hic,
haec. hoc./Gen. Hujus./ Dat. Huic./ Acc. Hunc, hanc, hoc./
Voc. Caret./||/LONDON: Printed and Sold for the Benefit of
the Comedi-/ans of the NEW THEATRE in the Hay-market./
MDCCXXXI./[Price One Shilling and Sixpence.]
8vo. Title p [i]. Blank p [ii]. Introduction pp iii-vii. Dramatis
Personæ p [viii]. Text pp 9-64.
In the Bodleian.

THE/GRUB-STREET/OPERA./As it is Acted at the/
THEATRE in the HAY-MARKET./||/By SCRIBLERUS SECUNDUS./||/
Sing. Nom. Hic, Hæc, Hoc./Gen. Hujus./Dat. Huic./Accus.
Hunc, Hanc, Hoc./Voc. Caret. Lil. Gram. quod vid./||/To which
is added,/THE/MASQUERADE,/A/POEM./Printed in
MDCCXXVIII./||/LONDON,/Printed, and sold by J. ROBERTS, in
Warwick-lane./MDCCXXXI./[Price One Shilling and Six-pence.]
8vo. Title p [i]. Blank p [ii]. Dramatis Personæ p [iii]. Blank
p [iv]. Introduction pp [v-vii]. Blank p [viii]. Text pp [i]-56.
In the Bodleian.

THE/LOTTERY./A/FARCE./As it is Acted at the/Theatre-
Royal in Drury-Lane,/BY/HIS MAJESTY's Servants./||/With
the MUSICK prefix'd to each SONG./||/LONDON:/Printed for J.
WATTS at the Printing-Office in Wild-Court near Lincoln's-Inn
Fields./||/MDCCXXXII./[Price One Shilling.]
8vo. Title p [i]. Advt pp [ii-v]. Prologue p [vi]. "A Table of
the Songs" p [vii]. Dramatis Personæ p [viii]. Text pp [i]-31.
Epilogue [i] p.
In the Bodleian and the British Museum.

OTHER EDITIONS

LONDON.

1732 (Second Edition). 1732 (Third Edition). 1733. 1748 (Fourth Edition). 1761. 1779. 1784 (Supplement to Bell's *British Theatre*, Vol 2).

GLASGOW.

1758.

DUBLIN.

1759.

EDINBURGH.

1786 (*The British Stage. A Collection of the Most Esteemed Farces*, Vol. 2). 1792.

THE/*MODERN HUSBAND.*/A/COMEDY./As it is Acted at the THEATRE-ROYAL/ in DRURY-LANE./By His MAJES-TY's Servants./|/Written by *HENRY FIELDING*, Esq;/| |*Haec ego non credam Venusinâ digna Lucernâ?*/*Hâec ego non agitem?— ——*/*Cùm Leno accipiat Mœchi bona, si capiendi*/ *Jus nullum Uxori, doctus spectare Lacunar,*/*Doctus & ad Calicem vigilanti stertere Naso.* Juv. Sat. 1./[ornament]/ *LONDON:*/Printed for J. WATTS at the Printing-Office in *Wild-Court* near *Lincoln's-Inn Fields*/|/MDCCXXXII. [Price 1s. 6d.]

8vo. Title p [i]. Blank p [ii]. Dedication "To the Right Honourable Sir Robert Walpole." pp [iii-v]. Prologue p [vi]. Epilogue p [vii]. Dramatis Personæ p [viii]. Text pp [1]-81. Epilogue [2] pp. Advt [5] pp.

In the Bodleian.

London 1732 (Second Edition). Dublin 1732.

German translation, Strasburg 1781.

Another German translation, Mannheim (no date).

THE/*Old DEBAUCHEES.*/A/COMEDY./As it is Acted at the THEATRE-ROYAL/in DRURY-LANE./By His MAJESTY'S Servants./|/By the Author of the MODERN HUSBAND./|[ornament]/*LONDON*:/Printed for J. W. And Sold by J. ROBERTS in/*Warwick-Lane*, MDCCXXXII./[Price One Shilling.]

8vo. Title p [i]. Blank p [ii]. Prologue p [iii]. Dramatis Personæ p [iv]. Text pp [1]-40.

In the British Museum and the Bodleian.

Title changed to "The Debauchees: or The Jesuit Caught" and the play reprinted London 1745, 1746, 1750 and 1780.

THE/*COVENT-GARDEN*/TRAGEDY./As it is Acted at the THEATRE-ROYAL/in DRURY-LANE./By His MAJESTY's Servants./||/—*quæ amanti parcet, eadem sibi parcet parum./ Quasi piscis, itidem est amator lenæ: nequam est nisi recens./ Is habet succum; is suavitatem; eum quovis pacto condias;/Vel patinarium vel assum: verses, quo pacto lubet./Is dare volt, is se aliquid posci, nam ubi de pleno promitur,/Neque ille scit, quid det quid damni faciat; illi rei studet:/Volt placere sese a micæ, volt mihi, pedissequæ,/Volt famulis, volt etiam ancillis: & quoque catulo meo/Subblanditur novus amator, se ut quum videat, gaudeat./* Plautus. Asinar./||/*LONDON*:/Printed for J. WATTS, and Sold by J. ROBERTS/in *Warwick-Lane*./||/MDCCXXXII./[Price One Shilling.]

8vo. Title p [i]. Blank p [ii]. Prolegomena pp 1-3. "A Criticism on the Covent-Garden Tragedy," originally intended for the Grub Street Journal pp 4-11. Prologue [1] p. Epilogue [1] p. Dramatis Personæ [1] p. Text pp [1]-32.

In the Bodleian and the British Museum.

OTHER EDITIONS

London 1754 and 1780.

THE/MOCK DOCTOR:/OR/*The* DUMB LADY *Cur'd.*/A/ COMEDY./Done from *MOLIERE.*/As it is Acted at the THEATRE-ROYAL/in DRURY-LANE,/By His MAJESTY's Servants./||/*With the* MUSICK *prefix'd to each* SONG./||/[ornament]/*LONDON*:/Printed for J. WATTS at the Printing-Office in/*Wild-Court* near *Lincoln's-Inn Fields.*/||/MDCCXXXII. [Price One Shilling]

8vo. Title p [i]. Blank p [ii]. Dedication "To Dr. John Misaubin" pp [iii-v]. Preface p [vi]. "A Table of the Songs" p [vii]. Dramatis Personæ p [viii]. Text pp [1]-32.
In the Bodleian.

OTHER EDITIONS

LONDON.

1732 (Second Edition, with additional songs and alterations.) 1734. 1742 (Third Edition). 1753 (Fourth Edition). 1760. 1761. 1779. 1784 (Supplement to Bell's *British Theatre*, vol 1). 1794. 1806 (Cawthorn's *Minor British Theatre*, Vol 3). 1811 (*The Modern British Drama*, Vol. 5. Operas and Farces). 1815 (T. Dibdin. *The London Theatre*, Vol 20). 1815 (Mrs. Inchbald's *Collection of Farces*, etc., Vol 5). 1824 (*The British Drama*, Vol 1). 1824 (*The London Stage*, Vol. II). 1856 (*The Irish Doctor or the Dumb Lady Cured. A Farce*... Altered from Fielding's translation of Molière's *Malgre Lui* by G. Wood. Lacy's Acting Edition of Plays, Vol. 27). 1883 Dick's *Standard Plays*. No. 200). 1893 (*Plays from Molière by English Dramatists*. Lubbock's *Hundred Books*. No. 61).

DUBLIN.

1735. 1752.

BELFAST.

1763.

EDINBURGH.

1782. 1786 (*A Collection of the Most Esteemed Farces*, Vol. I). 1792.

THE/MISER./A/COMEDY./*Taken from* PLAUTUS *and* MOLIERE./As it is Acted at the THEATRE-ROYAL in/*Drury-Lane*, by His Majesty's Servants.///By *HENRY FIELDING*, Esq;///*Servorum ventres modio castigat iniquo,*/*Ipse quoque esuriens: neque enim omnia sustinet unquam*/*Mucida cœrulei panis consumere frusta,*/*Hesternum solitus medio servare minutal*/*Septembri; nec non differe in tempora cœnæ*/*Alterius, conchem æstivi cum parte lacerti*/*Signatam, vel dimidio putríque siluro,*/

Filáque sęctivi numerata includere porri.|Invitatus ad hæc aliquis de ponte negabit.|Sed quò divitias hæc per tormenta coactas?| Cùm furor haud dubius, cùm sit manifesta phrenesis,| Ut locuples moriaris, egenti vivere fato? Juven./|||/*LONDON:*/Printed for J. WATTS at the Printing-Office in *Wild-Court* near *Lincoln's-Inn Fields.*/||/MDCCXXXIII. Price 1s. 6d.

8vo. Title p [i]. Blank p [ii]. Dedication "To His Grace Charles Duke of Richmond and Lenox," pp [iii-vi]. Prologue p [vii]. Epilogue p [viii]. Advt pp [ix-xi]. Dramatis Personæ p [xii]. Text pp [1]-87. Advt. [1] p.

In the Bodleian and the British Museum.

OTHER EDITIONS

EDINBURGH.

1733. 1768. 1774.

DUBLIN.

1733. 1741. 1762. 1788.

LONDON.

1744 (Second Edition). 1754 (Third Edition). 1761 (Fourth Edition). 1769 (Fifth Edition). 1775 (Sixth Edition). 1776 (Bell's *British Theatre*, Vol 6). 1776 (*The New English Theatre*, Vol 1). 1792. 1802. 1807. 1811 (*The Modern British Drama*, Vol 4, Comedies). 1815 (T. Dibdin, *The London Theatre*, Vol 24). 1818 (*The New English Drama*. Edited by W. H. Oxberry, Vol 11). 1824 (*The London Stage*, Vol 1). 1829 (Cumberland's *British Theatre*, Vol xxxv). 1850 (Lacy's *Acting Edition of Plays*, Vol 103). 1884 (Dicks' *Standard Plays*, No. 146). 1893 (*Plays from Molière by English Dramatists*. Lubbock's *Hundred Books*, No. 61).

GLASGOW.

1748. 1755. 1769.

Deborah, or A Wife for You All. By Henry Fielding. 1733. Never Printed.

THE/Intriguing Chambermaid. /A/COMEDY /Of TWO ACTS./As it is Acted at the/THEATRE-ROYAL in *Drury-Lane,*/

By His MAJESTY's Servants.///Taken from the *French* of REGNARD,/By *HENRY FIELDING, Esq*;///*Majores nusquam ronchi: juvenésque senésque,/Et pueri nasum Rhinocerotis habent.* Martial.///*LONDON:*/Printed for J. WATTS at the Printing Office in *Wild-Court* near *Lincoln's-Inn Fields*/// MDCCXXXIV./[Price One Shilling.]

8vo. Title p [i]. Blank p [ii]. "An Epistle to Mrs. Clive" pp [iii-vi]. Verses addressed "To Mr. Fielding, occasioned by the Revival of the Author's Farce. Sent to the Author by an unknown Hand," pp [vii-viii]. Prologue, pp [ix-x]. Epilogue, pp [x-xi]. Dramatis Personæ, Table of the Songs p [xii]. Text pp [1]-40.

In the Bodleian.

OTHER EDITIONS

DUBLIN.

1748. 1758.

LONDON. 1750. 1761. 1776. 1780. 1784 (Supplement to Bell's *British Theatre*, Vol 3). 1790 (altered). 1806 (Cawthorn's *Minor British Theatre*, Vol 6). 1811 (*The Modern British Drama*, Vol 5. Operas and Farces). 1824 (*The British Drama*. Vol 2).

CORK.

1765.

EDINBURGH.

1783. 1786 (*A Collection of the Most Esteemed Farces*, Vol III)

MANNHEIM.

1782 (German Translation).

DON QUIXOTE/IN/*ENGLAND*./A/COMEDY./As it is Acted at the/NEW THEATRE in the *Hay-Market.*///By *HENRY FIELDING*, Esq;///*—facilé quis/Speret idem, sudet multúm, frustráque laboret,/Ausus idem*—Hor.////*LONDON*:/ Printed for J. WATTS at the Printing-Office in/*Wild-Court* near *Lincoln's-Inn Fields.*///MDCCXXXIV./[Price One Shilling and Six Pence]

8vo. Title p [i]. Blank p [ii]. Dedication, "To the Right Honourable Philip Earl of Chesterfield " pp [iii-viii.] Preface pp [ix-xi]. "A Table of the Songs "p [xii]. Dramatis Personæ p [xiii]. Introduction pp. [xiv-xvi]. Text pp [1]-64. In the British Museum and the Bodleian.

OTHER EDITIONS
LONDON.

1754. 1772 (*Squire Badger*, a burletta in two parts (in verse) altered from Fielding's *Don Quixote in England*). 1775 (*The Sot*, a burletta in two parts, altered from Fielding's *Don Quixote in England*, by T. T. Arne). 1777.
EDINBURGH.

1760.

AN/OLD MAN *taught* WISDOM;/ OR, THE/ VIRGIN UN-MASK'D./A/FARCE./As it is Perform'd/By His MAJESTY's Company of/COMEDIANS at the THEATRE-/ROYAL in *Drury-Lane*./||/With the MUSICK *prefix'd to each* SONG./||/ *LONDON*:/ Printed for JOHN WATTS at the Printing-Office/ in *Wild-Court* near *Lincoln's-Inn Fields*./||/MDCCXXXV./Price One Shilling.

8vo. Title p [i]. Blank p [ii]. Table of the Songs p [iii]. Dramatis Personæ p [iv]. Text pp [1]-34. Song [2] pp.
In the Bodleian.

OTHER EDITIONS
LONDON.

1735 (Second Edition). 1742 (Third Edition). 1749 (Fourth Edition). 1770. 1777. 1784 (Altered. Supplement to Bell's *British Theatre*, Vol 2). 1786 (*A Musical Entertainment in one Act* . . . With Alterations). 1787. 1791. 1815 (T. Dibdin, *The London Theatre*, Vol 23). 1824 (*The London Stage*, Vol 3).
DUBLIN.

1740. 1747. 1762.
GLASGOW.

1761.

CORK.

1762.

EDINBURGH.

1782. 1786 (*A Collection of the Most Esteemed Farces*, (Vol 2).

THE/*UNIVERSAL GALLANT*:/OR, THE/DIFFERENT HUS-BANDS./A/COMEDY./As it is Acted at the/THEATRE-ROYAL in Drury-Lane./By His MAJESTY's Servants.///By *HENRY FIELDING*, Esq;////*Infœlix, habitum temporis hujus habe.* Ovid.///*LONDON*:/Printed for JOHN WATTS, at the Print-ing-/Office in *Wild-Court* near *Lincolns-Inn-Fields*/// MDCCXXXV./[Price One Shilling and Six Pence]

8vo. Title p [i]. Blank p [ii]. Dedication, "To His Grace Charles Duke of Marlborough," pp [iii-v]. Advertisement p [vi]. Prologue p [vii]. Dramatis Personæ p [viii]. Text pp [1]-82. Epilogue [2] pp.

In the British Museum.

PASQUIN./A DRAMATICK/SATIRE on the TIMES:/ BEING THE REHEARSAL of Two PLAYS,*viz.*/*A*COMEDY call'd,/THE ELECTION;/And a TRAGEDY call'd,/*The* LIFE *and* DEATH *of*/COMMON-SENSE./As it is Acted at the THEATRE in the/*HAY-MARKET.*///By HENRY FIELD-ING, Esq;////*LONDON*:/Printed for J. WATTS at the Print-ing Office in/*Wild-Court* near *Lincoln's-Inn Fields.*/// MDCCXXXVI./[Price One Shilling and Six Pence.]

8vo. Title p [i]. Blank p [ii]. Advt. p [iii]. Dramatis Personæ p [iv]. Text pp [1]-64. Epilogue [1] p. Advt. [3] pp.

In the Bodleian and the British Museum.

OTHER EDITIONS

LONDON.

1737. 1738. 1740 (Second Edition). 1754 (Third Edition)

DUBLIN.

1736.

TUMBLE-DOWN DICK:/or,/PHAETON *in the* SUDS./
A/Dramatick Entertainment of Walking,/in Serious and Foolish
Characters:/Interlarded with/Burlesque, Grotesque, Comick
Interludes,/CALL'D,/HARLEQUIN A PICK-POCKET./As it is
Perform'd at the/New Theatre *in the Hay-Market.*/Being ('tis
hop'd) the last Entertainment that will/ever be exhibited on any
Stage./Invented by the Ingenious/MONSIEUR *SANS
ESPRIT.*/The Musick compos'd by the Harmonious/SIG-
NIOR *WARBLERINI.*/And the Scenes painted by the
Prodigious/MYNHEER *VAN BOTTOM-FLAT.*/|| *Monstr'
horrend' inform.*—/||/*LONDON*:/Printed for J. WATTS at
the Printing-Office in/*Wild-Court* near *Lincoln's-Inn Fields.*
/MDCCXXXVI./[Price Six Pence.]

8vo. Title p [i]. Blank p [ii]. Dedication, "To Mr. John
Lun, Vulgarly call'd Esquire," pp [iii-vi]. "The Argument"
p [vii]. Dramatis Personæ p [viii]. Text pp [1]-19.

In the Bodleian.

Another Edition, London, 1744. 8vo.
In the British Museum.

EURYDICE,/A/FARCE://As it was d—mned/AT THE/
THEATRE-ROYAL/in DRURY-LANE.

Probably first published in the *Miscellanies* of 1743. The title,
as above, is reproduced from the *Miscellanies*, Vol. II.

THE/HISTORICAL REGISTER,/For the YEAR 1736./As it is
Acted at the/NEW THEATRE/In the *HAY-MARKET.*/
To which is added a very Merry TRAGEDY, called/EURY-
DICE HISS'D,/or,/A WORD *to the* WISE./Both written by
the Author of *Pasquin.*/To these are prefixed a long Dedication
to the/Publick, and a Preface to that Dedication./|||/*LONDON*,/
Printed: And sold by *J. Roberts* near the *Oxford-*/Arms-Inn in
Warwick-Lane./[Price 1s. 6d.]

8vo. Title p [i]. Blank p [ii]. "Preface To The Dedication"
pp [iii-iv]. "Dedication To The Publick" pp [v-xiv]. Blank
p [xv]. Dramatis Personæ p [xvi]. Text pp [1]-33.

In the Bodleian.
This is evidently the second edition of the play though not so
named. A copy of the first edition is in Yale.[1]

OTHER EDITIONS

DUBLIN.
1737.
LONDON.
1741. 1744 (Third Edition).

|EURYDICE HISS'D,/OR,/*A* WORD *to the Wise.*||
Sewed with *The Historical Register For the Year* 1736
(Second Edition).
8vo. Half Title p. [35]. Dramatis Personæ p [36]. Text
[37]-48.
In the Bodleian.

MISS *LUCY*/ IN TOWN./A/SEQUEL/TO/*The Virgin Unmas-
qued.*/A/FARCE;/WITH SONGS./As it is Acted at the THEA-
TRE-ROYAL/In DRURY-LANE,/By His MAJESTY's
Servants./|||/*LONDON*:/Printed for A. MILLAR, against
St *Clement's*/Church in the *Strand*. 1742./[Price OneShilling.]
8vo. Title p [i]. Blank p [ii]. A Table of the Songs p [iii].
Dramatis Personæ p [iv]. Text pp [1]-44.
In the Bodleian.
Second Edition, London, 1756.
Third Edition, London, 1764.

THE/WEDDING-DAY./A/COMEDY,/As it is Acted at the
/THEATRE-ROYAL/IN/*DRURY-LANE,*/By His MA-
JESTY's Servants./||/By HENRY FIELDING, Esq;/||/[orna-
ment]/||/*LONDON,*/Printed for A. MILLAR, opposite to
Catharine-/*Street* in the *Strand.* MDCCXLIII.
8vo. Title p [i]. Dramatis Personæ p [ii]. Prologue, "Writ

[1]Wilbur L. Cross. *The History of Henry Fielding.* Vol 3, p 3c1

and Spoken by Mr. Macklin," pp [iii–iv]. Text pp 1–82.
Epilogue [2] pp.

In the British Museum.

Published in the *Miscellanies*, London, 1743, Vol II.

OTHER EDITIONS

DUBLIN.

1743.

COPENHAGEN.

1759.

BERLIN AND LEIPZIG.

1764 (German Translation).

MANNHEIM.

1781 (German Translation).

THE/FATHERS:/OR,/The Good-Natur'd Man./A/COMEDY.
/As it is Acted at the THEATRE-ROYAL,/IN/DRURY-
LANE./BY THE LATE/HENRY FIELDING, ESQ./
AUTHOR OF TOM JONES, ETC.///LONDON:/PRINTED FOR
T. CADELL, IN THE STRAND./MDCCLXXVIII/[Price
One Shilling and Six Pence.]

8vo. Title p [i]. Advertisement p [ii]. Dedication, "To His
Grace the Duke of Northumberland," pp [iii]–iv. Prologue pp
[v]–vi. Epilogue pp [vii]–viii (Prologue and Epilogue written
by Garrick). Text pp [1]–111. Advt [1] p.

In the Bodleian and the British Museum.

OTHER EDITIONS

DUBLIN.

1779.

LONDON.

1783.

OTHER WORKS

OTHER WORKS

THE/CHAMPION; [woodcut]/OR,/*British* MERCURY. / | | *By*
Capt. *HERCULES VINEGAR*, of *Pall-mall.*/||/SATURDAY,
December 29, 1739.|(*To be continued every* Tuesday, Thursday,
and Saturday *Morning*)/|

First number, Thursday, November 15, 1739. Nos. 1 to 63
issued in the morning under the above title. Size about 15½ ins.
by 10 ins. Single sheet with first title, "The Champion," at the
head of the first page on the left; next to the first title, in the
middle, at the top of the first page, a woodcut representing
Hercules slaying the Hydra; next to the woodcut, to the right,
on the top of the first page, the alternative title, "British Mercury." Three columns on each page.

Colophon (in the numbers, down to 63, preserved in the
Bodleian) varies, the following being most frequent:

LONDON: Printed for C. CORBET, at *Addison's Head*,
against St *Dunstan's* Church, in *Fleet-street*; where Advertisements, and/Letters to the AUTHOR are taken in.

From the sixty-fourth number the *Champion* became an
evening paper with the title, *The Champion; or, the Evening
Advertiser* with the woodcut of Hercules slaying the Hydra
appearing between the first and the alternative titles as before.

The paper was now issued as a double sheet size about 13 ins.
by 9¾ ins. It came out, as before, on Tuesdays, Thursdays and
Saturdays. No. 64 of the *Champion* contains some paragraphs
complaining of " piracies" of the contents of the paper by many
of the country journals. The following words occur in these
paragraphs:

"Rather, therefore, than give way to such piracies any longer,
it has been thought expedient to alter the time of publishing this
paper, called the Champion, from Tuesday, Thursday and
Saturday mornings to the evenings of the same days, when it

293

will be punctually sent to such public or private houses, as shall order it in."

The Colophon in these subsequent numbers varies, the following being the most frequent:

LONDON: Printed for J. GRAHAM, under the *Inner Temple Gate*, opposite *Chancery-Lane*, in *Fleet-street*; where Advertise-ments/and Letters to the AUTHOR are taken in.

LONDON: Printed for J. SUMPTER, in *Apollo-Court*, over-against the *Middle-Temple-Gate*, in *Fleet-street*; where Ad-vertisements/and Letters to the AUTHOR are taken in.

LONDON: Printed for J. SHELLEY, at the *Bible* in *Ship-Yard*, near the *Ship Tavern*, without *Temple-Bar*; where Advertise-/ments and Letters to the AUTHOR are taken in.

LONDON: Printed for C. CHANDLER, at the *Bible* in *Ship-Yard*, near the *Ship-Tavern*, without *Temple-Bar*; where Advertise-/ments and Letters to the AUTHOR are taken in.

LONDON: Printed for J. Huggonson, in *Sword-and-Buckler Court*, over against the *Crown Tavern* on *Ludgate Hill*; where Advertisements/and Letters to the Author are taken in.

Original issues of Nos. 20-24 (Dec. 29, 1739—Jan. 8, 1740), Nos. 26-38 (Jan. 12, 1740—Feb. 9, 1740), Nos. 40-63 (Feb. 14, 1740—April 8, 1740), Nos. 64-158 (April 10, 1740—Nov. 15, 1740) and No. 509 (March 10, 1742) in the Bodleian.

No. 126 (Sept. 2, 1740), No. 213 (March 24, 1741), No. 237 (May 19, 1741), No. 265 (July 23, 1741), No. 295 (Oct. 1, 1741), No. 301 (Oct. 15, 1741), No. 305 (Oct 24, 1741), Nos. 308-375 (Oct. 31, 1741—April 10, 1742), Nos. 379-383 (April 20, 1742—April 29, 1742), Nos. 385-387 (May 4, 1742—May 8, 1742), No. 389 (May 13, 1742), Nos. 391-396 (May 18, 1742—May 29, 1742), No. 401 (June 10, 1742), No. 402 (June 12, 1742), Nos. 404-410 (June 17, 1742—July 1, 1742), Nos. 412-415 (July 6, 1742—July 15, 1742), Nos. 417-422 (July 20, 1742—July 31, 1742), No. 426 (Aug. 10, 1742), Nos. 428-430 (Aug. 14, 1742—Aug. 19, 1742), No. 432 (Aug. 24, 1742), No. 434 (Aug. 28, 1742) and No. 435 (August 31, 1742) in the British Museum.

of/TRUE GREATNESS./An Epistle to/The Right Hon-
ourable/*GEORGE DODINGTON*, Esq;/||/By HENRY
FIELDING, *Esq*;/|[ornament]/|||/*LONDON*:/Printed for C.
Corbet, at *Addison's Head* against St *Dunstan's*/Church, in
Fleet street. 1741./[Price One Shilling.]

Fol. Title p [i]. Blank p [ii]. Preface pp [3]-4. Text pp 5-16.
In the Bodleian.

*ΤΗΣ ΟΜΗΡΟΥ VΕΡΝΟΝ-ΙΑΔΟΣ, ΡΑΨΩιΔΙΑ ή
ΓΡΑΜΜΑ Α'*/||/the VERNON-IAD./done into *ENGLISH*
/From the original greek/of/HOMER/.Lately found at
CONSTANTINOPLE./with/NOTES in usum, &c./||/book
the first./|||/*LONDON*:/Printed for Charles Corbett, at
Addison's Head/against St *Dunstan's* Church; *Fleet-street*./||/
MDCCXLI./[Price is. 6d.]

8vo. Title p. [i] Blank p [ii]. Text pp [1]-37.
In the British Museum.
Another Edition, Dublin, 1741.

an/APOLOGY/for the/LIFE/of/Mrs. Shamela Andrews./In which, the many notorious Falsehoods and/
Misrepresentations of a Book called/*PAMELA*,/Are
exposed and refuted; and all the matchless/Arts of that young
Politician, set in a true and/just Light./Together with/A full
Account of all that passed between her/and Parson *Arthur
Williams*; whose Character/is represented in a manner something different/from what he bears in *PAMELA*. The/whole
being exact Copies of authentick Papers/delivered to the
Editor./||/Necessary to be had in all Families./||/By Mr.
CONNY KEYBER./||/*LONDON*:/Printed for A Dodd, at
the *Peacock*, without *Temple-bar*./M.DCC.XLI.

8vo. Half Title p [i]. Blank p [ii]. Title p [iii]. Blank p [iv].
Dedication, "To Miss Fanny, etc." pp [v]-xii. "Letters to the
Editor " pp [xiii-xv]. Blank p [xvi]. Text pp [1]-59.
In the British Museum.
Another issue, London, 1741. 8vo. In the British Museum.

Another Edition, Dublin, 1741. 12mo. In the British Museum.

Another Edition with an Introduction by R. Brimley Johnson. The Golden Cockerel Press. 1926.

THE/CHAMPION:|CONTAINING/A SERIES of PAPERS,/ HUMOROUS, MORAL, POLITICAL,/ and CRITICAL./To each of which is added,/A proper Index to the Times./||/*Quem legis ut nôris, accipe.* OVID./||/VOL I [II]/|/[ornament]/||/*LONDON:*| Printed for J. HUGGONSON, in *Sword and Buckler/Court*, over-against the *Crown-Tavern* on *Ludgate-/Hill./*MDCCXLI.

8vo. Vol. I. Title p [i]. Blank p [ii]. Dedication "To the New Members " pp [i-ix]. "Advertisement" p [x]. Text pp [1]-360.

Vol. II. Title p [i]. Blank p [ii]. Text pp [1]-360.

Contain leading articles, etc., together with selections from the news and other items in the paper, from the first number dated November 15, 1739, to the ninety-fourth dated June 19, 1740. Of the ninety-four leading articles, etc., reprinted in these two volumes fifty-nine have the letters C or L at the end to indicate that they were written by Fielding. The first four, though not marked by any distinctive sign or letter, exhibit all the characteristic features of Fielding's style. In the British Museum.

This collection with the same title page, dedication, advertisement and pagination was also issued the same year with an index at the end of each volume. Vol I of this issue has an index of 26 pages and is in the Bodleian.

Second Edition, "With the addition of a large Table of Contents in each Volume." London, Printed for H. Chapelle at Sir Isaac Newton's Head, in Grosvenor Street. MDCCXLIII.

Third Edition. Printed for T. Waller, opposite Fetter-Lane, Fleet Street. MDCCLXVI.

THE/HISTORY/OF THE/ADVENTURES / OF / *JOSEPH ANDREWS,*/And of his FRIEND/Mr. *ABRAHAM ADAMS.*

/Written in Imitation of/The *Manner* of CERVANTES,/Author of *Don Quixote.*/|/IN TWO VOLUMES./|/VOL I [II]./| /LONDON:/Printed for A. MILLAR, over against/*St. Clement's Church*, in the *Strand.*/M.DCCXLII.

12mo.

Vol. I Title p [i]. Blank p [ii]. Preface pp iii-xix. Errors p [xx]. Text pp [1]-306 (misprint for 308).

Vol. II. Title p [i]. Blank p [ii]. Text pp [1]-310.

[The title page of the second volume omits the words "In Two Volumes."]

OTHER EDITIONS AND TRANSLATIONS

LONDON.

1742 (Second Edition. "Revised and Corrected with Alterations and Additions by the Author." Printed for A. Millar. In two vols, 12mo). 1743 (Third Edition, illustrated with Cuts. Printed for A. Millar. In two vols, 12mo). 1743 (French Translation by Pierre Desfontaines). 1749 (Fourth Edition. Revised. 2 vols, 12mo). 1750 (French Translation). 1751 (Fifth Edition Revised and Corrected. 2 vols, 12mo). 1752. 1762 (Sixth Edition. Revised and Corrected with 12 plates by T. Hullett. 2 vols, 12mo). 1768. 1769. 1769 (Abridged Edition. F. Newbery). 1778. 1780. 1781 (A Millar. 2 vols, 12mo.) 1781 (Harrison and Co. 2 vols, 8vo). 1783. 1784 (Abridged Edition. F. Newbery). 1785. 1788. 1790. 1793 (Cooke's *Select British Novels.* Vols 6 and 7). 1794. 1808. 1809. 1810 (*The British Novelists.* Edited by Mrs. Barbauld. Vol XVIII. With a biographical and critical essay on Fielding). 1815. 1818 (In Walker's *British Classics*). 1820. 1822. 1823. 1825. 1831 (In the *Novelists' Library.* Edited by T. Roscoe. With Illustrations by Cruikshank.). 1832. 1833. 1834. 1857. 1868. 1874. 1876 (Bohn's *Novelists' Library*). 1882 (*Library Edition.* Routledge). 1885. 1889. 1892 (Dicks' *English Novels*). 1894 (*The Caxton Novels.* Routledge). 1902. 1904 (*Classic Novels.* Hutchinson. Illustrations by Cruikshank). 1904 (*The York Library*). 1904 (Abridged Edition). 1906 (*The Empire Library,*

Routledge). 1906 (Bell). 1910 (*Everyman's Library*. Introduction by G. Saintsbury). 1913 (Bohn's *Popular Library*). 1925 (Harrap's *Standard Fiction Library*).

DUBLIN.
   1742. 1747.

AMSTERDAM.
   1744. 1764. 1775 (French Translation by Pierre Desfontaines. 2nd Edition).

DANZIG.
   1745.

BERLIN.
   1746. 1765. 1770. 1776. 1784. 1786.

COPENHAGEN.
   1749.

VENICE.
   1752-53 (with engravings).

EDINBURGH.
   1770. 1792. 1805.

PARIS.
   1779. 1833.

DRESDEN.
   1783.

RHEIMS.
   1784.

FRANKFURT and LEIPZIG.
   1784.

LIPSKAR.
   1787.

PHILADELPHIA.
   1791. 1794. 1836. 1847. 1853.

LEITH.
   1792.

GÖTTINGEN.
   1793 (In *The Novelist or A Choice Selection of the Best Novels*. By J. H. Emmert (Abridged Edition). Vol II).

New York.

1816. 1852. 1857. 1861. 1902. 1903. 1905.
Brunswick.

1840. 1848.

A full/VINDICATION/of the/Dutchess Dowager/of/ *MARLBOROUGH*:/both/With regard to the Account lately/Published by /HER GRACE,/and to/Her Character in general;/against/The *base* and *malicious* Invectives contained /in a late *scurrilous* Pamphlet, entitled/REMARKS on the Account, &c.///In a Letter to the Noble AUTHOR/of those *Remarks.*////*LONDON*:/Printed for J. Roberts, in *Warwick-Lane.*/M.DCC.XLII.

8vo. Half title p [i]. Blank p [ii]. Title p [iii]. Blank p [iv]. Text pp [1]-40.

In the British Museum.

Second Edition. London, 1742.

PLUTUS,/the/God *of* Riches./a/COMEDY./Translated from the Original *Greek* of/*ARISTOPHANES*:/With Large notes Explanatory and/Critical.///By *HENRY FIELDING*, Esq;/and/The Revd. Mr. YOUNG.////*LONDON*:/Printed for T. Waller in the *Temple-Cloisters.*///MDCCXLII. [Price 2s.]

8vo. Title p [i]. Blank p [ii]. Dedication "To the Right Honourable the Lord Talbot" pp [iii]-vi. Preface pp [vii]-xv. Dramatis Personæ p [xvi]. Text pp [1]-112.

In the Bodleian and the British Museum.

MISCELLANIES,/by/*Henry Fielding* Esq;/In Three Volumes./[Ornament]./*LONDON*:/Printed for the AUTHOR:/ And sold by A. Millar, opposite to/*Catharine-Street*, in the *Strand.*/MDCCXLIII.

8vo. First Title p [i]. Blank p [ii]. Vol I. Title (same as the First Title except that it has "Vol I" in place of "In Three Volumes" and the ornament varies) p [i]. Blank p [ii]. "List of Subscribers " pp [iii-xxiv]. Preface pp [i]-xxvii (misprint for xxxvii). Blank p [xxxviii]. Title, "Of True Greatness, etc" [p [1]. Blank p [2]. Text pp [3]-114. Title, "An Essay on Conversation" p 115. Blank p [116]. Text pp 117-178. Title, "An Essay on the Knowledge of the Characters of Men" p [179]. Blank p [180]. Text pp 181-227. Blank p [228]. Title, "An Essay On Nothing" p [229]. Blank p [230]. Text pp 231-251. Blank p [252]. Title, "Some Papers Proper to be Read before the R——L Society etc." p [253]. Blank p [254]. Second Title of the same, "Philosophical Transactions For the Year 1742-3" p 254 [misprint for 255]. Blank p [256]. Text pp 257-277. Blank p [278]. Title, "The First Olynthiac of Demosthenes" p [279]. Blank p [280]. Text pp 281-294. Title, "Of the Remedy Of Affliction For the Loss of our Friends" p [295]. Blank p [296]. Text pp 297-332. Title, "A Dialogue Between Alexander the Great and Diogenes the Cynic" p [323]. Blank p [324]. Text pp 325-340. Title, "An Interlude Between Jupiter, Juno, Apollo and Mercury, etc.," p [341]. Blank p [342]. Text pp 343-354.

Vol. II. Title (has the words "A Journey from this World to the Next, etc" under "Vol II" and the ornament varies) p [i]. Blank p [ii]. Text, "A Journey From This World to the Next" pp 1-250. Title, "Eurydice, A Farce: As it was d——mned at the Theatre-Royal in Drury Lane" p [251]. Dramatis Personæ p [252]. Text pp 253-290. Title, "The Wedding Day. A Comedy, etc." p [291]. Blank p [292]. Prologue pp [293]-295. Dramatis Personæ p [296]. Text pp 297-420. Epilogue [2] pp.

Vol. III. Title (Has the words "The Life of Mr Jonathan Wild the Great" above the "Vol. III" and the words "By Henry Fielding, Esq" come under the latter. No ornament) p [i]. Blank p [ii]. Contents pp [iii-x.] Text pp [1]-421.

In the British Museum.

"Second Edition." London, 1743.

This was really a later issue from the same impression as the preceding, though the title page of Vols I and III of this issue

has the words "The Second Edition" on it. The title page of all
the three volumes has the words, "London:Printed for A.
Millar, opposite to Catherine Street in the Strand."

Miscellanies and Poems. Edited with Preface by J. P. Browne,
M.D. London, 1872. 8vo.

A SERIOUS/ADDRESS/TO THE/People of GREAT BRITAIN./
In which the/CERTAIN CONSEQUENCES/OF THE/PRESENT
REBELLION,/Are fully demonstrated./Necessary to be
perused by every LOVER/of his Country, at this Juncture./
//*Per Deos Immortales, vos ego appello, qui semper Domos,/Villas,
Signa, Tabulas vestras, pluris, quam rempublicam/fecistis: si ista
cujus cumque modi sint, quæ amplexamini,/retinere; si voluptatibus
vestris otium præbere, vultis:/expergiscimini aliquando, & capes-
site rempublicam. Non/nunc agitur de vectigalibus, non de Sociorum
Injuriis;/*Libertas & anima nostra in dubio est./SAL. BEL.
CATALIN./////*LONDON*:/Printed for M. COOPER, at the *Globe*
in *Pater-noster-/Row.* MDCCXLV./[Price One Shilling]
    8vo. Title p [i]. Blank p [ii]. Text pp 1-45.
    In the British Museum.
    Second Edition, Corrected, with Additions. London, 1745.
8vo.
    In the British Museum.

A/DIALOGUE/BETWEEN/The DEVIL, the POPE,/ AND
THE/PRETENDER./||/—*Comes additur una/Hortator Sce-
lerum.*/VIRGIL./|[Ornament]/|/*LONDON*:/Printed for M.
COOPER,/at the *Globe* in *Pater-noster-/Row.* MDCCXLV./
    8vo. Half Title p [i]. Blank p [ii]. Title p [iii]. Blank p [iv].
Text pp 5-44.
    In the British Museum.

The TRUE PATRIOT:/AND/The History of Our Own
Times./(To be Continued Every TUESDAY.)/||/TUESDAY,
NOVEMBER 5, 1745./|
    First number, Tuesday, November 5, 1745. Last, Tuesday,

June 10, to Tuesday, June 17, 1746. From the 13th number of the paper the whole week from Tuesday is given as the date, e.g., No. 13 has the date "From Tuesday, January 21, to Tuesday, January 28, 1746."

Double Sheet. Size (with margin) about 15 ins by 10½ ins. Three columns on each page. No woodcut or ornament at the top of the first page. The first letter of the first word in the leading article on the first page set in an ornamented square. "Price Three-Pence" printed at the bottom of the first page.

Nos. 17 and 18 have the following notice printed at the top of the first page under the date:

"Whereas we have been informed by several Persons, that they have not been able to procure the True Patriot at any Rate: And we have great Reason to believe that many malicious and base Endeavours have been used to suppress the Sale of this Paper, by some who are concerned in imposing on the Public, by propagating Lies and Nonsense, which we have endeavoured to detect and expose. If any Hawkers, or others, will acquaint Mr A. Millar, Bookseller, opposite Katharine Street in the Strand, with the Name of any Person who has bribed, or offered to bribe them to refuse delivering out the True Patriot to their Customers, they shall be well rewarded, and their Names, if they desire it, concealed.

"Gentlemen and Ladies may be furnished with this Paper, by sending their Names and Habitations to Mrs A. Dodd without Temple Bar; to Mr Chapelle in Grosvenor-street; or to M. Cooper in Pater Noster Row: By whom Hawkers, etc. may be constantly supplied with them."

Colophon for No. 1.

LONDON: Printed for M. Cooper, at the *Globe*, in *Pater-Noster-Row*; where Advertisements and Letters to/the Author are taken in.

Colophon No. 2 adds to the above:

" Where may be had, No. 1, containing an *Introductory Essay*, an *Apology for Scotland*,/a *New Loyal Song*, the *History of Europe, Great Britain*, &c."

Colophon for No. 3 adds:

And No. II containing *An Essay on Patriotism, an Apology/ for Roman Catholics*, &c.

Colophon for Nos. 4-18 changes the words "Where may be had, No. 1 etc." to "Where may be had the former Numbers"

Colophon for Nos. 19-32:

LONDON: Printed for M. COOPER, at the *Globe* in *Pater-Noster-Row*; And Sold by GEORGE WOODFALL, near/*Craig's Court, Charing-Cross.* At both which Places Advertisements, and Letters to the AUTHOR, are taken in./Where may be had the former Numbers.

Thirty-three numbers issued.

Nos. 1-32 in the Burney Collection in the British Museum. No. 28 in the Bodleian.

Extracts from Nos. 1, 4, 5, 7, 8, 20, 22, 23, 27, 28 and 29 printed in *The Gentleman's Magazine*, Dec. 1745, Jan., March, April and May, 1746. Extracts from Nos. 10, 14, 27, 28, 31 and 33 in *The London Magazine*, Jan., Feb., May and June, 1746.

THE/LOVER's ASSISTANT/ OR,/New Year's Gift;/BEING, A/ NEW ART of LOVE,/ADAPTED to the PRESENT TIMES./‖ Translated from the LATIN, with NOTES/BY THE LATE INGENIOUS/HENRY FIELDING Of FACETIOUS MEMORY./‖ /LONDON, Printed:/And *DUBLIN*, Re-printed, and sold by the Booksellers/‖/MDCCLIX./[Price a British Shilling.]

8vo. Title p [i]. Blank p [ii]. Preface pp iii-viii. Half Title, "Ovid's Art of Love Paraphrased," p [1]. Text pp 2-87.

In the British Museum.

A/DIALOGUE/BETWEEN A/GENTLEMAN of *LONDON*,/ Agent for two Court Candidates,/AND AN/HONEST ALDERMAN/ Of the Country Party./WHEREIN/The GRIEVANCES under which the/Nation at present *groans* are fairly and/impartially laid open and considered./Earnestly address'd to the/ELECTORS OF GREAT-BRITAIN./[Ornament]/*LONDON*:/Printed for M. COOPER, at the *Globe*, in *Pater-Noster-/Row.* 1747.

8vo. Title p [i]. Blank p [ii]. Text pp 1-91.

In the Bodleian.

Declared to be the work of Fielding in a note (p. 28) to *A Proper Answer To a Late Scurrilous Libel*, 1747.

Second Edition, London, 1747.

A PROPER/ANSWER/TO A LATE/Scurrilous Libel,/ENTITLED,/ *An Apology for the Conduct of a late/celebrated Second-rate Minister.*/By the AUTHOR of the *Jacobite's Journal.*/*Hic niger est, hunc tu, Romane, caveto.*/[Ornament]./*LONDON,*/Printed for M. COOPER in *Pater-noster-Row.*/MDCCXLVII./[Price One Shilling.]

8vo. Title p [i]. Blank p [ii]. "Advertisement" pp iii-iv. Text pp. 5-44.

In the Bodleian and the British Museum.

Second Edition. London, 1748. 8vo.

In the Bodleian.

THE/JACOBITE's JOURNAL./[woodcut]/|/|/*By* JOHN TROTT-PLAID, *Esq*;/|/SATURDAY, DECEMBER 5, 1747. NUMB. 1./|

First number, Saturday, December 5, 1747. Last, Saturday, November 5, 1748.

Double Sheet. Size varies. Nos. 1-12 and 15-16 are about 12½ ins. by 9 ins. Other numbers slightly larger. Three columns on each page. Picture at the top of the first page under the title in Nos. 1-12 only. The first letter of the first word in the leading article on the first page set in an ornamented square. Issued every Saturday.

Colophon for No. 1.

LONDON: Printed by W. STRAHAN, in *Wine-Office-Court, Fleetstreet*; and Sold by M. COOPER, in *Pater-/Noster-Row*, and G. WOODFALL, at *Charing-Cross*. Where ADVERTISEMENTS, and Letters to the AUTHOR/are taken in.

Colophon for Nos. 4-49.

LONDON: Printed for M. COOPER, in *Pater-Noster-Row*;

C. CORBETT, in *Fleet-street*; and G. WOODFALL,/at *Charing Cross*. Where ADVERTISEMENTS and Letters to the AUTHOR are taken in.

Colophon for Nos. 2-3 adds: "Mrs NUTT, at the *Royal Exchange*" after the words "C. CORBETT, in *Fleet-street*."

Forty-nine numbers issued. All these except No. 41 in the Burney Collection in the British Museum.

Extracts from Nos. 1, 5, 6, 7, 8, 10, 12, 16, 23, 24, 25, 31, 32, 33, 45 and 47 printed in *The Gentleman's Magazine* for Dec. 1747, Jan., Feb., March, April, May, July and Oct., 1748.

THE/HISTORY/OF/*TOM JONES,*/A/FOUNDLING./|/In SIX VOLUMES./||/By HENRY FIELDING, Esq;/||— *Mores hominum multorum vidit.*—/|||/*LONDON*:/Printed for A. MILLAR, over-against/*Catharine-street* in the *Strand.*/ MDCCXLIX.

12mo.

Vol I. Title p [i]. Blank p [ii]. Dedication, "To the Honourable George Lyttleton, Esq;" pp iii-xvi. Contents of the First Volume pp xvii-xxiv. Contents of the Second Volume pp xxv-xxxii. Contents of the Third Volume pp xxxiii-xl. Contents of the Fourth Volume pp xli-xlviii. Contents of the Fifth Volume pp xlix-lvi. Contents of the Sixth Volume pp lvii-lxii. Errata p [lxiii]. Blank p [lxiv]. Text pp [1]-214.

Vol. II. Title p [i]. Blank p [ii]. Text pp [1]-324.

Vol. III. Title p [i]. Blank p [ii]. Text pp. 1-370.

Vol. IV. Title p [i]. Blank p [ii]. Text pp 1-312.

Vol. V. Title p [i]. Blank p [ii]. Text pp 1-294.

Vol. VI. Title p [i]. Blank p [ii]. Text pp 1-304.

In the Bodleian.

Another Edition. In six volumes, 12mo [apparently taken in hand before the first was completed].

London: Printed for A. Millar, over-against Catharine Street in the Strand. MDCCXLIX.

Another. In four volumes, 12mo.

x

London: Printed for A. Millar, over against Catharine Street in the Strand. MDCCXLIX.

In the British Museum.

OTHER EDITIONS AND TRANSLATIONS.

LONDON.

1750 (Fourth Edition. In four vols, 12mo). 1750 (French version by M. de la Place). 1751 (M. de la Place's version. Third Edition). 1763 (Fifth Edition). 1765 (Sixth Edition. In four vols, 12mo). 1768 (Seventh Edition. In four vols, 12mo). 1773. 1774. 1778 (Abridged Edition). 1780 (In four vols, 8vo). 1780 (Vols 3-11 of the *Entertaining Museum*). 1780 (In three vols., 12mo). 1781 (*The Novelist'sMagazine*, Vol 3). 1782. 1783. 1783 (French Translation 5 tom., 12mo). 1786. 1787. 1789. 1791. 1792 (Vols 1-4 of Cooke's *Select British Novels*). 1792 (Murray). 1792 (Longman). 1794. 1798. 1801 (French Translation). 1807. 1808. 1809 (With a life of Fielding. In two vols, 12mo). 1810 (Cooke). 1810 (*The British Novelists*. Edited by Mrs. Barbauld. Vols XIX-XXI). 1811. 1816. 1818. 1819 (With a *Life of Fielding*. Walker's *British Classics*.) 1820. 1823. 1825. 1826 (the plates bear the date 1817). 1828. 1831. (In the *Novelists' Library*, Edited with a Memoir of Fielding by T. Roscoe. Illustrations by Cruikshank). 1832. 1834. 1844 (2 vols, 16mo. *Collection of British Authors*, Vols 60-61). 1847. 1857. 1867 (With a Memoir of Fielding by G. H. Townsend. Routledge's *Railway Library*). 1868 (Routledge's *Wide World Library*). 1874 (Routledge). 1874-78 (Bickers). 1876 (Bohn's *Novelists' Library*. With illustrations by Cruikshank). 1880. 1884. 1886 (Library Edition. Routledge.) 1888 (Dicks' *English Novels*). 1892. 1893. 1895 (*The Caxton Novels*. Routledge). 1896 (Abridged for the use of modern readers by J. E. M. Fielding, the novelist's great-granddaughter). 1897. 1899. 1900 (*The Library of English Classics*. Macmillan). 1902. 1904 (Abridged). 1904 (*Classic Novels*. Hutchinson. Illustrations by Cruikshank). 1905 (Methuen's *Standard Library*). 1905 (*The York Library*). 1907. 1908. 1909 (*Everyman's Library*. With an Introduction

by G. Saintsbury). 1910. 1913 (Bohn's *Popular Library*). 1915.
1925 (Harrap's *Standard Fiction Library*). 1926 (With a Memoir of Fielding. Routledge).

DUBLIN.

1749. 1759. 1766. 1767. 1818.

AMSTERDAM.

1750 (French version by M. de la Place. 4 tom., 8vo). 1763
(Dutch translation).

DRESDEN.

1750. 1764. 1773. 1774.

HAMBURG.

1750. 1758-9. 1771.

VENICE.

1757.

NAPLES.

1758.

BERLIN.

1764.

PARIS.

1762. 1764. 1767 (M. de la Place's version). 1770. 1775
1776-77. 1777. 1780.1784 (4 tom., 18mo. Three copies printed
on vellum. Part of the Collection printed by order of the
Count of Artois). 1788. 1794. 1796 (Traduction nouvelle par
le Citoyen Davaux). 1797. 1801. 1804. 1820. 1823 (Dalibon).
1823 (Parmentier). 1828. 1832. 1833 (Traduction nouvelle
et complète par Count de La Bédoyère). 1835 (Traduction
nouvelle par M. Defauconpret). 1841.

EDINBURGH.

1767. 1771. 1774. 1779. 1791. 1805.

ST. PETERSBURG.

1770-71. 1849.

LEIPZIG.

1771. 1786-88. 1826. 1844 (*Collection of British Authors*.
Tauchnitz Edition. Vols 60, 61).

PAISLEY.

1775.

NÜRNBERG.
   1780.
GENEVA.
   1782. 1796.
GÖTTINGEN.
   1792 (In *The Novelist, or A Choice Selection of the Best Novels.*
By J. H. Emmert (Abridged Edition). Vol I).
WARSAW.
   1783. 1793.
RHEIMS.
   1784.
VIENNA.
   1786-88 (Polish Translation). 1788 (German Translation).
MOSCOW.
   1787.
LIPSK.
   1787.
CARLSRUHE.
   1787-88.
BASLE.
   1791.
GOTHA.
   1791. 1804.
PHILADELPHIA
   1795
MADRID
   1796.
BRESLAU.
   1804.
MARBURG.
   1814
CHISWICK.
   1823.
NEW YORK.
   1836. 1879. 1882. 1892. 1904. 1906 (Burt). 1906 (Century). 1907. 1926 (*Borzoi Classics*

BRUNSWICK.

1840. 1841-42. 1848.

PESTH.

1853 (Bd III of *Neues Lese Kabinat für die reifere Jugend*).

COPENHAGEN.

1854-55.

STUTTGART.

1860. 1883.

HAARLEM.

1862.

PRAZE.

1872 (the cover has the date 1873).

CAMBRIDGE.

1903.

PLAYS, ETC., BASED ON "TOM JONES"

Tom Jones. Comédie Lyrique En Trois Actes. Imitée du Roman de M. Fielding.... par A. A. H. Poinsinet.

Paris, 1766.

Other Editions : Paris, 1767, 1773 and 1778. London, 1777 and 1778. Dresden, 1766. Amsterdam, 1767. Copenhagen, 1769. Avignon, 1772. Mannheim, 1772. Frankfort, 1773.

Thomas Jones, ein Lustspiel von fünf Aufzügen, nach der Grundlage des Herrn Fielding, von J. H. Steffens.

Zelle, 1765.

Tom Jones. Ein Lustspiel von fünf Aufzügen nach dem Englischen Roman. Von Franz von Heufeld.

Wien, 1767.

Tom, Jones, a Comic Opera. In three acts. By Joseph Reed.

London, 1769.

Tom Jones à Londres, Comedie en Cinq Actes, en Vers. Tirée du Roman de Fielding par M. P. J. B. Choudard-Désforges.

Paris, 1782. Other Editions, Paris, 1785, and 1789.

Tom Jones et Fellamar; Suite de *Tom Jones à Londres* Comédie en Cinq Actes et en Vers. Par M. Choudard-Désforges.

Paris, 1788.

The Tom Jones Natuck (in Bengali).

Calcutta, 1863.

Tom Jones, a Comic Opera written by A. M. Thompson and Robert Courtneidge; lyrics by Charles H. Taylor and H. Beswick; Music by Edward German.

London, 1909.

A/CHARGE/DELIVERED TO THE/GRAND JURY,/AT THE SESSIONS of the PEACE/HELD FOR THE/City and Liberty of *Westminster*, &c./On THURSDAY the 29th of June, 1749./By *HENRY FIELDING*, Esq;/CHAIRMAN of the said SESSIONS./ PUBLISHED/By Order of the COURT, and at the unanimous/ Request of the Gentlemen of the GRAND JURY./*LONDON*:/ Printed for A. MILLAR, opposite *Catherine-Street*, in/the *Strand*. 1749.

8vo. Title p [i]. Resolution of the Justices of the Peace for the City and Liberty of Westminster p [ii]. Text pp [7]-64.

In the Bodleian and the British Museum.

Reprinted Dublin, 1749.

A / TRUE STATE / OF THE / CASE / OF / *BOSAVERN PENLEZ*,/Who suffered on Account of the late/RIOT in the *STRAND*./IN WHICH/The Law regarding these Offences, and the/Statute of GEORGE the First, commonly/called the Riot Act, are fully considered./||/By *HENRY FIELDING*, Esq;/ Barrister at Law, and one of his Majesty's Justices/of the Peace for the County of *Middlesex*, and/for the City and Liberty of *Westminster*./||/*LONDON*:/Printed for A. MILLAR, opposite *Katherine-/street* in the *Strand*. 1749.[Price One Shilling.]

8vo. Title p [i]. Blank p [ii]. Text pp 1-54.

In the Bodleian and the British Museum.

AN/ENQUIRY/Into the CAUSES of the late/Increase of Robbers, &c./WITH SOME/PROPOSALS for Remedying this/ GROWING EVIL./IN WHICH/The Present Reigning VICES are impartially/exposed; and the Laws that relate to the/Provision for the POOR, and to the Punish-/ment of FELONS are largely and freely ex-/amined./*Non jam sunt mediocres hominum. libidines, non humanæ auda-/ciæ ac tolerandæ. Nihil cogitant nisi cædem, nisi incendia, nisi rapinas.* CIC. in Catil. 2da./By HENRY FIELDING, Esq;/Barrister at Law, and One of His Majesty's Justices/of the Peace for the County of *Middlesex*, and for/the City and Liberty of *Westminster*./LONDON:/Printed for A MILLAR, opposite to *Katharine-Street*,/in the *Strand*. M.DCC.LI./[Price 2s. 6d.]

8vo. Title p [i]. Blank p [ii]. Dedication, "To the Right Honourable Philip Lord Hardwick, Lord High Chancellor of Great Britain" pp [iii]-iv. Preface pp v-xv. Blank p [xvi]. Text pp [1]-127. "To the Public" [1] p.

In the Bodleian and the British Museum.

Second Edition : London, 1751.

AMELIA./BY/*Henry Fielding*, Esq;/||/*Felices ter & amplius*/ *Quos irrupta tenet Copula*./Γυναικὸς οὐδὲν χρῆμ᾽ ἀνὴρ ληΐζεται ᾽Εσθλῆς ἄμεινον, οὐδὲ ῥίγιον κακῆς.||/In FOUR VOLUMES./||/VOL. I. [II., III., IV.]/||/[ornament]./|||/*LONDON*:/Printed for A. MILLAR, in the *Strand*./M.DDC.LII.

12mo.

Vol I. Title p [i]. Blank p [ii]. Dedication, "To Ralph Allen, Esq;" pp [iii]-vi. Contents pp vii-xii. Text pp [1]-285.

Vol II. Title p [i]. Blank p [ii]. Contents pp iii-viii. Text pp. 1-262. Advertisements of the Universal Register Office [1] p.

Vol III. Title p [i]. Blank p [ii]. Contents pp iii-ix. Blank p [x]. Text pp [1]-323.

Vol IV. Title p [i]. Blank p [ii]. Contents pp iii-vii. Blank p [viii]. Text pp [1]-296.

In the British Museum.

OTHER EDITIONS AND TRANSLATIONS

DUBLIN.

1752. 1818.

HANOVER.

1752.

FRANKFORT and LEIPZIG.

   1752.

AMSTERDAM.

   1758.

LONDON.

   1760 (?) (Abridged. R. Snagg). 1775. 1780. 1785. 1790. 1793 (Cooke's *Select British Novels*). 1798. 1799. 1800. 1808. 1811. 1831 (In the *Novelists' Library*. Edited by T. Roscoe. Illustrations by Cruikshank). 1857. 1868. 1874. 1877 (Bohn's *Novelists' Library*. With illustrations by Cruikshank). 1882. 1884. 1893. 1894. 1902. 1905 (*Classic Novels*. Hutchinson. Illustrations by G. Cruikshank). 1906 (*The York Library*). 1914 Bohn's *Popular Library*).

PARIS.

   1762 (French Translation by Mme Riccoboni. 3 tom., 12mo). 1763. 1772. 1790. 1834.

FRANKFORT.

   1763. 1764. 1768.

LEIPZIG.

   1781. 1781-82. 1797.

MILAN.

   1782.

GENEVA.

   1782 (French translation).

RHEIMS.

   1784.

VENICE.

   1786.

MADRID.

   1795-96.

JENA and LEIPZIG.

   1801.

DRESDEN.

   1803.

NEW YORK.

   1837. 1852. 1882. 1886.

The Covent-Garden Journal./By Sir ALEXANDER DRAW-
CANSIR, Knt. Censor of GREAT BRITAIN./||/SATURDAY,
JANUARY 4. 1752. NUMB. 1./||/To be continued every TUESDAY
and SATURDAY./||

First number Saturday, January 4, 1752. Last, Saturday,
November 25, 1752. Up to No. 52 the paper was a bi-weekly
and the words "To be continued every Tuesday and Saturday"
occur under the date in every issue till the 52nd. From the 53rd
to the last number, the 72nd, the journal was issued once a
week and the words "To be continued every Saturday in the
Morning" occur under the date in each of these numbers.

Double sheet. Size (with margin) about 16½ ins by 10¾ ins.
The title, etc., printed without ornament. The first letter of the
first word in the leading article on the first page set in an
ornamented square. From the fifth number the words "Price
3d]" printed on the left between the lines containing the date.
Three columns on each page.

Colophon for No. 1
LONDON: Printed, and Sold by Mrs DODD, at the *Peacock,
Temple-Bar*; and at the UNIVERSAL REGISTER/OFFICE, oppo-
site *Cecil-street*, in the *Strand*; where ADVERTISEMENTS and
LETTERS to the AUTHOR are taken in.

Colophon for No. 2 adds: *"Where may be had the First
Number"* to the above.

Colophon for Nos. 3-26, 29-72 substitutes for the above
the words, *"Where may be had the former Numbers."*

Nos. 3-25 have the following at the bottom of the first page
in addition to the colophon as above:

*" All imaginable Care hath been taken to supply the Subscribers
with this Paper, but if notwithstanding this, any Gen-|tleman or
Lady should not have received it, on sending their Names either to
Mrs.* Dodd, *or to the* Universal Register/Office, *opposite* Cecil-
Street *in the* Strand, *they will be carefully supplied for the future."*

This is also the colophon for Nos. 27 and 28.

No. 28 has the words, LONDON: Printed and Sold by Mrs.
DODD, at the *Peacock, Temple-Bar*; and at the UNIVERSAL

REGISTER/OFFICE, opposite *Cecil-Street*, in the *Strand*; where
ADVERTISEMENTS and LETTERS to the AUTHOR are/taken in.
Where may be had the former Numbers, printed at the bottom of
the first page.

Nos. 32-72 have the following printed at the bottom of the
first page: " Note, *This* Paper *is to be had at the* Universal
Register Office, *next the Corner of* Bishopsgate-street, Cornhill."
Seventy-two numbers issued.

Original issues of Nos. 5-7 (Jan. 18—Jan. 25, 1752), Nos.
11-16 (Feb. 8—Feb. 25, 1752), Nos. 18-20 (March 3—March
10, 1752), No. 22 (March 17, 1752), Nos. 25-32 (March
28—April 21, 1752), No. 36 (May 5, 1752), Nos. 38-41
(May 12—May 23, 1752), No. 43 (May 30, 1752), Nos. 45-
46 (June 6—June 9, 1752), No. 50 (June 23, 1752), No. 52
(June 30, 1752), Nos. 57-58 (Aug. 1—Aug. 8, 1752), Nos.
62-70 (Sept 16—Nov. 11, 1752) in the Bodleian.

The Bodleian file containing these numbers has the signature
in ink, " Alexr Chalmers," on the flyleaf, and the following
words, also written in ink and initialled " P.V.H." (?) :

"This was Arthur Murphy's Copy, sold with rest of his
Library to Mr White of Fleet Street. The numbers are
wanting, which are printed in Fielding's Works: Murphy
appears to have sent them to press from this collection. See his
Life of Fielding, p 87, *Works*, Vol. 1, octo. Edit. 1786.

" The numbers by Fielding are all that are not in this volume
except Nos. 1 and 2 which are in neither. I bought this at
Alexr Chalmers' Sale 1835."

The British Museum has all the original numbers of *The
Covent Garden Journal* except No. 61 and parts of Nos. 71 and 72.

Most of Fielding's leading articles in the journal were
brought out in a paper printed in Dublin, the first seventy-six
numbers of which bear the title, " The Covent-Garden Journal.
By Sir Alexander Drawcansir, Knt. Censor of Great Britain.
(otherwise Henry Fielding, Esq;)." The first number of this is
dated Thursday, January 23, 1752. Nos. 77-82 of this paper
bear the title, "The Covent-Garden Journal: Or the Censor.

By Sir Alexander Drawcansir, Knt. (alias Henry Fielding, Esq;)." Nos. 83-86 of this paper have the title, "The Censor. Or, Covent-Garden Journal."

This paper came out as a double sheet, size about 11 ins. by 8 ins. with two columns on each page. The colophon varies, the form most frequent being:

DUBLIN: Printed by JAMES HOEY, at the Sign of *Mercury*, in *Skinner-Row*. Where may/be had the former Numbers. 1752.

Originals of Nos. 1-57 of this paper are in the Bodleian. The British Museum has Nos. 1-100 and some other odd subsequent issues.

THE/COVENT-GARDEN JOURNAL./BY/SIR ALEXAN-DER DRAWCANSIR, KNT./CENSOR OF GREAT BRITAIN.

12mo. Has no imprint or date.

Title p [1]. Blank p [2]. Text pp [3]-143.

Contains leading articles from the following numbers of the journal.

3, 4, 8, 9, 10, 17, 21, 23, 24, 33, 34, 35, 37, 42, 44, 47, 48 49, 51, 53, 54, 55, 56, 59, 60, 61.

As these are the same numbers from which leading articles were printed in the first collected edition of Fielding's Works, this collection seems to have been reprinted either from that or some subsequent edition of Fielding's Works.

In the Bodleian.

THE COVENT-GARDEN/JOURNAL/BY/SIR ALEXANDER DRAWCANSIR/KNT. CENSOR OF GREAT BRITAIN/(HENRY FIELD-ING)/EDITED BY/GERARD EDWARD JENSEN/VOLUME I [II] [ornament]/NEW HAVEN: YALE UNIVERSITY PRESS/LONDON: HUMPHREY MILFORD/OXFORD UNIVERSITY PRESS/MDCCCCXV.

In two volumes 8vo. With an Introduction, Notes and twelve illustrations. Reprints the leading articles, etc., in all the 72 numbers of the journal together with other items of special interest like the "Journal of the War," "Proceedings of Sir Alexander Drawcansir's Court of Censorial Enquiry," etc.

8vo.

Vol. I. Half Title p [i]. Blank p [ii]. Picture, View of Covent Garden, facing Title p [iii]. Imprint p [iv]. Dedication p [v]. Blank p [vi]. Preface pp [vii]-viii. Contents pp [ix]-x. List of Illustrations p [xi]. Blank p [xii]. Half Title p [xiii]. Blank p [xiv]. Introduction pp [1]-129. Blank p [130]. Half Title p [131]. Blank p [132]. Text pp [133]-368.

Vol. II. Half Title p [i]. Blank p [ii]. Portrait of Bonnell Thornton facing Title p [iii]. Imprint p [iv]. Contents pp [v]-vi. List of Illustrations p [vii]. Blank p [viii]. Half Title p [ix]. Blank p [x]. Text pp [1]-142. Notes pp [143]-275. Blank p [276]. Index pp [277]-293.

EXAMPLES / OF THE / INTERPOSITION / OF / PROVI-DENCE/IN THE/DETECTION and PUNISHMENT/OF/MUR-DER./CONTAINING,/Above thirty Cases, in which this dreadful/ Crime has been brought to Light, in the/most extraordinary and miraculous Man-/ner; collected from various authors, anti-/ ent and modern./WITH AN/INTRODUCTION and CONCLUSION,/ Both written/By HENRY FIELDING, Esq;/||/LONDON: /Printed for A. MILLAR, in the Strand./MDCCLII./[Price bound One Shilling, or Ten Shillings/a Dozen to those who give them away.]

12mo (5⅛ ins by 2⅞ ins.). Title p [i]. Blank p [ii]. Dedication, "To the Right Rev. Father in God, Isaac Lord Bishop of Worcester," pp i-iii. Blank p [vi]. Text pp [1]-94.

In the Bodleian.

OTHER EDITIONS.

DUBLIN.

1752. 1764.

LONDON.

1764 (In *A Right Pleasant and Famous Collection of Histories,* Vol V). 1799.

BATH.

1820.

A/PROPOSAL/FOR/Making an Effectual Provision/FOR THE/ POOR,/FOR/Amending their MORALS,/AND FOR/Rendering them useful MEMBERS of the SOCIETY./To which is added,/ A PLAN of the BUILDINGS proposed, with/proper Elevations./ Drawn by an Eminent Hand./By HENRY FIELDING, Esq;/Barrister at Law, and one of his Majesty's Justices of the/ Peace for the County of Middlesex./Ista sententia maximè et fallit imperitos, et obest sæpissime/Reipublicæ, cùm aliquid verum et rectum esse dicitur, sed/obtineri, id est obsisti posse populo, negatur./CIC. de Leg. lib. 3./LONDON:/Printed for A. MILLAR, in the Strand./MDCCLIII.

8vo. Title p [i]. "Explanation of the Plan " p [ii]. Folded plan of the proposed buildings. Dedication "To the Right Honourable Henry Pelham, Chancellor of his Majesty's Exchequer " pp [iii]-iv. Text pp [1]-91. Advt. [1] p.

In the Bodleian and the British Museum.

Another Edition, Dublin, 1753.

A/CLEAR STATE/OF THE/CASE/OF/ELIZABETH CANN- ING,/Who hath sworn that she was robbed and almost starved/ to Death by a Gang of Gipsies and other Villains in/January last, for which one MARY SQUIRES now/lies under Sentence of Death./||/Quæ, quia sunt admirabilia, contraque Opinionem/ omnium; tentare volui possentne proferri in Lucem, &/ita dici ut probarentur./CICERO. Parad./||/By HENRY FIELDING, Esq;/|||/LONDON:/Printed for A. MILLAR in the Strand./ M.DCCLIII./(Price One Shilling)

8vo. Title p [i]. Blank p [ii]. Text pp 1-62.

In the Bodleian and the British Museum.

Second Edition: London, 1753.

Other Editions: Dublin, 1753. London, 1754.

THE/LIFE/OF/Mr. JONATHAN WILD/THE GREAT./ A NEW EDITION/With considerable Corrections and Additions./||/ BY HENRY FIELDING, Esq;/||/LONDON:/Printed for A. MILLAR, in the Strand./||/MDCCLIV.

12mo. Title p [i]. Blank p [ii]. Advertisement From the Publisher to the Reader pp [iii-iv]. Contents pp [i]-vi. Advertisement of "Books printed for A. Millar, opposite Catharine-Street in the Strand " pp [vii-viii]. Text pp [1]-263.

In the British Museum.

First published in the *Miscellanies*, 1743. Vol. III

OTHER EDITIONS AND TRANSLATIONS.

COPENHAGEN.

1750 (German Translation). 1758 (German Translation).

AMSTERDAM.

1757 (Dutch Translation).

PARIS.

1763. 1784 (Part of the *Petite Bibliothèque de Campagne ou Collection de Romans*). 1834.

LONDON.

1763 (French Translation by C. Picquet). 1775 (With *A Journey From this World to the Next*). 1782. 1785(?). 1790. 1793. 1799 (Cooke's *Pocket Edition of Select Novels*). 1811. 1840 (Charles Daly. With a "Contemporary life of Jonathan Wild by H.D." and illustrations by "Phiz"). 1840 (Churton). 1842. 1845. 1886 (With *A Journey From this World to the Next*. Routledge. Library Edition). 1905 (With *A Journey from this World to the Next*. *Classic Novels*. Hutchinson. With Illustrations by "Phiz").

LAUSANNE.

1782.

RHEIMS.

1782. 1784

BERLIN.

1790.

LEIPZIG.

1800.

ZWICKAW.

1812.

HALIFAX.

1843. 1845.

NEW YORK.

1853. 1926 (With *The Life and Actions of Jonathan Wild by Daniel Defoe.*" Introduction by W. Follett.)

THE JOURNAL/OF A/VOYAGE to LISBON,/By the late/ HENRY FIELDING, Esq;/[ornament]/*LONDON*:/Printed for A. MILLAR, in the Strand./MDCCLV.

12mo. Half Title p [i]. Blank p [ii]. Title p [iii]. Blank p [iv]. "Dedication To The Public" pp [i]-iv. Preface pp [i]-xvii. Blank p [xviii]. Introduction pp [19]-41. Blank p [42]. The Journal pp [43]-198 (i.e. 246, pp 241-246 being incorrectly numbered 193-198).

In the Bodleian and the British Museum.

Sewed with the above:

A/FRAGMENT/OF A/COMMENT/ON /L. BOLINGBROKE'S ESSAYS./

12mo. Title p [247]. Blank p [248]. Text pp 201-228 (i.e. pp 249-276, these pages being incorrectly numbered].

This, the "edited" version of the Journal was first issued to the public. The other, fuller version was printed first but suppressed. It was, however, issued to the public by Millar in December, 1755. The title-page of this version is the same as that of the other, and the "Fragment of a Comment on L. Bolingbooke's Essays" was also sewed with the Journal, as in the edition first issued. The pagination of the version issued later varies from that of the first as the following details of the pagination of the "unedited" version will indicate:

12mo. Half Title p [i]. Blank p [ii]. Title p [iii]. Blank p [iv]. "Dedication To The Public" pp [i]-iv.Preface pp [i]- xv. Blank p [xvi]. Introduction pp [17]-37. Blank p [38]. The Journal pp [39]-219. "A Fragment of a Comment on L. Bolingbroke's Essays." Title p [221]. Blank p [222]. Text pp 223-245.

In the British Museum.

OTHER EDITIONS

DUBLIN.

1756 (Text of the " edited" version, first issued).

ALTONA.
   1764.
LAUSANNE.
   1783.
LONDON.
   1785 (Text of the "unedited" version). 1809 (In Mavor's *Voyages*, Vol. XI. Text of the "edited" version, first issued) 1887 (Cassell's *National Library*. Text of the "unedited" version). 1892 (Edited by Austin Dobson. Text of the "edited" version, first issued). 1893 (Text of the "unedited" version). 1907 (In the *World's Classics*. Edited by Austin Dobson. Text of the "edited" version first issued). 1907 (*Carlton Classics*, with a biographical introduction by Hannaford Bennett. Does not contain the Dedication To The Public and the Preface. Text of the "unedited" version).
BOSTON.
   1902 (Text of the "unedited" version).
CAMBRIDGE.
   1913 (Edited by J. H. Lobban. Text of the "edited" version first issued.)

COLLECTED EDITIONS OF WORKS

COLLECTED EDITIONS OF WORKS

The Works of Henry Fielding, Esq; with the Life of the Author. In four volumes.

London: Printed for A. Millar, opposite Catharine-Street, in the Strand. M.DCCLXII.

4to.

The first collected edition of Fielding's Works. Another edition in eight volumes octavo of the same was issued about the same time and this is described as the second edition on the title page.

Vol I has a portrait of Fielding facing the title page with the words "Wm. Hogarth, delin. James Basire sculp." It contains a dedication "To Ralph Allen, Esq"; An Essay on the Life and Genius of Henry Fielding, Esq, signed Arthur Murphy, Lincoln's Inn, March 25, 1762; *Love in Several Masques*; *The Temple Beau*; *The Author's Farce*; *The Coffee-House Politician*; *The Tragedy of Tragedies*; *The Letter Writers*; *The Grub Street Opera*; *The Lottery*; *The Modern Husband*; *The Mock Doctor*; *The Covent Garden Tragedy*; *The Debauchees*; *The Miser*; *The Intriguing Chambermaid*; *Don Quixote in England*; *An Old Man Taught Wisdom*.

Vol. II contains: *The Universal Gallant*; *Pasquin*; *The Historical Register*; *Eurydice*; *Eurydice Hiss'd*; *Tumble-Down Dick*; *Miss Lucy in Town*; *The Wedding-Day*; *Jonathan Wild*; *A Journey from this World to the Next*; *Joseph Andrews*; *Preface to David Simple*; *Preface to the Familiar Letters*.

Vol. III contains: *Tom Jones*; *Philosophical Transactions for the Year* 1742-3; *The First Olynthiac of Demosthenes*; *Of the Remedy of Affliction for the Loss of Our Friends*; *Dialogue between Alexander the Great and Diogenes the Cynic*; *Interlude between Jupiter, Juno, Apollo and Mercury*; *The True Patriot* Nos. 1, 3, 4, 7, 9, 10, 11, 13, 23 and 24; *The Jacobites' Journal*, Nos. 15 and 34.

Vol. IV contains: *Amelia*; *An Essay on Conversation*; *An Essay on the Knowledge of the Characters of Men*; *The Covent Garden Journal*, Nos. 3, 4, 8, 9, 10, 17, 21, 23, 24, 33, 34, 35, 37, 42, 44, 47, 48, 49, 51, 53, 54, 55, 56, 59, 60 and 61; *The Charge to the Westminster Grand Jury*; *The Journal of the Voyage to Lisbon*; *Comment on Lord Bolingbroke's Essays*; *Enquiry Into the Causes of the late Increase of Robbers*.

In the British Museum.

OTHER EDITIONS OF THIS

LONDON.

1766 (Third Edition. 12 vols, 12mo). 1769. 1771 (8 vols 8vo). 1771 (12 vols, 12mo). 1775 (12 vols, 12mo). 1780. 1783 (12 vols, 12mo. Which adds, in Vol IV, *The Fathers or the Good Natur'd Man* to the plays). 1784 (10 vols, 8vo). 1806 (10 vols, 8vo. Edited by Alexander Chalmers). 1821 (10 vols, 8vo). 1871 (10 vols, 8vo. Edited by James P. Browne, M.D. A supplementary volume to this Edition: *Henry Fielding. Miscellanies and Poems*. Edited with a preface by James P. Browne, M.D. London, 1872).

EDINBURGH.

1767. 1771.

GENEVA.

1781-82.

Oeuvres Complètes de Fielding. Paris, 1804. 23 tom., 12mo. Tom. XI-XIV contain *Aventures de Roderick Random* and Tom. XVIII-XX, *David Simple*

The Works of Henry Fielding. Complete in one volume. With Memoir of the Author. By Thomas Roscoe.

London : Printed for Henry Washbourne; H. G. Bohn; Scott, Webster and Geary; L. A. Lewis; John Chidley; William Gilling; and R. Griffin and Co., Glasgow. 1840. With portrait of Fielding engraved by Samuel Freeman facing title page and a facsimile of a letter to Nourse. 8vo.

Reprinted several times.

The Works of Henry Fielding, Esq. Edited with a Biographical Essay by Leslie Stephen. London. Smith, Elder & Co., 15 Waterloo Place. 1882.

In 10 vols, 8vo.

The Works of Henry Fielding. Edited by George Saintsbury. London. Published by J. M. Dent and Co. At Aldine House in Great Eastern Street. 1893.

In 12 vols, 12mo.

The Works of Henry Fielding. With an Introduction by Edmund Gosse. Westminster: Archibald Constable and Co. New York: Charles Scribner's Sons. 1899.

In 12 vols, 8vo.

The Temple Edition of the Works of Henry Fielding. Edited by George Saintsbury.

London: 1902. Published from Aldine House by J. M. Dent and Co.

In 12 vols, 16mo.

The Complete Works of Henry Fielding, Esq. With an Essay on the Life, Genius and Achievement of the Author, by William Ernest Henley, LL.D. . . . Illustrated with Reproductions of Rare Contemporary Drawings and Original Designs by E. E. Carlson and E. J. Read.

Printed for Subscribers only by Croscup and Sterling Company, New York [1903].

In 16 vols, 8vo.

The Works of Henry Fielding. Edited by G. H. Maynadier. Illustrated.

London: Gay and Bird, 22 Bedford Street, W.C. (1903-1905.)

In 12 vols, 8vo.

COLLECTED EDITIONS OF NOVELS

COLLECTED EDITIONS OF NOVELS

The Novels of Henry Fielding, Esq., viz: 1, *Joseph Andrews*, 2 *Tom Jones*, 3 *Amelia* and 4 *Jonathan Wild*. Complete in one volume. To which is Prefixed a *Memoir of the Life of the Author* [by Sir Walter Scott].
Ballantyne's *Novelists' Library*. Vol. I.
London: Published by Hurst, Robinson and Co., 90 Cheapside. Printed by James Ballantyne and Company, at the Border Press for John Ballantyne, Edinburgh. 1821. 8vo.

The Writings of Henry Fielding Comprising His Celebrated Works of Fiction. Carefully Revised and Collated with the Best Authorities. With a Memoir by David Herbert. Edinburgh. William P. Nimmo. 1872.
In one volume. 8vo.

The Works of Henry Fielding.
London: Jarrold and Sons. [1917.]
Part of the *International Library*.
In 6 vols, 8vo.

The Works of Henry Fielding. Edited by George Saintsbury. Illustrated by George Cruikshank.
London: The Navarre Society, Ltd., 23 New Oxford Street, W.C. [1926.]
In 12 vols, 8vo.

The Shakespeare Head Edition of Fielding's Novels.
Oxford: Basil Blackwell. Publisher to the Shakespeare Head Press of Stratford-upon-Avon. 1926.
In 10 vols, 8vo.

SELECTIONS, Etc., FROM FIELDING'S WORKS

SELECTIONS, Etc., FROM FIELDING'S WORKS

Illustrations of Smollett, Fielding and Goldsmith, in a series of forty-one plates designed and engraved by G. Cruikshank. Accompanied by descriptive extracts.
London: 1832.
The Beauties of Fielding. Consisting of Selections from his Works. By Alfred Howard, Esq.
London. [1834?].
Vol. XXIX of Howard's *Beauties of Literature.*
Episodes of Fiction or Choice Stories from the Great Novelists. With Biographical Introductions and Numerous Original Illustrations by Eminent Artists Engraved on Wood by R. Paterson.
Edinburgh: William P. Nimmo. 1870.
[*Henry Fielding,* pp. 51-67.]
Selected Essays of Henry Fielding. Edited with Introduction and Notes. by Gordon Hall Gerould. Athenæum Press Series. Boston and London. 1905.
Wise Sayings and Favourite Passages from the Works of Henry Fielding, including his Essay on Conversation. Cedar Rapids, Iowa. The Torch Press. 1909.
Masters of Literature. Fielding. Edited by George Saintsbury
London: George Bell and Sons. 1909.
The Fielding Calendar. A quotation from the works of Henry Fielding for every day in the year. Selected by John Kirby.
London. 1913.
Fielding. Selections, with Essays by Hazlitt, Scott, Thackeray. With an Introduction and Notes by L. Rice-Oxley.
Clarendon Press. 1923.

BIOGRAPHIES

BIOGRAPHIES

An Essay on the Life and Genius of Henry Fielding, Esq. By Arthur Murphy. Prefixed to the *Works of Henry Fielding.* First published London, 1762.

In *The Companion to the Playhouse,* or An Historical Account of all the Dramatic Writers . . . that have appeared in Great Britain and Ireland from the Commencement of our Theatrical Exhibitions down to the present year, 1764. By D. E. Baker, Vol II. London. 1764.

In Dr. John Aikin's *General Biography.*
London. 1799-1815.

The Life of Henry Fielding, Esq. With observations on his character and writings. By William Watson.
Edinburgh. 1807.

Biographical and Critical Essay by Mrs. Barbould, prefixed to *Joseph Andrews* in the *British Novelists,* Vol XVIII.
London. 1810.

Biographical and Critical Preface by William Mudford to the *British Novelists,* Vols IV and V.
London. 1811.

In Dr. Alexander Chalmers' *General Biographical Dictionary.*
London. 1812-1817.

A Memoir of the Life of Fielding, by Sir Walter Scott. Prefixed to the novels of Henry Fielding in Ballantyne's *Novelists' Library.* Vol. I. 1821. Published also in *Lives of the Novelists.* A. and W. Galignani. Paris. 1825. Reprinted in the *World's Classics.* 1906.

A Memoir of Fielding, by Thomas Roscoe. Prefixed to *The Works of Henry Fielding.*
London and Glasgow. 1840.

In *A Third Gallery of Portraits.* By George Gilfillan.
Edinburgh and London. 1854.

z

The Life of Henry Fielding; with Notices of his Writings, his Times and his Contemporaries. By Frederick Lawrence, Barrister-at-Law.

London. 1855.

"The Life and Writings of Henry Fielding," by Thomas, Keighley. In *Fraser's Magazine*, January and February, 1858 and Postscript, June, 1858.

In *Memoirs of Celebrated Etonians*. By J. H. Jesse. Vol I.
London. 1876.

A Biographical Essay by Sir Leslie Stephen. Prefixed to the *Works of Henry Fielding, Esq*. London, 1882.

Henry Fielding, a Memoir. By Austin Dobson.
London, 1900.

"Henry Fielding." By Austin Dobson. In Chambers' *Cyclopædiæ of English Literature*. Vol II.
London. 1902.

In *Some XVIII Century Men of Letters*. By the Rev. Whitwell Elwin. Vol II.
London. 1902.

"An Essay on the Life, Genius and Achievement of Henry Fielding." By William Ernest Henley. Prefixed to the *Complete Works of Henry Fielding Esq*.
London and New York. 1903.

"Fresh Facts about Fielding." By Austin Dobson. *Macmillan's Magazine*. April, 1907.

Henry Fielding. A Memoir, including newly discovered letters and records with illustrations from contemporary prints. By Miss G. M. Godden.
London. 1910.

The History of Henry Fielding. By Wilbur L. Cross. In three volumes.
New Haven. 1918.

CRITICISM

CRITICISM

An Examen of the History of Tom Jones a Foundling. By "Orbilius."
London. 1750.

An Essay on the New Species of Writing founded by Mr. Fielding. With a word or two upon the modern state of Criticism.
London. 1751.

Observations on Mr. Fielding's Plan for a Preservatory and Reformatory; to which is added, A Scheme for establishing and perpetuating this Charity.
London, 1758.

"Standard Novels and Romances." By William Hazlitt. In the *Edinburgh Review*, February, 1815.

Lectures on the English Comic Writers. By William Hazlitt.
London, 1818.

The English Humourists of the Eighteenth Century. By W. M. Thackeray.
London. 1853.

"Fielding's Novels." By Sir Leslie Stephen. In the *Cornhill Magazine*, February, 1877.

Henry Fielding in *Hours in a Library* (Third Series). By Sir Leslie Stephen.
London. 1879.

Fielding. By Austin Dobson. English Men of Letters Series.
London. 1883.

Two English Bookmen. By Austin Dobson.
London. 1894.

Henry Fieldings Dramatische Werke. Litterarische Studie von Felix Lindner.
Leipzig and Dresden. 1895.

Henry Fielding . . . The Pickering Club Booklets. No. 1.
London. 1904.

"Henry Fielding." By J. H. Lobban. In *Blackwood's Magazine.*
April, 1907.

Entstehungsgeschichte von Fieldings Joseph Andrews. By E.
Bosdorf.
Berlin. 1908.

Henry Fielding. His Works. An Independent Criticism. By
Emanuel Green.
London. 1909.

Fielding's Jonathan Wild. By G. T. Bispham. In *Eighteenth
Century Literature.* An Oxford Miscellany.
Oxford. 1909.

"Fielding's Political Purpose in Jonathan Wild." By John
Edwin Wells. In the *Publications of the Modern Language
Association of America.* Vol XXVIII.

Fielding and Smollett, By Harold Child. In *The Cambridge
History of English Literature.* 1913.

Les Romans de Fielding. Par Aurélien Digeon. Paris, 1923.
English Translation. London. 1925.

Le Texte des Romans de Fielding. Par Aurélien Digeon.
Paris. 1923.

Fielding the Novelist. A Study in Historical Criticism By
Frederic T. Blanchard.
New Haven. 1926.

Henry Fielding als Kritiker. By Karl Heinrich Bruno
Radtke.
Leipzig. 1926.

DATE DUE